I0119955

Seams of Empire

UNIVERSITY PRESS OF FLORIDA

Florida A&M University, Tallahassee
Florida Atlantic University, Boca Raton
Florida Gulf Coast University, Ft. Myers
Florida International University, Miami
Florida State University, Tallahassee
New College of Florida, Sarasota
University of Central Florida, Orlando
University of Florida, Gainesville
University of North Florida, Jacksonville
University of South Florida, Tampa
University of West Florida, Pensacola

# Seams of Empire

Race and Radicalism in Puerto Rico
and the United States

CARLOS ALAMO-PASTRANA

University Press of Florida
Gainesville · Tallahassee · Tampa · Boca Raton
Pensacola · Orlando · Miami · Jacksonville · Ft. Myers · Sarasota

Portions of chapters 1 and 2 appeared previously in "Dispatches from a Colonial
Outpost: Puerto Rico as Schema in the Black Popular Press." *Du Bois Review* 9, no. 1
(Spring 2012): 201–25. Reprinted by permission of the *Du Bois Review: Social Science
Research on Race*.

Published in the United States of America. Printed on acid-free paper.

This book may be available in an electronic edition.

First cloth printing, 2016
First paperback printing, 2019

24  23  22  21  20  19    6  5  4  3  2  1

Library of Congress Cataloging-in-Publication Data
Names: Alamo-Pastrana, Carlos, author.
Title: Seams of empire : race and radicalism in Puerto Rico and the United
    States / Carlos Alamo-Pastrana.
Description: Gainesville : University Press of Florida, [2016] | Includes
    bibliographical references and index.
Identifiers: LCCN 2015040943 | ISBN 9780813062563 (cloth : alk. paper)
ISBN 9780813064253 (pbk.)
Subjects: LCSH: Puerto Rico—Race relations. | United States—Race relations.
    | Radicalism—United States. | Radicalism—Puerto Rico.
Classification: LCC F1983.A1 A43 2015 | DDC 305.80097295—dc23
LC record available at http://lccn.loc.gov/2015040943

The University Press of Florida is the scholarly publishing agency for the State
University System of Florida, comprising Florida A&M University, Florida Atlantic
University, Florida Gulf Coast University, Florida International University, Florida
State University, New College of Florida, University of Central Florida, University of
Florida, University of North Florida, University of South Florida, and University of
West Florida.

University Press of Florida
2046 NE Waldo Road
Suite 2100
Gainesville, FL 32609
http://upress.ufl.edu

For my wamus

# Contents

List of Figures   ix

List of Abbreviations   xi

Acknowledgments   xiii

Introduction   1

1. The Puerto Rican Blueprint   17

2. Dispatches from the Colonial Outpost   38

3. The Living Negro in Latin America   61

4. The Republic of the Penniless   86

5. You Are Here to Listen   117

Conclusion   149

Notes   155

Bibliography   185

Index   203

# Figures

2.1. "Puerto Rico Will Choose," by Wilbert L. Holloway  55

4.1. "Do not let the dollar emigrate from your country"  90

4.2. Child in workers' quarter of Puerto de Tierra  91

4.3. Water supply in the workers' quarter  92

4.4. Negro workers in front of their homes near Ponce  96

4.5. Portrait of Edwin and Louise Rosskam  101

4.6. Sugar worker taking a drink of water  105

5.1. Members of Proyecto Piloto  118

5.2. Proyecto Piloto members at a news conference in Barrio Tortugo
    following their arrest  133

5.3. Proyecto Piloto Comic: "Época del saqueo"  138

5.4. Proyecto Piloto Comic: "Manela"  141

# Abbreviations

| | |
|---|---|
| ABB | African Blood Brotherhood |
| AFL | American Federation of Labor |
| ASNLH | Association for the Study of Negro Life and History |
| CAL | Comandos Armados de Liberación (Armed Commandos of Liberation) |
| CGT | Confederación General de Trabajadores (General Confederation of Workers) |
| CIO | Congress of Industrial Organizations |
| CIS | Centro de Investigaciones Sociales (Social Science Research Center) |
| CIT | Confederación Interamericana de Trabajadores (Inter-American Confederation of Workers) |
| CPUSA | Communist Party of the United States of America |
| CTAL | Confederación de Trabajadores de América Latina (Confederation of Latin American Workers) |
| DIVEDCO | División de Educación de la Comunidad (Division for Community Education) |
| FALN | Fuerzas Armadas de Liberación Nacional (Armed Forces for National Liberation) |
| FLT | Federación Libre de Trabajadores (Federation of Free Workers) |
| FSA | Farm Security Administration |

| | |
|---|---|
| FUPI | Federación de Universitarios Pro-Independencia (Federation of Pro-Independence University Students) |
| HUAC | House Committee on Un-American Activities |
| IASB | International African Service Bureau |
| ICP | Instituto de Cultura Puertorriqueña (Institute of Puerto Rican Culture) |
| IWW | International Workers of the World |
| JMPI | Juventud del Movimiento Pro-Independencia (Youth of the Pro-Independence Movement) |
| MPI | Movimiento Pro-Independencia (Pro-Independence Movement) |
| NAACP | National Association for the Advancement of Colored People |
| NAM | Non-Aligned Movement |
| OIPR | Office of Information for Puerto Rico |
| OPA | Office of Price Administration |
| PIP | Partido Independentista Puertorriqueño (Puerto Rican Independence Party) |
| PNP | Partido Nuevo Progresista (New Progressive Party) |
| PPD | Partido Popular Democrático (Popular Democratic Party) |
| PRERA | Puerto Rico Emergency Relief Administration |
| PRLRA | Puerto Rico Labor Relations Act |
| PRPC | Puerto Rico Policy Commission |
| PRRA | Puerto Rican Reconstruction Administration |
| ROTC | Reserve Officer Training Corps |
| SNCC | Student Nonviolent Coordinating Committee |
| UN | United Nations |
| UNIA | Universal Negro Improvement Association |
| UPR | University of Puerto Rico |

# Acknowledgments

Writing and research is difficult and isolating work. Even when our intentions are to capture the aspirations and plans of collective activity, we are often left to read and compose these stories secluded from the rest of the world. This kind of separation from our communities stands in stark contrast to how many of the people we write about think about the kind of world they desire to live in. I have been most fortunate to have a highly committed group of accomplices and beloveds in my life, who never left me to travel alone on this journey. These people have lovingly inserted themselves into my life to speak truths, humor, and justice when I felt most isolated and unsure of the direction of this project. I am forever indebted to all of you for your collective love and wisdom.

I am thankful to my parents, Ramon and Nivea Alamo, for their unconditional love and support. I hope this book makes you as proud of me as I am of all of your accomplishments and to call you my parents. Thanks also to my brother, Ramon Alamo, and his beautiful family (Leslie, Luiz, Micaela, and Nayeli) for their continuous encouragement, love, and laughter. I love all of you deeply and am so fortunate to have you in my life.

This project would have never been completed without the support of my extended family in Puerto Rico. A thank-you goes to Carmen and Carlos Ramírez for their willingness to take me into their home as their own son. I am particularly grateful for my uncle and aunt, Félix Alamo and Ivette Rodríguez, for allowing me to use their beautiful condo in Fajardo while I wrote extensive portions of this manuscript and for always making me laugh to the point of tears. The large and extensive Alamo clan were my strongest supporters as I worked on this project over the course of ten years. Gracias. My abuelita Dolores Pastrana provided the meals and smiles that sustained me in between many trips to the archive. I owe a note of appreciation to my cousins Ricardo Alamo and Antonio Soisa for their endless companionship, bantering, and teasing about the mysterious book project I was working on, and for their willingness to reach out to people on my behalf.

The seeds of this project started many years ago when I was still a graduate student in California. While at Santa Barbara, I had the privilege of having the best group of advisors, including Avery Gordon, George Lipsitz, Jon Cruz, and Ana Yolanda Ramos Zayas. Their mentoring and lessons have served me well as I have navigated the academy. I especially want to thank Avery for her willingness to read endless drafts and have long phone dates across continents. This project is inspired by the ways you have taught me to think about history and sociology. Your mentorship and friendship mean so much to me, and I am eternally indebted to you.

I am very lucky to call the Department of Sociology at Vassar College my professional home. The intellectual sustenance they provide me never ceases to amaze me. I am especially grateful to William Hoynes for his friendship and for volunteering to read various drafts of the manuscript and provide thoughtful feedback. I am also profoundly appreciative of my other accomplices at Vassar, including David Bradley, Lisa Brawley, Light Carruyo, Terri Cronk, Eve Dunbar, Maria Hantzopoulos, Katherine Hite, Hua Hsu, Luis Inoa, Amitava Kumar, Kiese Laymon, Eileen Leonard, Zachariah Mampilly, Seungsook Moon, Hiram Perez, and Eréndira Rueda. I also want to give a special acknowledgment to Vassar librarian Carol Lynn Marshall for her invaluable help in locating and sorting through materials in the Black press.

I have had the privilege of having some of the best students and research assistants while at Vassar. Raymon Azcona, Angélica Aurora Gutiérrez, and Jennifer Lopez provided instrumental assistance during the early stages of the project as I combed through vast amounts of information. Nicole Wong's brilliance, energy, and endless knowledge helped bring this project to an enjoyable close. Thank you very much to the wonderful students in my "Race and Popular Culture" and "Racial Borderlands" classes for helping me to think through many parts of this book. You have all taught me to be a better listener and teacher.

I am also grateful for the extended community of people that have nourished me with their friendship over the years. Thank you so much to Mona Ahamad Ali, Frances Aparicio, Robert Bixler, Karl Bryant, Krista Bywater, Ginetta Candelario, Clayton Childress, Dana Collins, Sylvanna Falcón, Zaire Dinzey-Flores, Tyrone Foreman, José Fuste, Lorena Garcia, Rudy Guevarra, Tiffany Willoughby Herard, Gaye Theresa Johnson, Aldo Lauria Santiago, Marisol Lebrón, Helene Lee, Erik Love, Neda Maghbouleh, John Miller, Nancy Mirabal, Jesse Moya, Bob Ngo, César Rodríguez, Mérida Rúa, Alberto Sandoval-Sánchez, Molly Talcott, Michelle Tellez, Arlene Torres, Evelyn Velazquez, Charles Venator Santiago, Carmen Whalen, and all the members of the New England Consortium of Latina/o Studies.

A special thank-you to Sonia Tycko for her motivation, revisions, and guidance as I prepared the manuscript for submission. I am lucky to have sent this manuscript to Sian Hunter at the University Press of Florida. She immediately understood my project and why it mattered. Thank you.

Various research centers and people helped me gather invaluable amounts of data for this project. Thank you to Miguel Vega Rivera for all his help at the Colección Puertorriqueña at the University of Puerto Rico, Río Piedras.

Dax Collazo's endless assistance at the Fundación Luis Muñoz Marín made the process of sifting through material there so much easier. The staff at the Centro de Estudios Puertorriqueños at Hunter College helped me fill in key parts of my chapters, especially when I was unable to travel to Puerto Rico. I am extremely grateful for the assistance of the Robert E. Howard Foundation and Rob Roehm. Roehm's archives were essential in helping me piece together and make sense of Harold Preece's multifaceted life.

I am greatly indebted to lawyer Rafael Anglada López and professor Aarón Gamaliel Ramos for putting me in touch with members of Proyecto Piloto and other key members of the Puerto Rican Left. Similarly, I am grateful to Efraín Negrón and Rafael Mayfield for sharing Dr. Ana Livia Cordero's personal papers with me.

As I conducted research on Ana Livia Cordero I came across Sandy Placido, a brilliant graduate student at Harvard University also working on Ana Livia Cordero's legacy. I encourage those interested in knowing more about Ana Livia Cordero's life to look up Sandy's pending dissertation, which delves much deeper into many aspects of Cordero's career that I only hint at within my chapter.

Finally, and most important, I want to express my deep love and appreciation for my wife, Tanya Smallwood, and our beautiful son, Félix. Your unconditional *amor*, laughter, and honesty over the years have made this book so much easier to write. We often joke that there is way too much love in our house. All three of us know there is no such thing and would have it no other way. This book is dedicated to both of you.

# Introduction

In the spring of 2011, government officials in Puerto Rico scrambled to have decaying public housing structures painted, roads cleaned, and meeting venues secured. The frantic arrangements occurred in preparation for U.S. president Barack Obama's official state visit to the island on June 14 of that year. Local authorities strived to present the commonwealth in as flattering a light as possible. The last time a sitting U.S. president traveled to Puerto Rico on official state business came in 1961 with the visit of John F. Kennedy. Local resident Juanita Seguinot noted in the island's most circulated newspaper, *El Nuevo Día*, that Puerto Ricans from all walks of life were honored to greet the American president. But she also insisted that President Obama "be taken through the poorer areas" of the island. Seguinot demanded that he "not just [be taken] through the main avenues," which had been aesthetically groomed for his visit, because "he also needs to see the poverty here and [see] that the money is kept by the well-off and the poor never see any of it."[1] Poverty continues to plague an overwhelming number of island residents and serves to illustrate the continued failure of colonial policies. As of 2010, Puerto Rico's per-capita income of $16,560 amounted to just a little more than half that of the poorest state in the American union.[2]

But Seguinot's comments also hinted at a larger critique of the image of Puerto Rico that local government officials and elites presented to President Obama and the larger American public. Seguinot insightfully recognized that the president would not meet the island's poor, who "never see" the more than $21 billion in federal expenditures sent to the island in 2009 alone.[3] More simply, Seguinot cautioned against believing the façade of Puerto Rican prosperity created by local elites.

Through her critique, Seguinot implicitly asked readers and President Obama to think more deeply about the things and people we *do not* see, or what sociologist Avery Gordon refers to as structural hauntings and the ghosts they animate. According to Gordon, a haunting hints at the ways "abusive systems of power make themselves known . . . when their oppressive nature is denied" historically or contemporarily through narratives created by those in power. Seguinot directed *El Nuevo Día's* audience to consider the "seething presence" of ghosts that haunted the dominant narrative about the island created for the presidential procession.[4]

Local politicians also used Obama's visit as an opportunity to tell their own ghost stories about race and sovereignty. The internationally recognized artist and former political prisoner Pablo Marcano García bought a full-page ad in *El Nuevo Día* to publish a letter addressed to President Obama. Marcano García's letter called on Obama to resolve the island's continued colonial status and to remove the travel restrictions imposed on those who elect Puerto Rican over limited U.S. citizenship.[5] More striking, however, were the ideas about race Marcano García discussed in his letter.

Marcano García, a self-described Black Puerto Rican, made his appeal for Puerto Rican independence to Obama by drawing on a racialized vision of the Americas. Using important twentieth-century figures, among them Arturo (Arthur) Schomburg, Martin Luther King Jr., and Langston Hughes, Marcano García highlighted the spatial and temporal connections between himself, the (self-identified) African American president, Puerto Ricans, and the larger Black diaspora. Marcano García argued that because Obama was "looked upon by the world as a brother by faith and race," he was morally and ethically bound to create political opportunities for Puerto Rico's decolonization.[6]

In the same newspaper renowned conservative Tomás Rivera Schatz, president of the Puerto Rican senate and advocate for Puerto Rican statehood, took out his own two-page advertisement, entitled "Igualdad [equality]: Come Home!" He too demanded decolonization as he urged President Obama to resolve the island's status by making it the fifty-first U.S. state. Like Marcano García, Rivera Schatz referred to prominent African Americans, including Martin Luther King Jr. and Rosa Parks. Unlike Marcano García, however, Rivera Schatz shied away from a hemispheric vision of the Americas, opting instead to center on the American Union through a focus on Abraham Lincoln's Gettysburg Address (1863). Drawing parallels between the status of Black American slaves and contemporary Puerto Ricans, Rivera Schatz wrote that just as President Lincoln once defended the rights of African Americans, so should President Obama stand up for Puerto Rican statehood.

Rivera Schatz blamed Puerto Rico's continued colonial predicament on a small group of "anti-Hispanics" (*antihispanos*) in Washington who opposed granting statehood to a "Hispanic" territory. Anti-Hispanics and those who remain neutral in Puerto Rico's status debate (by implication, supporters of commonwealth status), wrote Rivera Schatz, are "just like the slave masters of the 18th and 19th centuries." Conflating Obama's Black heritage and the U.S. history "of overcoming discrimination" against these slave masters, Rivera Schatz argued Obama's election as president should give all Puerto Ricans the hope that they too would one day enjoy the same citizenship and rights demanded and won by African Americans.[7]

Thus, the president's visit to Puerto Rico incited average residents and prominent public figures to strategically link the status of Puerto Ricans with that of African Americans. Their letters hint at the ways ideas about race are invoked and deployed strategically to organize political debates in Puerto Rico around decolonization, economic development, and national culture. They also show how Puerto Ricans make sense of U.S. racial history. Yet these comparative narratives about racial history obscure more than they reveal about transnational and trans-local structures of inequality within Puerto Rico's racial regime. The parallels to U.S. racial history in both preceding examples serve not only to highlight Puerto Rico's colonial status, but also to mark race and racism as social phenomena found only in the United States and not in Puerto Rico. As such, the connective histories of race and empire between both national spaces haunt these narratives.

At the same time, the stories told by Seguinot and Marcano García are part of a rich but often overlooked Black radical tradition that studies and observes racial regimes inside and outside the United States. W.E.B. Du Bois, Ida B. Wells, Julia de Burgos, C.L.R. James, Arturo Schomburg, James Baldwin, Richard Wright, and Toni Morrison are just a few of the Black intellectuals and activists who have provided valuable insights on the exclusionary practices and violence experienced by the Black diaspora.

In spite of their continued marginalization within traditional disciplines, an extensive group of cultural workers has productively shaped and pushed the contours of Black social and political life.[8] Black writers have effectively drawn connections between their own histories of subjugation and the everyday experiences of people of color around the world. Writers in the transnational Black radical tradition have thus also demonstrated a profound sensitivity to and understanding of the imposition of imperialism across the globe.

*Seams of Empire* examines the neglected exchanges between cultural and political actors in the United States and Puerto Rico, each of whom draws on ideas about race and empire to make sense of local conditions and accomplish diverse sociopolitical objectives. These overlooked histories disrupt dominant narratives about race, colonialism, and cultural practices in both Puerto Rico and the United States. Responses to institutionalized racism and colonialism have produced an oft-overlooked corpus of texts demonstrating the symbolic and material connections between marginalized subjects in both national spaces. In other instances, the corpus shows traces of the ways in which white liberalism in the United States strategically used the island to envision a political future free of significant racial strife. Since the end of the Spanish-American War in 1898, the United States has forcefully held Puerto Rico as a colonial possession. Given Puerto Rico's distinctive colonial history under Spain and then the United States, the island offers a valuable space in which to examine how ideas about empire and race have been activated, understood, and challenged.

Uncovering the overlooked stories of journalists, writers, and activists in Puerto Rico and the United States challenges the prevailing comparative frames of what political scientist Cedric Robinson terms racial regimes. According to Robinson, racial regimes are "constructed social systems in which race is proposed as a justification for the relations of power . . . a makeshift patchwork masquerading as memory and the immutable."[9] This makeshift patchwork (structure) upon which racial regimes are built is difficult to chart. The difficulty arises primarily from the unwillingness of racial regimes to openly exhibit their hostility toward difference and their investment in what political scientist Claire Jean Kim terms racial power. Instead, such regimes often use misdirection to divert our attention from unequal or violent structural arrangements. Equally important, these institutional arrangements are masked in ways that cast them as natural and incontestable.[10]

National myths produced by powerful political and cultural brokers discursively reinforce the naturalness of racial regimes. Despite their best efforts to conceal themselves, racial regimes possess a history that is traceable and can be studied. *Seams of Empire* uncovers the confluent histories about race and power among Puerto Ricans, the Black diaspora, and U.S. liberalism from 1940 to 1972.

This period of roughly three decades is significant because it spans the era leading up to the formal establishment of Puerto Rican Commonwealth colonial status in 1952. This period also covers the twenty-year Partido Popular Democrático (PPD) control of the governorship before it lost the 1968 gubernatorial elections to the statehood party, the Partido Nuevo Progresista (PNP). In part, I suggest that the establishment of the PPD and of commonwealth rule during this period were not inevitable outcomes of U.S. colonial policy. Instead, the PPD's ascendency was due to the direct challenge and strategic deployment, at times aided by proponents of sovereignty themselves, of anticolonial narratives focused on a critical assessment and reimagining of the relationship between race and empire.

Equally significant, the curtailment of Black and Puerto Rican radicalism—which led to a racially unified labor movement in the United States and Puerto Rico—was not an inherently natural conclusion to the events of the era. Instead, this book presents the missed opportunities to radically reshape social and institutional arrangements in both national spaces that occurred between 1940 and 1972. The encounters between racial regimes during this thirty-two-year era ruptured the apparently natural order of colonial and racial difference in Puerto Rico and the United States.

## Colonialism and the Comparative Method

Forged through military conquest and political maneuvering, the colonial relationship between Puerto Rico and the United States bridges nationalist ideologies, diverse populations, and heterogeneous cultures. Despite the relational nature of these exchanges, most scholarship about race in Puerto Rico uses a comparative approach. This method obsessively focuses on race and operationalizes racism in Puerto Rico and in the United States as distinct problems. This analytic approach has the specific intention of minimizing the prevalence of racism in Puerto Rico and essentializing its manifestation in the United States. Such comparisons contribute to a distorted historiography of what is, in fact, an intimate relationship between the Puerto Rican and American racial regimes.

Ethnic studies scholar Lisa Lowe suggests that the dissimilarities observed through comparison literally produce "deviations" that "institutionaliz[e] difference as a modern apparatus for apprehending and disciplining otherness." These deviations are viewed as social formations that threaten the nation-state rather than as potential meeting points of unforeseen and productive transformations. Accordingly, they are relegated to being social outliers in need of assimilation or banishment. As discussed later, the production of comparative difference between Puerto Rican and U.S. racial regimes ultimately re-centers whiteness and white supremacy in both national contexts.[11]

The deviations created by the comparative method haunt two key aspects in the study of the relationship between race and empire in Puerto Rico: the production of Puerto Rican racial difference and the myth of racial democracy. Historically the United States approached Puerto Rican racial difference as a non-normative social formation in need of colonial discipline. Using white patriarchal normativity as their comparative frame, American academics and government officials—whether they opposed or favored American colonial expansion—depicted Puerto Rican colonial subjects as deviant, non-normative, and Black.[12] Even before the United States invaded the island in 1898, popular depictions characterized Puerto Rico as a backward society inhabited by Black children. American institutions and the spirit of democracy could not flourish in this imagined Puerto Rico.[13]

Opponents of the war bolstered their anticolonialism with normative morality and constitutionality. But underlying their opposition lay a fear of the culturally and racially deviant colonial subjects that the United States would have to contend with should the war end in conquest. Stanford chancellor David Starr Jordan, a former vice president of the Anti-Imperialist League, weighed the institutional and racial consequences that would come with the new territories. "Our question is not what we shall do with Cuba, Porto Rico and the Philippines," but rather, opined

Jordan, "it is what these prizes will do to us."[14] Jordan cautioned that, unlike previous groups of marginalized others, Puerto Rico's new colonial subjects would bring financial and social burdens to the U.S. nation:

> Wherever we have inferior and dependent races within our borders to-day, we have a political problem—"the Negro problem," "the Chinese problem," "the Indian problem." These problems we slowly solve. Industrial training and industrial pride make a man of the Negro. Industrial interests may even make a man of the Chinaman, and the Indian disappears as our civilization touches him. But in the tropics such problems are perennial and insoluble.[15]

The comparative interpretation of non-normative, racial, and colonial formations as social problems worked as a constitutive strategy that defined and secured white supremacy in nineteenth-century America. According to sociologist Moon-Kie Jung, the United States is an "empire-state" organized through comparative and legally sanctioned differentiations premised on the elusive acquisitions of property, whiteness, and citizenship.[16] The exclusions promoted by white supremacy prove that the United States has never been an egalitarian nation-state.

Despite its discursive and state-sanctioned assertions, the idea that Puerto Rico is a racially democratic nation is also a lie.[17] American, white, patriarchal normativity mediated through property ownership and citizenship only accounts for half of the distortions created by comparative approaches to racial difference. Puerto Rican *criollo* (creole) elites responded to their designation as non-normative by discursively and symbolically celebrating the island's African, indigenous, and Spanish heritages.[18] Racial democracy, or the "racial triad," is the other prominent comparative frame from which Puerto Rican racial difference is imagined vis-à-vis the United States. Puerto Rican elites have been the main promoters of racial democracy, but it permeates every facet of Puerto Rican race relations and popular life. Both nationalists and annexationists use racial democracy as an anticolonial strategy from which Puerto Rican cultural and political formations are disentangled from those in the United States. Pivoting from this comparative strand are two forms of racial exceptionalism. On the one hand, Puerto Rican elites and intellectuals assert the uniqueness of the American racial regime as the sole arbiter of racial violence and exclusion. On the other, they commend Puerto Rico as a racially tolerant society. In this way, they effectively disavow Puerto Rico's own history of legally (i.e., slavery) and socially (i.e., segregation) sanctioned racial exclusions.[19]

Over the span of the twentieth century, Puerto Rican intellectuals and politicians bolstered claims of Puerto Rican racial inclusivity in contrast to the aberration of racism found in the United States. In 1909, José Celso Barbosa, founder of the statehood party and the island's most revered Black politician, articulated this troubling comparative stance. Writing in his newspaper, *El Tiempo*, Barbosa asserted that racism never had existed and never would exist in Puerto Rico, in contrast to "some states in the Union, to the shame and embarrassment of the most democratic nation in the world."[20]

Nationalist writers, including members of the literary *generación de los treinta* such as Tomás Blanco and Antonio Pedreira (discussed in chapters 3 and 4, respectively), followed Barbosa's comparative lead.[21] Their nationalist sympathies and the larger populism sweeping Latin America in the 1930s and 1940s profoundly influenced these intellectuals. They described Puerto Rican culture in ways that were unevenly white, Eurocentric, and dismissive of Puerto Rican racism, even as they reproduced racist tropes in their own writing. Pedreira, for example, alleged that in order to be "capable of the grandest and most heroic feats," Puerto Ricans needed to rely on their European "blood." Showing his nationalist anxieties and investment in biological determinism, Pedreira lamented that Puerto Ricans remained "drenched under waves of African blood," leading them to be "indecisive, almost stupefied by the colors and threatened by the cinematic vision of witches and ghosts."[22]

The establishment of the Institute of Puerto Rican Culture (ICP) in 1955 cemented these inherently derogatory comparative musings about race and democracy. Through the ICP's historical scholarship and cultural programming the racial triad ultimately became an unquestioned cornerstone of Puerto Rican culture and national identity. A central facet of the cultural nationalist wing of the ruling PPD, the ICP implemented initiatives that helped suture racial democracy to the party's cultural politics. The discursive and political use of the racial triad helped the PPD to secure the support of the party's politically radical yet culturally conservative members. This powerful wing of the PPD worried about being culturally assimilated into American society should annexation ever occur.[23] The invention of racial democracy as a discursive and cultural production demonstrated the PPD's efforts to protect the uniqueness of the "Puerto Rican personality" even as it endorsed the island's status as a colonial commonwealth of the United States.[24]

While racial democracy has been used to culturally distinguish Puerto Rico from the imperialist and assimilationist impulses of the United States, such comparisons also regulate and silence internal heterogeneity across a variety of demographics and reduce understandings of Blackness. According to anthropologist Isar Godreau, Blackness in Puerto Rico is imagined only as a premodern *fact* shared by a few "happy and rhythmic [Black] tradition bearers who still inhabit homogenous and harmonious communities." Blackness is therefore confined to a folk realm while its contemporary and heterogeneous manifestations are obscured.[25] By insisting on the veracity of its racially inclusive model, the ICP maligned any criticisms of Puerto Rican race relations from inside or outside of Puerto Rico as moot and unfounded.[26]

Even when Puerto Rican writers tried to break away from the "seductive archaeology" of Puerto Rican racial democracy, they remained bound to reproduce its distorted logics.[27] Writing against earlier generations of Puerto Rican writers in the 1970s, Eduardo Seda Bonilla cautioned against the valuing of whiteness and whitening (*blanqueamiento*) that he observed among Puerto Ricans.[28] Seda Bonilla argued that *blanqueamiento* and Latin American somatic understandings of race were different from and, in part, a response to U.S. norms of hypodescent and blood quantum. Although he recognized the prevalence of "pseudo-ethnic" racism in Puerto Rico, in his later scholarship Seda Bonilla shockingly located the origins of this deviation among Puerto Ricans in the United States. He claimed that members of the Puerto Rican diaspora acted as conduits who imported this American brand of racism back to the island.[29]

Rejecting movement toward assimilation with the United States, Seda Bonilla and some of his contemporaries cast return migrants as deviants or "confused migrants" who local ruling elites pitted against other Puerto Ricans in an attempt to "denationalize" all Puerto Ricans. Seda Bonilla went so far as to use the characters in novelist Pedro Juan Soto's *Ardiente suelo fría estación* as evidence of the racialized discourse of the Puerto Rican diaspora. An *independentista*, Seda Bonilla condescendingly dismissed the isolation and alienation that migrants experienced upon their return to the island as the result of cultural illiteracy and racialized psychosis: "If someone had explained the concept of culture to them they would have mastered the skills necessary for their [re]insertion into the authentic Puerto Rican existentiality. The pseudo-ethnic hallucination prevents them from seeing things as they are. They think they are rejected because of prejudice just like when they were in the 'ghetto.'"[30]

In emphasizing the individualized nature of the "pseudo-ethnic hallucinations" that haunted Puerto Ricans from the diaspora, Seda Bonilla concealed structural manifestations of racism in Puerto Rico. More importantly, he located the links between racism, cultural dissonance, and urban poverty exclusively in the American ghetto. Taken together, the creative comparison of Puerto Rican and U.S. racial formations by intellectuals and institutions implicitly promoted a version of Puerto Rican political and cultural nationalism that re-centered white and nationalist normativity. The domestic emphasis on a Eurocentric and patriarchal nationalism was a direct response to the racialization of Puerto Ricans by colonial powers.

The cultural workers profiled in this book worked against these simplistic comparative tropes about race and colonialism. Instead, these writers harnessed Black radicalism and critical examinations of the material conditions of Black life on the island and in the United States to more accurately interpret their political milieus and possibilities. Other writers struggled to envision what role progressive white Americans could play in facilitating the visions of freedom and racial justice prominent among some sectors of the American Left during the middle decades of the twentieth century.

### Haunting *La Gran Familia Puertorriqueña*

Avoiding the exclusionary framework of comparative analysis is difficult but not impossible. Given comparative analysis's reliance on large social units such as the nation-state, challenging the method necessarily requires rethinking the categories of analysis and meaning created by the state. Confronting the comparative method necessitates a focus on the subjects, social formations, and stories the state treats as insignificant or as deviations within the fissures of history.

A return to Gordon's concept of haunting is instructive in this regard.

As mentioned, hauntings point to the signs, ideas, people, and histories only hinted at within dominant historiography. The writers and activists uncovered in *Seams of Empire* are the "striking impressions" (ghosts) created and continuously banished to the margins of comparative-analysis-driven Puerto Rican and U.S. history. But, as Gordon reminds us, it is not sufficient to think of a ghost as someone or something that is missing. A ghost is more broadly a "social figure" that can teach us about the "dense site where history and subjectivity make social life." These apparently isolated aberrations emerge as "singular and yet repetitive instances when home becomes unfamiliar."[31] More simply, the recurrent instances of structural hauntings demand an intervention that critically interrogates comparative histories about race and empire.

Not coincidentally, within the field of Puerto Rican studies, especially in literature, "the familiar" or "the family" operates as the major trope for framing the island's racial heterogeneity.[32] The great Puerto Rican family (*la gran familia puertorriqueña*) discursively constructs Puerto Rico as a patriarchal, inclusive, and mestizo nation.[33] In her monumental essay on race, anthropologist Arlene Torres notes that despite its use as a seemingly inclusive metaphor, the trope of the Puerto Rican family benefited only a small segment of the island's *criollo* elite while it whitened, disciplined, and silenced Puerto Rico's largely Black and biracial laboring classes.

Torres challenged scholars in Puerto Rican studies to account more adequately for the ways in which discursive and material constructions of the Puerto Rican national family stifle Blackness and difference. By recounting the repeated encounters among journalists, artists, and activists in the United States and Puerto Rico, *Seams of Empire* takes up this challenge. But the chapters that follow show that it is not sufficient to chart or acknowledge Blackness as a living or dynamic presence within Puerto Rican historiography. I do not wish to simply complement, revise, or enhance *la gran familia puertorriqueña*. Rather, in this book I ask that Puerto Rican studies scholars banish it as an analytic lens.[34]

At a basic level *la gran familia puertorriqueña* restricts the scope of the social formations and identities we consider within the parameters of the nation-state. Migrants to Puerto Rico from the Dominican Republic, Haiti, and parts of Asia have historically been shunned from the "family" or relegated to tokenization. Furthermore, treating Blackness as the corrective additive to a grotesque nationalist historiography only fetishizes

Blackness. It also subscribes to assimilationist or pluralist myths about the perfectibility of the nation-state without challenging the premises under which that nation is imagined and constituted. Puerto Rican nationalism often counters colonial exclusion with its own troubling forms of marginalization, including the disavowal of queer subjects and members of the diaspora.

*Seams of Empire* rethinks race and nation in Puerto Rico by decentering these dangerous nationalisms that reproduce discourses of exclusion.[35] Approaching material culture as a site of contestation, rather than simply as a site where domination is enacted, I explore the contradictions and unforeseen identifications between Puerto Rican activists and African American and white American liberal writers in the middle decades of the twentieth century.[36] Resisting the lure of comparative approaches that conceal and reduce these identifications and contradictions, I instead propose racial imbrication as a theoretical and methodological concept for studying race within Puerto Rico's colonial relationship with the United States.

In architecture or botany, *imbrication* describes the arrangement of tiles, roof shingles, leaves, or flower petals so that their outer edges overlap with one another. I first encountered the word in Lisa Lowe's essay "Insufficient Difference," where she notes that *imbrication* and other terms such as *encounters, entanglements,* and *intimacies* offer possibilities to "excavate what has been suppressed under the rubric of [comparative] difference."[37] Although Lowe does not expand upon the term, I argue that racial imbrication occurs at the structured and relational meeting points along the margins of racial regimes.

But racial imbrication eschews simplistic and celebratory readings of relational exchanges. In imbrication, a part of the subject of study is necessarily hidden from view at the point of structural overlap. Unless these points of imbrication are exposed under duress, they must be actively sought out and assessed. Not to do so risks leaving the social haunting unaccounted for even as it repeats itself in the same observable pattern. The concept of imbrication therefore reveals the contradictory meanings and social formations produced at the political edges of racial regimes while also exposing what the overlapping connections concealed from view.

The chapters that follow use racial imbrication in two interrelated ways. First, racial imbrication is a methodological tool that enables sociologists to make specific linkages among varying and diverse racial regimes. As a methodological concept racial imbrication directs scholars to the unexpected yet organized points of overlap among seemingly diverse points of difference. As a sociological method, racial imbrication requires that these areas of convergence be rigorously questioned and analyzed. When used properly, racial imbrication tracks and explicates the historical hauntings within dominant scholarly literature.

But imbrication involves more than the structured connections between racial regimes. It is also the process through which people understand and contest social structures. The writers and activists in this study looked to other national spaces to constitute new meanings about race in their local and national contexts. Although the marginalization of antiracist and anticolonial activists such as Ana Livia Cordero by nationalists in the 1960s (discussed in chapter 5) can be interpreted as an intentional act of erasure, I do not wish to imply that the cultural workers profiled in this book always deliberately undertook acts of imbrication. In general, they made these linkages without consciously understanding the full ramifications and meanings behind their actions. Nonetheless, their political and cultural work highlights how imbricative practices helped imagine and create new class, racial, national, and gendered arrangements.

Secondly, as a theoretical lens, racial imbrication facilitates a more complete understanding of social movement histories and their contradictory relationship with race, diaspora, and gender. Rethinking the historiography of the political Left in Puerto Rico and the United States exposes the hidden encounters of marginalized subjects within the very spaces popularly conceived of as liberal or progressive. In particular, racial imbrication helps to explain how progressive Puerto Rican and U.S. intellectuals on the island and within the continental United States mobilized understandings about diaspora and gender through a racial lens. Nationalist representations of the diaspora, for example, illustrated the dangers of colonialism in ways that ultimately were tacitly racist and undergirded by bigoted assumptions about Black urban life. Moreover, racial imbrication helps us to make sense of the radical antiracist work undertaken by a community of activists led by Ana Livia Cordero, who had been cast out of the broader *independentista* movement.

Historically, Black writers across disciplines have also been excluded from a canon dominated by writings that made Eurocentric, normative, and patriarchal formations central to their analyses. Using a version of what W.E.B. Du Bois termed double consciousness,[38] Black writers effectively articulated from the margins distinct theoretical insights that breathed new life into social movements even if they ultimately failed or remained hidden. Despite their limited success, this cluster of marginalized intellectuals and activists created a substantial body of work that demands our attention. It is in these spaces of racial imbrication that radical alternatives to racism and imperialism are produced, challenged, and reconfigured. Looking at these points of imbrication, the subsequent chapters offer a critical reading of the array of racial hauntings that trouble nationalist narratives of U.S. and Puerto Rican racial formations.

## Organization of the Book

Chapters 1 and 2 examine the writings of African American journalists who visited Puerto Rico beginning in the 1940s. The interest in Puerto Rico that Black journalists expressed was not accidental or merely the random musings of tourists passing as journalists in the tropics. Chapter 1 shows that the rapid deterioration of economic and social conditions in Puerto Rico coincided with two significant sociopolitical forces in the Black community in the United States. The first was the rise of Black radicalism among large segments of Black laborers as well as intellectuals. In spite of the increased activism and solidarity within the Black Left, Blacks remained marginalized within larger Leftist political organizations such as the Communist Party. At the same time, Black Leftists modeled and aligned their political demands within the broader coalitional politics of Black internationalism developing at the time. Nonetheless, because most African Americans in that era did not have the material resources to travel or move outside the United States, Black internationalism remained a limited lens for making sense of and radically altering the conditions that the domestic Black community faced at the time.

The second social formation, the Black press, wrote through this tension. In chapter 2 I analyze the writings of *Chicago Defender* journalist Deton Brooks and *Pittsburgh Courier* guest contributor Dr. George Little, both of whom visited Puerto Rico in 1942 and 1943. Using the island's colonial status, Puerto Ricans' citizenship status, and their construction as racialized subjects as points of departure, Brooks and Little wrote about

Puerto Rico's massive land and economic reforms and critically investigated how the same reforms might be implemented in the U.S. South to empower African Americans. Puerto Rico became an important lens through which marginalized groups thought about their relationship to U.S. racial capitalism and how to labor against it. In spite of these positive relational affinities between Puerto Rico and African Americans, Black journalists also produced their own problematic readings of race in Puerto Rico, as this chapter documents.

Similar to Black journalists, progressive white Americans also reflected and wrote about Puerto Rico's colonial and racial politics. Chapters 3 and 4 tell the stories of little-known liberal white writers who analyzed the material conditions of Black labor and poverty in the United States and Puerto Rico. Using the island's class-based racial structure, these writers aligned Puerto Rico's presumed racial democracy with U.S. liberal (colorblind) ideologies of race.

A self-described "ex-Nordic," southern liberal Harold Preece made labor and antiracist organizing part of his life's work. Between 1943 and 1946 Preece wrote two nationally syndicated columns in the Black press. The first, "The Living South," radically reimagined a new racial order in the U.S. South built around class-based alliances between poor white and Black laborers. In his efforts to visualize what this new racial order might look like, Preece simultaneously penned "The Living Negro in Latin America." In this extensive and never before analyzed series, Preece detailed the history, traditions, and politics of the Black diaspora in Latin America. Using his writings about Puerto Rico, I show in chapter 3 that Preece hoped to use Latin American racial formations as a model for the U.S. South. Driven by his desire to create a broad transnational, multiracial, and class-based social movement, Preece ultimately succumbed to reducing race and labor relations in Latin America to fit under the umbrella of racial democracy.

Edwin Rosskam worked as a photographer for the Farm Security Administration (FSA) during the New Deal before serving in a variety of roles within the Puerto Rican government throughout the 1940s and 1950s. In 1964 Rosskam published *The Alien,* a novel based on his time in Puerto Rico. A white liberal like Preece, Rosskam depicted Puerto Rico as a space where American progressives could comfortably settle without having to be burdened by the cultural and political baggage of U.S. race relations. Chapter 4 illustrates how Rosskam used popular sociological mechanisms to sidestep race-based connections between the continental United States and the island. While Rosskam's novel explored the productive possibilities of class-based coalitions, its emphasis on a colorblind politic reinforced whiteness and characterized the Puerto Rican diaspora as a contaminated and racialized class of outsiders to the nation.

In the final chapter I consider the silences created by the connective political affinities between the Puerto Rican Left and Pan-Africanist internationalism. As the fractured *independentista* Puerto Rican Left looked to redefine itself during the late 1950s and 1960s, it built strategic alliances with Black radicals working in the United States and internationally. *Independentista* Ana Livia Cordero, a doctor and the wife of African American author Julian Mayfield, worked in Ghana as a physician and researcher from 1963 to 1967. Influenced by her interactions with prominent radical Black intellectuals in Ghana and the United States, Cordero spent the rest of her life in Puerto Rico building an anticolonial project centered on Puerto Rican Blackness. In chapter 5 I argue that Cordero's efforts were severely undermined and constrained not only by harsh police repression but also by the patriarchal structure of the larger Puerto Rican nationalist movement and its unwillingness to engage Puerto Rican racism.

The conclusion discusses how these hidden histories of racial imbrication help to make sense of the recent migration trends of Puerto Ricans and the island's contemporary political and racial climate. Thereby, I pursue the concerns expressed by Juanita Seguinot and Pablo Marcano García. Their thinking is part of a larger Black radical tradition that rethought the stories we are told about race and empire. They demonstrate that we cannot be content to be driven down the main avenues of history to see only those things the people in power would have us see. Instead, we must also learn to venture into the spaces of racial imbrication that both enact and oppose racial power.

# The Puerto Rican Blueprint

A tired Deton Brooks sat down on an early July 1943 morning to type his first column for the *Chicago Defender* from a desk in San Juan, Puerto Rico. Getting to San Juan had proved arduous for the reporter. Days earlier, Brooks had left Chicago on a two-day trip to Miami, Florida, where he boarded a Pan American Airlines flight to the island. The difficulty of Brooks's trip to Miami had nothing to do with the distance he traveled. Rather, as Brooks made his way by train to the southernmost point in the continental United States he witnessed and felt the harsh realities of Jim Crow segregation. These experiences reminded him of his standing as a second-class citizen in the United States. The dehumanizing encounters extended beyond his segregated train ride and his housing at Miami's all-Black Lowrie Hotel.[1]

In Miami, waiting to board his flight, matters got worse for Brooks. Because he would be traveling to Latin America, workers questioned whether or not Brooks had a right to eat his complimentary breakfast in the same dining area as whites. To resolve the issue, a manager escorted Brooks to a side room and said she hoped he understood enough English to read the menu.[2] By the time Brooks boarded his flight to San Juan, his marginal status within the United States had come into even sharper focus. Not only did Brooks require "separate but equal" accommodations, he no longer even appeared to belong in the United States.

All of this weighed on Brooks's mind as he typed away in the humid San Juan summer. Puerto Rico presented its own challenges for Brooks. "Color is a delicate problem to the Spanish-Speaking American" on the island, he wrote in one of his first articles after arriving in Puerto Rico.[3] Witnessing family members with different complexions and features walking alongside each other on the streets of Puerto Rico and entering the same social spaces shocked Brooks. Based on his experience in the continental United States, Brooks speculated that "color" must be something Puerto Ricans "keep in the background."[4] This observation fascinated Brooks so much that he believed the success of Puerto Rico to be critical to the larger war effort. In order for the United States to accomplish its goals in World War II—including projecting itself as a beacon of equality in the face of fascism—Brooks felt that Americans had to learn a lot from tiny Puerto Rico.

U.S. military brass and government officials, however, viewed the island with greater uncertainty. For its part, the U.S. military intended to use the island as a strategic colonial outpost for its wartime military maneuvers in the Atlantic. Puerto Rico and the larger Lesser Antilles served as tactical points of entry into the Caribbean and, more importantly, the Panama Canal Zone. Throughout World War II, German submarines exacted a huge toll on ships in the region, sinking almost 350 ships carrying food and oil supplies.[5] Puerto Rico's earlier colonial relationship to Spain also complicated the island's role in the war. Puerto Ricans continued to object to the U.S. colonial occupation of the island throughout the 1930s, with some opting to remain loyal to Spain and retain their Spanish citizenship. Found mostly in the upper echelons of Puerto Rican society, Spanish loyalists on the island faithful to military dictator Francisco Franco proved to be a security nightmare for U.S. military intelligence given Spain's ideological and material support of the Axis nations.[6]

Puerto Rico was also in the midst of a major political transition. Just two years earlier, in 1940, the Partido Popular Democrático (PPD), led by the charismatic senator Luis Muñoz Marín, assumed the presidency of the Puerto Rican Senate—at the time the highest political office for which Puerto Ricans could vote. Muñoz Marín and several others founded the PPD in 1938 shortly after their expulsion from the Liberal Party for challenging the monopolization of the sugar industry on the island. The PPD organized its party platform to appeal to Puerto Rico's class of rural proletariat farmers and peasants (jíbaros). Muñoz Marín ran primarily on the promise of major land reforms that would empower the proletariat as small landowners, a goal perfectly captured in the party's slogan of "Pan, Tierra, y Libertad" (Bread, Land, and Liberty).

The bulk of these reforms consisted of the development of farming cooperatives and the enforcement of a provision in the Organic Act of 1900 (more commonly known as the Foraker Act) that restricted ownership of land by corporations to five hundred acres. Muñoz Marín, the son of a prominent politician, campaigned by traveling from town to town, often by foot and on horseback, through the Puerto Rican countryside. During his town meetings and conversations, Muñoz Marín listened to local farmers tell of their daily struggles and needs. He hoped that by paying close attention to this rural class of agricultural laborers he might ultimately mobilize them as a large political bloc. Despite his early *independentista* sympathies, Muñoz Marín avoided the issue of the island's colonial status, believing it might internally fracture his new party. Instead, Muñoz Marin and the PPD focused on the wide-scale poverty on the island and proposed social and economic reforms rooted in the radical transformation of traditional arrangements of landownership.

Given this historical background, in this chapter I move between the island and the United States, exploring how the practice of racial imbrication was expressed in writings about Puerto Rico that appeared in the Black press in the 1940s. Reporters for the Black press facilitated a high level of synergy between Black radical thought and the practices of Black intellectuals and labor organizers. Specifically, the mid-twentieth century brought increased interest in Black sovereignty and internationalism, on which basis African Americans rethought their own subjugation and exclusion in the U.S. racial regime. Ideas about (internal) colonialism served as a crucial pivot point around which Black writers considered the unequal application of political rights and uneven economic development experienced by African Americans in the United States vis-à-vis Puerto Rico. The search for new political models outside the United States was a direct indictment of the inability of the American Left to properly address racism in its everyday organizing and institutional life.

Maintaining a race-conscious agenda that fostered some of this race radicalism, the Black press operated at the margins of the mainstream media, struggling to secure enough advertising revenue to maintain its operations. As this chapter shows, in spite of the challenges of writing from the margins, the Black press made significant interventions in the study of U.S. race relations through its coverage of diasporic racial regimes that more effectively linked racism and imperial endeavors. Specifically, looking to Puerto Rico helped African Americans bridge their domestic political and economic struggles with a growing (Black) international-ism. Puerto Rico's colonial status enabled the Black press to make larger connections between racism, imperialism, and global capitalism. Using Puerto Rico as their point of reference, Black journalists made invaluable connections between the practices of the U.S. racial regime and of colo-nialism even as they imagined new conditions for Black life based on the island's radical land reform program.

## Unfinished Reconstruction and the Rise of Black Radicalism

Northwest and across the Atlantic Ocean from Puerto Rico in the U.S. South, land reform remained an unfulfilled promise. In 1935 W.E.B. Du Bois published *Black Reconstruction in America*, his classic treatise on the post–Civil War moment when the United States could have permanently altered the racialized dimensions of economic inequality in the antebel-lum South. The radical structural transformations he proposed included building schools for Black children, electing African American legislators to state senates, and passing major pieces of legislation rooted in prin-ciples of land reform.

However, the structural gains made in the first decade following the Civil War proved difficult to maintain in the face of White resentment and violence.[7] Du Bois concluded that the "lawlessness" that never ceased in the South following the Civil War undermined the radical projects un-dertaken by African Americans and white progressives. During the early twentieth century white laborers and violent clandestine groups like the Ku Klux Klan perpetrated much of this lawlessness. Du Bois documented that white labor "joined the white landholder and capitalist and beat the black laborer into subjection through secret organizations and the rise of a new doctrine of race hatred."[8]

The need for industrial labor created by the advent of World War I cou-pled with the failure of Reconstruction ultimately pushed millions of Afri-can Americans north. Between 1910 and 1935 more than 200,000 African Americans settled in Chicago alone.[9] While migration provided greater work opportunities, it did not mean an escape from racism or racialized terror. African Americans migrating north to cities like Chicago faced re-strictive racial covenants that prevented the renting or sale of housing to nonwhites.[10] The Chicago race riots of 1919, for example, reminded these migrants that violence remained a looming threat against African Americans regardless of where in the United States they lived.

Given these circumstances it is not surprising that radicalism flourished among Black workers and intellectuals in the first decades of the twentieth century. Political scientist Cedric Robinson defines the Black radical tradition as the Black diaspora's historical negotiation and analysis of Western racial capitalism and imperialism, and its own resistance to what Patricia Hill Collins refers to as the "matrix of domination."[11] Du Bois and his contemporaries, including Booker T. Washington and Ida B. Wells, wrestled with the outcomes of the failed period of Reconstruction and how African Americans might radically rework their place in American society.[12] These prominent Black thinkers thought of the workplace as a pivotal location where African Americans valiantly proved their worth and value to the nation. Between 1910 and 1920 the number of Black industrial workers almost doubled, from 550,000 to more than 900,000.[13] Industrial factories and mills were not the only places where African Americans proved their worth to the nation. During the same period another half million African Americans joined the ranks of the U.S. Armed Forces.[14] One month before the United States entered World War I, Puerto Ricans were granted a form of U.S. citizenship under the terms of the Jones-Shafroth Act of 1917, enabling their conscription into the Armed Forces. These Puerto Rican troops contained a significant number of segregated units that often served alongside African Americans.

Like Reconstruction, the end of World War I proved to be a difficult time of disillusionment for African Americans. Despite having fought for freedom on their country's behalf, they continued to experience daily threats of racial violence and discrimination. Feeling that black workers had displaced them from jobs in factories and on shipping docks, resentful white soldiers returning from the war openly clashed with African American industrial workers and soldiers. For African American soldiers, their time abroad had imbued them with a stronger sense of their rights as members of U.S. society. In a context of growing discrimination, violence, and unemployment, African Americans developed and turned to other models of social life as a way to counter the increasing threats against Black personhood in the United States. Marcus Garvey's Universal Negro Improvement Association (UNIA), Cyril Briggs's African Blood Brotherhood (ABB) and the International Workers of the World (IWW) emerged as vital Black nationalist or socialist organizations where African Americans confronted and proposed alternative models of Black life.[15] Other segments of the U.S. Left at the time, most notably the U.S. Communist Party (CPUSA), did not look kindly upon Garvey's brand of Black nationalism. For his part, Garvey harbored an even stronger dislike for communism and socialism and maintained a relative faith in Western capitalism.

In spite of these disagreements, the CPUSA made significant efforts to attract the growing black industrial class to its ranks, and offered an appealing political organization for African American workers. One of the more prominent strategies of the CPUSA was to center Black oppression within its political platform. Though mostly symbolic, this approach provided an important tool to work against racism not only in general but within the party rank and file.

The CPUSA stance on Black oppression ("the Negro Question") focused on the reformulation of the communist position on nationalism (chauvinism) and the right to self-determination. Specifically, chauvinism and self-determination would only compromise the success of the larger class struggle by promoting the national interests of the dominant bourgeois class. Yet the CPUSA had to contend with the reality that racism flourished within the ranks of its own party, while many African American workers were dissatisfied with the overall emphasis on class struggle as the official party doctrine. This approach asked African Americans to suppress their criticism of the racialized nature of Western capitalism even as they continued to face racial violence and discrimination in their everyday lives and within the CPUSA.[16]

Working to counter this deterrent, Vladimir Lenin broke with the party line organized exclusively around a politics of class and argued instead that self-determination was a key component of the larger struggle against imperialism and should be used to unite the international laboring class. Historian Robin Kelley notes that Lenin's position "created an opening for African Americans to articulate nationalist ideologies in spite of the Party's formal opposition to Negro Nationalism."[17] Lenin's reconsideration of the nationalist question perhaps unintentionally created an opportunity for Black workers to reassess their exclusive commitment to the radical work of Black nationalist organizations such as the UNIA and the ABB, both of which garnered strength from notions of Pan-Africanism and internationalism more generally. "The Communist movement's internationalism," argues Kelley, "not only appropriated the familiar idioms of Pan-Africanism, but in many ways it cleared the way for a vision of black anti-imperialism that could transcend without negating a completely racialized worldview."[18] Kelley's point is instructive because it highlights the ways in which Black radical thought unified the intimately related processes of colonialism, capitalism, and global racism.

The CPUSA's platform of Pan-Africanist internationalism rooted in the right to self-determination culminated in 1928 during the Sixth World Congress of the Comintern with the party's recognition of the Black Belt theory. The Black Belt theory contended that African Americans constituted an oppressed majority in the U.S. South. As such, African Americans were a nation within a nation, entitled to the right of self-determination. This configuration of Black nationhood served as the first full articulation of what later Black thinkers would label internal colonialism as a description of the ways in which African Americans constituted a dominated and exploited social group within the United States.[19]

The Black Belt theory also recognized that African Americans, in addition to being a numerical majority in the U.S. South, were descendants of a unique intellectual and cultural tradition that further substantiated their claim to nationhood. For the CPUSA and Lenin, the cultural autonomy of African American workers constituted an even more significant rationale for the right of Black self-determination.[20] This emphasis resulted in the reification and essentialization of Black culture and ultimately eviscerated the political components of Black sovereignty. Because of this emphasis on Black culture and the already undergirding emphasis on class within the Communist Party, Black national sovereignty remained an under-theorized and abstract political claim. Accordingly, the Black Belt theory as a political model for Black nationhood never found any real traction at the local level of the CPUSA.

The closure of Black self-determination as an avenue of redress for African Americans resulted in a turn toward Black internationalism. Through a Black internationalist frame African Americans hoped to move across national and cultural spaces in order to challenge the essentialism found within the CPUSA.[21] The turn toward internationalism in African American political thought shaped an analysis of the relationship between local formulations of Black dispossession and Black cultural and political subjugation across the globe from the period of the Great Depression through the end of World War II. The shift toward internationalism brought a more radical edge to Black activism as it considered the ways in which Black American politics and identity intersected with the larger Black diaspora in different parts of the globe.[22] During the 1930s and 1940s internationalism among African Americans did not necessarily result in tangible political and economic changes for Blacks residing *within* the United States.

Richard Wright's important 1937 essay "Blueprint for Negro Literature" takes on this glaring deficiency through a discussion of the divide existing between Black radical theory and everyday life. Wright's essay pushed Black authors toward a Marxist framework for their writing in order to avoid the pitfalls of nationalist rhetoric and focus instead on the "complexity" and "magic wonder" of Black personhood that thrived even under the "most sordid existence."[23] The motivation behind Wright's essay stemmed from his personal distaste for the majority of writing appearing by and about African Americans during this time. Wright remained skeptical of writers content simply to illustrate the humanity of African Americans while refusing to delve deeper into the textured richness of cultural and political life found among the Black proletariat. "Shall Negro writing," asked Wright, "be for the lives and consciousness of the Negro masses, moulding those lives and consciousness towards new goals, or shall it continue begging the question of the Negroes' humanity?"[24]

Wright believed the development of new writing directed toward the mobilization of the Black masses to be more than "propaganda" or the selling of a Black tradition.[25] Even though Wright remained skeptical of the use of Black nationalism he did not entirely abandon it, seeing it instead as a potential frame for organizing the Black diaspora. Drawing from the Leninist reconfiguration of the Negro Question discussed in the previous section, Wright understood Black nationalism not as an "inherent trait of the Negro" but as a "reflex expression whose roots are deeply imbedded in Southern soil" and the "Jim Crow system of the South . . . built upon a plantation feudal economy." Wright's reformulation of nationalism in response to Western racial capitalism provided a space for Black writers to understand the strengths and limitations of Black nationalism while still aiming for "the highest pitch of social consciousness."[26]

Wright identified the void that Marxist theory created between Black intellectuals and labor organizers as another practical limitation to any radical reimagining of U.S. race and class relations. "After Marxism [had] laid bare the skeleton of society," Wright charged that Black writers still remained responsible for "plant[ing] flesh upon those bones out of the plentitude of his will to live."[27] In taking on this assignment Black writers would confront more than the history of Western racial capitalism. They would also document the material conditions of new alternative schemas that the Black masses might use as models for living differently, or what Wright loosely termed "perspective." Defined as "an intellectual space where writers stand to view the struggles, hopes and suffering of their people,"[28] Wright's "perspective" is an emphatic call to "movement."[29] Wright demanded that Black writers ally themselves with international social movements aimed at transforming the unequal structural conditions produced by colonialism and capitalism.[30]

As Cedric Robinson notes, "words" were crucial "vitalizing tools of the radical (Black) intelligentsia."[31] For Wright and Robinson, words served as the medium for new radical imaginings rooted in the politics of struggle, labor, and everyday life. On a much deeper level, perspective exposed the commonalities among oppressed groups, or what cultural historian Gaye Johnson terms "constellations of struggle."[32] Perspective empowered Black writers to look "upon the harsh lot of their race and [compare] it with the hopes and struggles of minority peoples everywhere" until the "cold facts have begun to tell them something."[33] Wright's challenge to search for the "cold facts" was addressed to Black literary writers but was not exclusive to them. His call for a more radical form of Black imaginative writing extended to activists, academics, and, especially, to the work of the Black press.

### The Black Press in America

Most scholars trace the history of the Black press in the United States to the 1827 founding of Samuel E. Cornish and John B. Russwurm's *Freedom Journal*. Low levels of literacy among African Americans and lack of capital needed to run a national syndicate within the Black community posed major difficulties for early Black newspapers.[34] Nonetheless, the number of Black-owned periodicals continued to rise steadily through the rest of the nineteenth century, with several dozen in operation by the beginning of the Civil War. Publications picked up noticeably in the first decade of the twentieth century with the founding of what would become some of the largest Black periodicals, including the *Chicago Defender* (1905) and the *Pittsburgh Courier* (1907). Though based in northern urban centers, both newspapers had deep southern roots. Both founding editors, Robert Abbott (*Chicago Defender*) and Robert Vann (*Pittsburgh Courier*), migrated north after spending much of their early years in the South. Both men's early experiences with southern racism formed the political and social outlook that they brought to their respective papers. Abbott—the son of former slaves—worked arduously against the internalized racism in the southern Black community that valued lighter skin tones more than his darker complexion.[35]

Even as Black periodicals worked to produce a positive message around the question of race, the Black press did not share a universal message of racial uplift. Contradictory messages and stories flourished across different presses and even within a single periodical. The Black press's coverage of the Great Migration is one example of the mixed messages on racial pride. Based on the personal histories of their founding editors, several northern newspapers like the *Chicago Defender* encouraged the migration of southern Blacks to northern urban centers. Though this effort seemingly welcomed southern Blacks, historian Davarian Baldwin connects it with the simultaneous disciplining of these migrants, who were cast as "premodern." Baldwin shows that Chicago's Black middle class forced southern migrants to assimilate into traditional Victorian models of respectability and middle-class consumption habits if they expected to prosper and survive.[36]

The general task of the Black press was to maintain a delicate balance between supporting a race-conscious agenda while still attracting white advertisers in order to generate revenue.[37] Robert Abbott modeled the *Defender*'s journalistic approach on the sensationalistic tactics of William Randolph Hearst and Joseph Pulitzer, but with a greater emphasis on questions of racial justice.[38] Vann, for his part, translated his work as a defense lawyer for Black defendants into fodder for both the headlines in his newspaper and his reputation as a legal defender.[39]

The political and economic crises of the 1940s led the Black press to focus more on political issues. Described as the "golden age in Black American journalism," the war years brought the Black press unprecedented

growth in its readership and ideological reach.[40] Close to 150 Black newspapers existed in the United States in 1933, with a circulation of about
600,000. Just seven years later the number of Black newspapers soared
to 210, with a readership of 1,276,000.[41] Between 1940 and 1947 the *Pittsburgh Courier*, which expanded to open twelve branch offices across the
country, increased its circulation from 126,962 to 357,212, making it the
largest Black periodical in the country at the time.[42] The *Chicago Defender*
followed this trend, doubling its combined national and local subscrip-
tions during the same period to a high of 203,631 in 1946.[43] Historian Lee
Finkle attributes the rapid and sizable jump in circulation to the Black
press serving as a "vehicle to express the feelings of Blacks toward American society and as a means of obtaining information not found in the
white press or on the radio."[44]

But the *Courier*'s and *Defender*'s success during this period cannot
be explained simply as African Americans' desire for information or to
express their feelings. The growth of both newspapers is instead better
understood through the ways in which they situated local-level racism
within international happenings. The *Pittsburgh Courier*'s "Double Victory" (Double V) campaign against racism at home and fascism abroad is
perhaps the best example of this. The origins of the Double V campaign
are traceable to the *Courier*'s publication of a January 31, 1942, letter by
twenty-six-year-old Black service worker James G. Thompson. As the war
effort against the Axis nations ramped up, Thompson called for more critical reflection about the meaning and goals of the war. Reframing the tide
of jingoistic militarism sweeping the nation at the time, Thompson visualized both "victory over our enemies from without" and "victory over our
enemies from within."[45] Thus, adoption of the Double V campaign among
the larger Black press represented an attempt to use the war as a key opportunity to shine a global light on racial injustices on the home front.

The connection between local conditions and global formations evolved
as an extension of an earlier strategy to link local struggles to national and
global battles for racial justice. Earlier travel narratives by Black journalists focused on tours through other parts of the Americas and the United
States. For example, Robert Abbott spent much of 1923 traveling throughout Latin America, making numerous stops in Brazil, Peru, Panama, and
Cuba, among other countries.[46] Abbott's thirteen-part series on his experiences in Latin America detailed his impressions of the countries he

visited and the prevalence of prominent Black intellectuals throughout the Americas.[47] He also used the trip as an occasion to discuss race relations in the United States, most especially with Brazilian intellectuals and politicians. In spite of his positive impression of Latin American race relations, Abbott showed a larger predisposition to American exceptionalism and commitment to the U.S. racial project. In his final report Abbott noted that "no wholesale exodus of the American Negro is expected nor desired. The base of the future achievements of the Negro will remain, as now, in the United States."[48]

In 1926–27 George Schuyler, who went on to become associate editor of the *Courier*, also spent nine months touring thirteen states in the South to create a series that newspaper historian Patrick Washburn estimates increased the *Courier*'s readership by at least 20 percent.[49] Schuyler wrote extensively about the racism faced by Blacks throughout the region, as well as about the development of Black schools, businesses, and churches. Importantly, series like Schuyler's effectively connected African Americans across the United States, allowing them to draw parallels between their local plights and those of fellow Blacks in the rural countryside and in urban centers.

The *Defender* and *Courier* editors understood the appeal of such stories among their readerships and actively worked to continue providing more of them. This form of internationalist print capitalism, argues historian Penny Von Eschen, "can be observed in the sympathetic attention of the African American press to strikes across the Caribbean and West Africa."[50] By focusing on labor, the press effectively formulated economic critiques of colonial expansion alongside their analyses of race. As such, the Black press assertively took up Wright's challenge to search for "perspective." Not only did Black correspondents detail the material effects of inequality resulting from colonialism and racism, they also thought about these issues in relation to the plight of the Black community in their respective cities. Similar to Wright's position on Black nationalism, this relational approach cautiously avoided essentialist understandings of Blackness that bound Black cultural production to a single national space. By focusing on the interplay between race and political economy, Black journalists effectively imagined the plausibility of transposing different political and economic models from abroad into their local contexts.

### The Links between Freedoms

The linking of local battles for racial justice with a broader internationalism explains why the *Pittsburgh Courier* and the *Chicago Defender* each
published a series on Puerto Rico, in 1942 and 1943, respectively. In the
early months of 1942, the *Courier's* Dr. George Little departed on a three-
day boat ride to the island, where he spent about a month. Little published
his three-part special series on Puerto Rico in the *Courier* between February 21 and March 7, 1942, upon his return to Pittsburgh. The small amount
of archival documentation available on Little indicates that he moved to
Pittsburgh in the late 1930s or early 1940s. Ultimately, he settled in the
Pittsburgh suburb of Homestead in 1944 with his wife, Easter Little Baker,
and worked as one of the town's first African American physicians.[51] While
in Homestead, the Littles maintained an active profile within Pittsburgh's
elite Black social circles.[52] The limited number of articles Little published
in the *Courier* indicate that he did not work as a regular correspondent
for the paper. More than likely, Little wrote his series on Puerto Rico as
a guest contributor after visiting the island. Middle- and upper-class African Americans with enough capital to travel often published extensive
write-ups in the local Black press as a way of exposing the general readership to other parts of the world, especially to places where other members
of the Black diaspora lived.

A native of Chicago's South Side, *Defender* staff correspondent Deton
Brooks visited Puerto Rico almost a year later during an "extended tour
of the American outpost in the Caribbean."[53] After working for years as a
messenger for Union Tank Car and the Tivoli Theatre in Chicago, Brooks
planned an illustrous career in the U.S. military. In 1930 Brooks gained
admission into the U.S. Army Academy at West Point but the discovery
of a heart condition quickly ended any hopes for a career in the Armed
Forces. Brooks later attended the University of Chicago, where he majored
in mathematics and earned a master's degree in international relations
in 1937. After teaching for a short time, Brooks put his master's degree
to good use by accepting a position with the *Defender* as a foreign correspondent in 1942, following the U.S. entry into World War II.[54] In addition
to his work in Puerto Rico, Brooks spent extensive time as a journalist
in China and India throughout the duration of the war, culminating in

his witnessing of the Japanese surrender to General Douglas MacArthur aboard the USS *Missouri* in 1945.[55]

The insular government welcomed Brooks and Little to Puerto Rico with open arms. More than likely, prominent members of the government had extended invitations to both men—a common practice of the PPD administration at the time. University of Puerto Rico chancellor Jaime Benítez Rexach hosted and toured George Little around the island during his short visit. As an academic and a political moderate, Benítez emerged during the 1940s as an important collaborator within the PPD as it sought to promote Muñoz Marín's modernization project. In addition to Benítez, Little spent considerable time with renowned pianist Elsa Rivera Salgado and Felisa Rincón de Gautier (Doña Fela) who became the first female mayor in the Americas four years later.

Brooks did not specify whether a PPD politico hosted him, but it is hard to imagine an American journalist associated with such a popular press spending close to seven weeks on the island without some assistance from the insular government. In fact, throughout his stay in Puerto Rico Brooks interviewed prominent figures in the PPD-led government. One interview included the then president of the Puerto Rican Senate Luis Muñoz Marín, whose manner Brooks stated "resembled that of President Roosevelt" because of his "knack of talking in language that the 'man on the street' understands."[56]

Given his formal training with the *Defender*, it is not surprising that Brooks's series possessed a more rigorously journalistic tone than Little's writings. In the end, both accounts centered on the ways in which the struggle for freedom and democracy in Puerto Rico affected the plight of African Americans in the United States. "How could occurrences in a little subtropical island outpost 1,150 miles from Florida," asked Brooks in his first dispatch, "affect the condition of minorities here at home?" He concluded "the link between freedom for Puerto Rico and the freedom for the Negro is understandable."[57]

By contrast, Little did not immediately make the understandable "link" between Puerto Rico and African Americans that Brooks observed in his first post. Little's initial observations about Puerto Rico centered on the natural beauty of the island and its inhabitants. In fact, Little's first article included an inset entitled "Beautiful Señoritas a la Puerto Rican Style" featuring photographs of Puerto Rican "lovelies" demonstrative of the "beauty of the young women, rich and poor," on the island.[58] While a part of the larger travel narrative genre, Little's writings moved quickly beyond his initial sexist and gendered observations. By his second and third reports, Little was delving into more nuanced analysis of Puerto Rican politics and social customs.

An August 28, 1943, *Defender* editorial reveals that part of the paper's larger rationale for sending Brooks to Puerto Rico was to search for a solution to the state-sanctioned racism experienced by African Americans in the United States:

> To understand our problem [racism] in relation to world patterns is the first step in effecting a solution. Present day pressures won't let us withdraw into a shell to nurse our hurts. For a blow which looks as if it were aimed at the peoples of India, China, Africa or even at the *citizens* of the little American possession of Puerto Rico, may crush our protective covering, injuring us more deeply. Intelligent fighting of our problem, therefore requires that at times we fight the battle of others. And to do this the Negro people must be fully informed of the issues.[59]

The editorial underscored the connections between the effects of Jim Crow segregation and global patterns of inequality in far-off places like India and China. The problems found in a nearby place like Puerto Rico and its "citizens" merited equal amounts of attention. "It was this thought," reasons the editorial, "which prompted us to send an editor 2500 miles to the American possession of Puerto Rico, where with first hand information he [Brooks] has shown how certain anticipated repressive measures in that island are in part aimed at keeping *us down*."[60] The series on Puerto Rico aimed to think imaginatively about the island as an archetype illustrating a newfound perspective on the racial injustices experienced by African Americans.

Brooks and Little were moved by what they saw during their time in Puerto Rico. Little found the island an "invigorating" place and made special note of the people's numerous customs. He also made special mention of the "courtesy" Puerto Ricans extended him throughout his time on the island.[61] By giving their readers a sense of local customs and the treatment they received while in Puerto Rico Little and Brooks implicitly confirmed what African Americans back home already suspected: African Americans were treated with more dignity in *other* countries than in *their own*. Keeping the racialized violence and exclusion experienced by African Americans in mind gives a sense of why the customs and manners of Puerto Ricans mattered so much to both men.[62] But in order for Brooks and Little to fully capture the imaginative possibilities of a place like Puerto Rico for their readership, they needed to do more than talk about notions of respectability or propriety. As their readers (many of them southern Blacks who had migrated north) also knew, respectability had its limits. Not surprisingly then, Black journalists generally avoided essentialist understandings about the politics of race in the places they wrote about.

Brooks and Little devoted significant attention to the material conditions and political possibilities of the island. As discussed in the next chapter, both men wrote extensively about colonialism, Western racial capitalism, and land reform. All three variables remained important points of reference that shaped the creative possibilities for a different America. Penny Von Eschen argues that the similarities between African Americans and other populations in the Global South were not always predicated on the supposed biological characteristics they shared with one another.[63] Instead, the alignment of different but relationally situated communities was a result of the historical legacy of colonialism and the transatlantic slave trade that ultimately gave rise to capitalism. Simply stated, the perverse history of racial capitalism in the Americas was what bound African Americans and Puerto Ricans.

Black writers did not limit themselves to Puerto Rico when theorizing their relationship to imperialism and capitalism. Trinidadian writer and London correspondent for the *Defender* George Padmore devoted the majority of his analysis to British colonialism in the English-speaking Caribbean, Africa, and India. The son of a school headmaster in Trinidad, Padmore developed a distaste for imperialism in his early years as a writer under Edward J. Partridge, "an Englishman who demanded subservience from his Black staff."[64] The Italian invasion of Ethiopia in 1935 motivated Padmore and fellow Trinidadian radical C.L.R. James to found the International African Service Bureau (IASB), a Pan-African advocacy organization devoted to class struggle and national liberation. In its early years the IASB openly lobbied for a proletarian revolution among colonies in Africa, though its position shifted in later years to achieving independence through nonviolence and reform.

Though typically emphasizing British colonialism, Padmore's reports in the *Defender* portrayed colonialism as a tool deployed by all global powers and one that decimated populations throughout the third world. One place where Padmore expressed the intimate relationship between U.S. and British colonialism was in regard to the Atlantic Charter. Agreed to by Franklin Roosevelt and Winston Churchill, the Atlantic Charter affirmed principles of international justice and human rights. Though not a formally binding treaty, the charter expressed certain rights of all nations, including the right to self-determination, and called for an end to territorial expansion.

In the pages of the *Defender* Padmore harshly reprimanded Churchill once the prime minister began to backtrack on these commitments by arguing that the charter applied only to the regions of Europe ravaged by Hitler, not to the "regions and peoples which owe allegiance to the British Crown."[65] As Britain vacillated, Padmore argued that at least the United States—through its interactions with Puerto Rico—appeared to take the words of the charter seriously. Referring to the then recent announcement that in 1948 Puerto Ricans would be empowered to elect their own governor, Padmore cited a local paper that wrote the United States was "setting an example in liberalizing colonial administration and accepting the right of peoples freely to choose their own governments."[66]

Padmore and other Black journalists also focused on various crises and revolutions taking place in the Americas and beyond, including Mexico, Brazil, Cuba, and the Philippines. The American popular imaginary racialized the populations of these different spaces much as they did African Americans—as children of the tropics dependent on the United States for their moral, political, and social development. At the same time, these national spaces also represented useful points of imbrication for African Americans contemplating their standing in the United States. Discussing the Spanish-American War of 1898, cultural historian Amy Kaplan notes that the "negative identification of the Cubans . . . and the Filipinos as 'colored' found contradictory political interpretations among African Americans." Kaplan shows that within the U.S. imperialist project, African Americans played the role of "mediators" between the U.S. government and its new racialized colonial subjects. But Kaplan also uncovers why these new colonies—imagined as free of racial strife—functioned as valuable models for African Americans.[67]

Though the United States controlled several territories after the Spanish-American War, most had limited appeal to African Americans: the Teller Amendment of 1898 prohibited the United States from annexing Cuba and the Jones Act of 1916 limited Filipinos to the status of "wards without citizenship rights."[68] There is also no record of African Americans ever migrating en masse to live in any of the new colonial territories the United States acquired by force during the Spanish-American War. As a result, Puerto Rico's importance for Black journalists stemmed from its possibility as a space to bridge internationalist and domestic political struggles. The island's continued colonial status, meanwhile, also facilitated their ability to draw larger connections among imperialism, racism, and global capitalism. The granting of citizenship to Puerto Ricans on the island allowed Black correspondents to map the limits and the possibilities of American citizenship.

Following the Spanish-American War, the citizenship status of Puerto Ricans remained unclear. The Foraker Act of 1900 served as a temporary agreement establishing a military regime on the island—led by a governor handpicked by then U.S. president William McKinley—while Congress debated whether to annex the island or grant it independence. The Foraker Act granted Puerto Ricans the appearance of a representative democracy, establishing a Puerto Rican house of representatives whose thirty-five members were popularly elected. It did not, however, extend citizenship to Puerto Ricans or formally incorporate the island into the United States.[69] Accordingly, the Foraker Act is one of the earliest indications of the U.S. government's intent to place the island in an ambiguous and precariously defined political and legal status.

Racialized understandings of Puerto Ricans as immoral and lacking intelligence account for much of the early ambiguity around the territorial status of the island. George Milton Fowles's ethnographic account *Down in Porto Rico* (1906) is one of the earliest racialized portrayals of Puerto Ricans following the U.S. occupation of the island.[70] Fowles, who spent a year in Puerto Rico, sought to provide readers with a "picture of Porto Rican life as it now exists" without attempting to "cover up the mistakes and shortcomings of Porto Ricans, Spaniards, or Americans."[71]

Emphasizing his own Protestant individualism and the "shortcomings" of Puerto Ricans, Fowles argued that Puerto Rican deficiencies evolved from the island's relationship with the Spanish colonial regime and

Spanish traditionalism. Even so, Fowles also made it abundantly clear that there were few Spaniards, or "pure whites," in Puerto Rico; a "large percentage of persons of mixed blood" who "cannot eradicate the unmistakable signs of the negro race" permeated Puerto Rican society.[72] Fowles's general observations thus define clear distinctions among Puerto Ricans on both class and racial lines.

In spite of this racialized context, the Jones Act of 1917 unilaterally conferred U.S. citizenship upon Puerto Ricans (without their input). This U.S. citizenship was limited, however, in that the Jones Act granted Puerto Ricans neither formal representation in Congress nor the right to vote in presidential elections. As Representative James Harvey Davis of Texas animatedly summed up during the 1916 congressional hearings, "The fact that [Puerto Ricans] are under the flag does not mean much except that you are American citizens and that we have our paws on you."[73]

The institutionalized and racialized nature of the second-class citizenship imposed upon Puerto Ricans made them valuable points of imbrication for Black journalists like Brooks and Little. More precisely, the very nature of Puerto Rico's subjugated status *within* the United States engendered new re-imaginations of citizenship among African Americans. As John Robert Badger noted in the *Defender*'s regular "World View" column: "It is difficult to overestimate Puerto Rico's significance in the struggle for a democratic America, with which the Negro's whole quest for first class citizenship is inextricably linked. More than we think, the Puerto Rican question plays a key role in the domestic politics of the United States."[74] Although countries such as Ethiopia, Algeria, and India functioned as useful international points of reference to discuss Pan-Africanism or Black personhood, they still remained *outside* the formal political and legal jurisdiction of the United States. This legal externality severed the possibility of transposing Pan-African schemas to the U.S. racial regime.

On the other hand, Puerto Rico's dual status as both foreign and domestic (albeit colonial) presented African Americans with a tangible link to claims about Black nationhood and citizenship.[75] Referring to the Atlantic Charter in another report, Badger explicitly connected Puerto Rican colonialism with the demand for Black sovereignty within the United States. Alluding to Churchill's and Roosevelt's convenient omissions of application of the charter, Badger commented, "Churchill made a mental omission of Africa and India, while Mr. Roosevelt's cronies back home would like to forget Puerto Rico and the 'home colonials' of America, the 13,000,000 Black Americans."[76] Just as Padmore had done, Badger exposed the selective application of the Atlantic Charter. However, he also importantly expanded earlier imaginings of the Black Belt theory and notions of domestic colonialism. That is, he extended the call for Black self-determination and nationhood beyond the South and to the larger population of Black "home colonials."

Regardless of Badger's radical reimagining of Black nationhood, the significance that African American intellectuals attached to the granting of U.S. citizenship represents their continued investment in ideas about democracy at the domestic and international levels. Discussing Pan-Americanism at the onset of World War II, journalist Frank Bolden noted,

> At the same time we must eliminate color discrimination at home or these Pan-American allies will not be sold on the United States' ideas of democracy, and that indeed would prove fatal to the cause for which we are fighting. It is being proved daily that the 'white democracies' cannot persecute this war to a desirable finish without giving recognition and assurance to the colored people of the world that they TOO ARE WELCOME AT HOME AND ABROAD.[77]

That is, principles of inclusion and freedom outlined in the U.S. Constitution remained unfulfilled and contradictory promises for African Americans and other marginalized populations in the U.S. national body.

## Conclusion

Recognizing the overlapping relationship between the plight of African Americans and Puerto Ricans and the efforts of the U.S. government to dismantle socialism and communism in the United States during the war years made a turn toward Puerto Rico as a model for change a worthy endeavor for African American writers. Coverage of Puerto Rico by the Black press corps enabled a deep synergy and overlap between Black radical thought and the political possibilities of a place like Puerto Rico. "The fate of the Negro, the Jew, the laboring classes, in fact most of America's minorities," proclaimed Brooks in his July 31 report, "will be decided by what happens in Puerto Rico."[78] Puerto Rico's colonial status emerged as a key variable that allowed Black intellectuals and writers to consider the domestic inequality in application of rights and economic development to African Americans. The study and use of Puerto Rico by these thinkers simultaneously served to rebuke the larger white U.S. Left and its failures to adequately address racism discursively and, more importantly, in its organizational practices.

The popularity and importance of the Black press in the Black community made it an ideal location to draw broader connections between different racial regimes and the Black diaspora. Its discussions of imperialism, racism, and global capitalism in Puerto Rico bridged the U.S. Black diaspora with an emergent Black internationalism. But the forms of imbrication between Puerto Rico and Black communities in the United States were not limited to abstract political connections about imperialism or even democracy.

As I discuss in the next chapter, the reorganization of Puerto Rico's insular government and economy around a program of land reform during the 1940s represented an important material and structural point of reference for Black journalists. Specifically, racial imbrication requires more than acknowledging encounters of difference that exist at the margins. It also requires an understanding of the material conditions of how those margins are conceptualized. Drawing on the massive land and economic reforms the PPD implemented in the 1940s, Brooks and Little discovered the material forms of "perspective" that Puerto Rico could provide. Detailed analysis of these material forms helped these Black journalists to rethink and challenge the failures of U.S. policy with respect to African Americans and how Puerto Rico's land reforms might be implemented in the southern United States.

# 2

# Dispatches from
# the Colonial Outpost

Optimism reigned supreme in early-1940s Puerto Rico. Deton Brooks had the utmost confidence in Luis Muñoz Marín and his recently founded PPD. In his second report from Puerto Rico, dated July 3, 1943, Brooks described the "Populars" (Populares) as a party that had "sprung from the discontent of hungry, poverty-stricken farmers and came to power in two short years." Muñoz Marín's leadership, Brooks opined, endowed Puerto Rico's displaced and landless proletariat with "hope for a better way of life."[1] But there is a deeper history behind Brooks's faith in the PPD and the conflicts that arose about the party's reform program. The story behind both narratives can be traced back to Franklin D. Roosevelt's only presidential visit to the island nearly a decade earlier. During this visit, in July 1934, President Roosevelt seemed mildly surprised by the progress the island had made since the first years of the twentieth century. Roosevelt noted in his arrival speech that housing, health, and work conditions for the island's inhabitants could be improved through an application of the New Deal policies he had implemented in the United States. Ever the optimist, Roosevelt stated Puerto Rico's best days were yet to come.[2]

Muñoz Marín expressed admiration for Roosevelt's New Deal and his interest in the island as he welcomed the president to Puerto Rico. The Puerto Rican senator described Roosevelt's presidential visit as "justification" and a "seal and a pledge" that the people of Puerto Rico should have hope for the future. Just as the president had done, Muñoz Marín envisioned Puerto Rico progressing. But he expressed the idea of progress differently than the U.S. president who spoke before him had. Commenting on the "progress" Roosevelt had alluded to, Muñoz Marín countered "there has been a very noticeable progress along one line, and an undeniable increase in human suffering along another line."[3] He cited advances in road construction and minor gains in sanitation control as things to be proud of. Yet human misery had also *progressed* on the island: "The increase in human suffering has been in the lives of the mass of people—in the loss of the lands which they owned and cultivated; in the passing of their control of these lands to great corporations, mostly absentee owned."[4] The concentration of wealth in the hands of sugar monopolies remained an impediment to Puerto Rico's modernization project.

The Black press noted the extreme concentrations of wealth against widespread poverty as a glaring contradiction in the island's efforts at modernization. This chapter explores the material connections that Deton Brooks and George Little made between Puerto Rico and the American South. More specifically, their imbricated readings of Puerto Rico's economic and social reforms organized around land redistribution facilitated a radical reimagining of land tenure and citizenship in the southern United States. Equating Puerto Rico's displaced proletariat with southern sharecroppers, Brooks and Little highlighted the connection between race and uneven capitalist development in both spaces.

At the end of the chapter, however, I also illustrate how racial imbrication accounts for the traps and shortcomings that Black journalists fell into when documenting race on the island. At times their desire to establish affinities between African American and Puerto Rican political and economic struggles obscured or severely limited their analyses of local manifestations of racial difference. Lastly, I demonstrate how the PPD's economic and social reforms—once thought of as radical—were transformed as the party moved beyond the margins. As the PPD ascended to the dominant ruling bloc, many of their progressive reforms wilted and were left by the wayside. Prominent Black thinkers who felt betrayed by the PPD's drastic political shift retaliated quickly, ultimately ending the brief moment where Black and Puerto Rican radical imaginaries coalesced along the axis of race and empire.

### Plan Chardón: Reform and Opposition

In the early months of 1934, Congress approved the Jones-Costigan Act, more commonly referred to as the Sugar Act, which increased the amount of sugar produced domestically in the United States. The implementation of the Sugar Act exposed the Puerto Rican economy's vulnerability to market fluctuations under sugar monoculture. Under the hotly contested terms of the Sugar Act, Puerto Rico lost its privileged U.S. market status.[5] Instead, the island found itself behind the sugar-beet-producing states in the western United States, and even behind other sugar-producing colonies within the U.S. empire. Cuba and the Philippines far outpaced Puerto Rico with quotas of 1,902,000 and 1,015,000 tons of sugar, respectively.[6] Puerto Rico's quota of 802,000 tons even fell behind Hawaii (917,000 tons), which had recently been formally annexed as a U.S. territory.[7] The Puerto Rican "sugar kingdom" had begun its steep decline.[8]

With sugar production no longer a dependable source of revenue or employment, Roosevelt signed Executive Order 7057 in May 1935, establishing the Puerto Rican Reconstruction Administration (PRRA). The PRRA replaced the Puerto Rico Emergency Relief Administration (PRERA) established two years earlier. PRERA had implemented many of the same New Deal programs enacted in the continental United States, in an effort to curtail the widespread misery brought on by the Great Depression. The PRRA continued much of this work with a focus on combating poverty and increasing the island's dismal unemployment rate. A PRRA research report indicated that in 1934 unemployment on the island directly or indirectly affected close to 75 percent of the total population.[9]

Families also struggled to keep up with the growing cost of living on the island, given the meager earnings available in the deteriorating agricultural sector. The ever-increasing cost of many basic necessities that were imported to the island added to the already difficult burden on families.[10] A Federal Relief Administration study calculated that, in 1935, a weekly income of $7.14 was needed in order to pay for basic subsistence needs, including food and shelter. However, in 1936 agricultural workers cultivating coffee and sugar still averaged only between $3.00 and $4.90 weekly, respectively.[11]

The PRRA, under inaugural director Ernest H. Gruening, was part of the Department of the Interior. A liberal firmly in line with many of Roosevelt's New Deal policies, Gruening strongly supported land redistribution and opposed large private monopolies.[12] Within the PRRA, Gruening established the Puerto Rico Policy Commission (PRPC), which worked to counter the crippling effects of the Sugar Act by developing a more dynamic and balanced local economy. Headed by University of Puerto Rico chancellor Carlos Chardón, the PRPC published a plan of economic reforms, approved in 1935, popularly known as the Plan Chardón.

The Plan Chardón diversified economic development through the state-mandated appropriation of some of the island's largest sugar mills. The plan had two primary objectives. The first and arguably most important entailed a permanent reduction in sugar production—by as much as 150,000 tons in the third year of the program—in order to stabilize global markets. The plan aimed to achieve this reduction through state confiscation and redistribution of land currently under the control of absentee sugar barons. Such redistribution would create more than 24,000 new homesteads for displaced Puerto Rican agricultural laborers.[13] These small famers were to use their newly acquired land for small-scale agricultural production for family subsistence and sales in local markets. In a letter to Senator Millard Tydings, chairman of the Committee on Territories and Insular Affairs, Chardón estimated that under his plan close to 172,000 Puerto Rican workers could be taken off of federal relief rolls.[14] Because it broke the sugar and coffee monopolies, Chardón's plan appealed both to Puerto Rican laborers and to American politicians looking to significantly cut relief subsidies to the island.

Enforcement of the land reform clauses in the Plan Chardón became the central policy piece for Muñoz Marín and the PPD as they broke away from the Liberal Party in 1938. For Black journalists, the PPD's massive program of land redistribution in a colonial territory of the United States had all the makings of a revolutionary project that could ameliorate the severe poverty plaguing the island. But in the eyes of Brooks and Little, it also offered African Americans an important model for instituting the similar economic reforms and land redistribution within the colonial metropolis. Muñoz Marín understood the real and symbolic importance of Puerto Rico as a bridge between the United States and countries in the global South. In an interview, Muñoz Marín reminded Brooks of the importance of his journalistic coverage of the island's economic reforms:

Some way, somehow, you correspondents must convey to the American people the shocking effect any undemocratic Congressional action down here will have on the rest of the Americas. Puerto Rico by its geographical location is the link between North and South. It has a close affinity with the South by common language and culture. These countries are watching to see if the United States seriously means what it says [sic] that it is fighting for the democratic principles to which all of the American countries are committed.[15]

As early as 1934, during early congressional deliberations on the Plan Chardón, Muñoz Marín realized the plan faced stiff opposition. In particular, he worried about the plan's "economic enemies" and the "political lackeys" in Congress and in the insular government.[16]

Puerto Rican businessman Jorge Bird Arias counted himself among these enemies. With Charles P. Armstrong, Bird Arias cofounded the Fajardo Sugar Company in 1905 and developed it into one of the largest sugar corporations on the island. On hearing about Plan Chardón's goal of land redistribution, Bird Arias wrote an open letter in the Puerto Rican newspaper El Imparcial addressed to southerner Blanton Winship, governor of the island at the time. Government purchase and operation of sugar factories, wrote Bird Arias, seemed like a very "dangerous" idea—though he did not explicitly state what he considered dangerous about the plan. In the next sentence, he called government operation and ownership of factories "unethical due to the competition that the plan threatens to establish against the sugar companies."[17]

Bird Arias also did not appreciate the permanent reduction in Puerto Rico's sugar quota proposed in the plan. Based on a market-driven understanding of fairness, Bird Arias described the sugar restriction as an "abusive discrimination against Puerto Rico."[18] Nowhere in his letter did Bird Arias acknowledge either his own economic interests as a sugar baron or the devastating effects of sugar production on Puerto Rico's landless proletariat. He only briefly mentioned that he wished "the best for Puerto Rico and for the welfare and happiness of the majority of its inhabitants."[19] Undoubtedly, Bird Arias did not note the cruel irony of his words as thousands of Puerto Ricans died around him of malnutrition and disease—the direct result of the monoculture economic dependency that his business practices supported.

Senator Arthur Vandenberg (R-Mich.) requested that Bird Arias's letter in El Imparcial be entered into the Congressional Record. Vandenberg had worked as a newspaper editor in Michigan prior to his long career in Congress. A strong proponent of U.S. isolationism in his early years,

Vandenberg also fervently opposed many of Roosevelt's New Deal policies. Not surprisingly, Vandenberg disagreed with what the Plan Chardón envisioned for Puerto Rico, going so far as to call it a "socialistic enterprise."[20] Vandenberg's opposition was shared by a larger group of senators, who worked against many of the tenets of the Plan Chardón. Their efforts came to a head in 1943 with the establishment of the Bell Committee.

## The Bell Committee

As Muñoz Marín, the PPD, and Rexford Tugwell, whom Roosevelt appointed governor of Puerto Rico in 1941, faced mounting congressional opposition to their reform program, the Black press quickly came to their defense. "Why should American interests be so intent in strangling reforms within the island," asked Deton Brooks. "Because they are afraid that some of them will eventually infiltrate into the United States jeopardizing their vested interests."[21] As Muñoz Marín had predicted, the number of enemies to his program of economic reforms continued to grow. Among those who opposed various facets of the PPD's program were Michigan congressman Fred Crawford, Louisiana congressman James "Jimmy" Domengeaux, and Mississippi congressman Dan McGehee. Like Vandenberg, all three representatives opposed land reform in Puerto Rico, but for different reasons.

A longtime Michigan banker and businessman, Crawford worked in the agricultural industry for many of his early years as the owner of several sugar beet mills. Crawford believed that the reforms—approved by voters in Puerto Rico during the 1940 elections—were unconstitutional. As such, he worked to have them repealed, even drafting a resolution to have them overturned. "The action proposed by Crawford," argued Muñoz Marín, "is particularly outrageous when it is considered that the legislation referred to [in Puerto Rico] has been . . . in effect in the United States."[22] Crawford's stance on the reforms in Puerto Rico stemmed from imperialist maneuvering among Republican congressmen who opposed the New Deal. In other words, Republicans would make an example of Puerto Rico as they aimed to curtail the expansion of the New Deal.

Brooks deemed Crawford's ties to the sugar beet industry to be a conflict of interest and clear evidence of how Puerto Rico's colonial dependence often conflicted with the economic interests of businessmen and congressmen. While the PPD's vision of land reform required an initial curtailment of the sugar quota, as the market stabilized over time the volume would increase again. At that point, independent farmers and the Puerto Rican government stood to gain the most. "The sugar interests naturally don't want to see [the land reform] succeed. And they are using every possible technique to kill it," Brooks claimed.[23] He connected Crawford's advocacy for Puerto Rico's current sugar monopolies with his personal financial interests as both a banker and a representative of the sugar lobby.

Brooks also suggested that the large multinational sugar trusts shared a natural affinity with the interests of politicians like James Domengeaux, who had deep southern roots. Hailing from Lafayette, Louisiana, Domengeaux worked as an attorney before and after his time in Congress. Domengeaux is often celebrated as a francophone traditionalist who in his later years sought to preserve the French language in Louisiana. A true social conservative, Domengeaux also aimed to preserve Jim Crow segregation. Throughout the 1940s, Domengeaux identified politically as a Southern Dixiecrat opposed to racial integration, and he viewed anyone who challenged the Southern racial order as a "self-seeking demagogue." In his retirement speech on leaving Congress in 1944 he worried that these demagogues might "lure [Blacks] by false promises to hope for a status they know [they] can never attain."[24]

A fellow Dixiecrat, Mississippian "Smiling Dan" McGehee mirrored the political and economic trajectory of Crawford and Domengeaux. A conservative constitutionalist and opponent of centralization McGehee served six terms in the U.S. House of Representatives. McGehee also shared strong ties to the southern agricultural industry, having made his fortune as a businessman and banker.[25] Although, like Domengeaux, McGehee believed in segregation, he imagined the South as a space rife with opportunity for African Americans and quickly demonized anyone who dared to say otherwise.[26]

All three congressmen served on the Bell Committee, which investigated the social and economic conditions on the island.[27] Commissioned in April 1943 by House Resolution 159, the Bell Committee—named for its chairman, Missouri congressman Charles Jasper Bell—worked under the umbrella of the larger Committee of Insular Affairs. Bell had been a lawyer then a judge in Kansas City, Missouri, before representing Missouri's fourth congressional district.

The Bell Committee worked from May to July 1943, gathering data, reading reports, and holding hearings. Not published until 1945, the committee's final report detailed a variety of recommendations that, taken as a whole, aimed to repeal many of the policies of the PPD and specifically the Plan Chardón. Preempting their findings, the committee offered to hold private sessions for those who feared Muñoz Marín and Tugwell, whom the committee described as "dye[d] in the wool communists."[28] The committee's massive report is sprinkled with various insinuations that Tugwell, Muñoz Marín, and the PPD had ulterior political motives for enacting the reforms. Committee member Sterling Cole, a Republican from New York, even went so far as to accuse Tugwell of fomenting "national socialism" comparable to "communism in Russia, fascism in Italy, Falangism in Spain, and Nazism in Germany."[29]

Among the Bell Committee's most interesting findings was its characterization of the PPD's reforms as following the "patterns used by fascists in Italy to control every avenue of commercial activity."[30] In particular, the committee strongly opposed the PPD's following the Chardón Plan by enforcing land restrictions on sugar monopolies and concurrently redistributing land to workers. The committee resolved that instead of redistributing land, the insular government should support the sugar industry, which they described as the "backbone of the Puerto Rican economy."[31] Furthermore, the committee proposed that the local government should encourage out-migration in order to deal with the island's growing population. Perhaps not surprisingly, however, members of the committee did not encourage Puerto Rican migration to the United States.[32]

Not surprisingly neither members of the PPD nor Tugwell viewed favorably the committee's ostensible efforts to help the people of Puerto Rico. Muñoz Marín referred to members of the Bell Committee as a "firing squad" intent on blocking the PPD reforms. He and other PPD leaders believed the committee to be full of political reactionaries with underlying racist and self-serving economic motives.[33] Puerto Ricans witnessed and experienced committee member James Domengeaux's bigotry firsthand when he visited Puerto Rico in 1943 as part of the Bell delegation. During his trip Domengeaux "managed to fondle women, get drunk, curse out

Governor Tugwell and racially abuse the speaker of the insular House, Ramos Antonini." Upon seeing Ernesto Ramos Antonini, a Black Puerto Rican, it is reported that Domengeaux said, "It's pretty dark in there. Come
out so that I can see."[34]

### The Puerto Rican Model(s)

In some ways the Bell Committee ushered in an era in which Puerto Rico's
strategic importance for the United States began to shift. Outlandish
though they were, the Bell Committee's accusations about Puerto Rican
fascism were symbolic of the competing visions of Puerto Rico in the
American imagination. In addition to the work of the Black press, the
early- to mid-1940s ushered in an intense period of research and observation in Puerto Rico. A host of researchers, policymakers, and foreign
diplomats swarmed to Puerto Rico to experience firsthand the reforms
being undertaken on the island. Prominent social scientists from American institutions such as the University of Chicago, Dartmouth College,
and Columbia University worked out of the University of Puerto Rico to
assist in the launching of the island's modernization project. During and
after the war, the U.S. government effectively modeled Puerto Rico as a
"showcase" of democratic development. In the face of other countries ex-
perimenting with alternative political and economic models, officials in
the United States promoted Puerto Rico's modernization project as one
that could be undertaken anywhere.

Despite these forms of "intellectual imperialism," the U.S. government
never fully controlled the meanings and uses of its cultural and political
missions abroad.[35] As the work of the Black press shows, Puerto Rico did
not serve just as a research laboratory for U.S.-sponsored capitalism and
development. Black journalists like Brooks and Little used Puerto Rico to
understand the challenges of Black social life and as a basis for making
demands from the U.S. government. The similarities between the island's
economy and that of the U.S. South, the second-class nature of Puerto
Rican citizenship, and the Puerto Rican race and class structure served as
key points of reference for these journalists and their large readerships.

Whereas U.S. citizenship granted Puerto Ricans certain privileges and
mobility between the island and the continental United States, it did not

translate into upward economic mobility for the vast majority of Puerto Ricans. In fact, poverty and disease remained widespread throughout the island almost thirty years after the granting of American citizenship. As sociologist Kelvin Santiago-Valles notes, the poverty and disease running rampant within the population were central concerns for social scientists and government officials. Concurrently, these two issues, along with concerns about criminality, developed into the key discursive tropes used to cast Puerto Ricans as a "subject people."[36]

Brooks studiously listed a number of the key causes of Puerto Rico's poverty, including the aforementioned sugar monopolies as well as overpopulation. In one of his final reports, however, Brooks settled on colonialism as the primary cause: "For over 430 years Puerto Rico has been a colony, first of Spain and then since 1898 the United States. Regardless of the use of the less objectionable term 'possession' or 'territory' or the half-hearted grant of home rule flowing from the organic act of 1917, its administration follows this pattern. This is just as true today as in the years gone by."[37] Brooks could not help but see the granting of U.S. citizenship as an empty and purely symbolic gesture. American citizenship and limited autonomy were insufficient to offset the uneven economic colonial relationship that failed to improve the material conditions under which the majority of Puerto Ricans on the island lived.

The Black press continually pointed out that U.S. citizenship did not better the everyday lives of most Puerto Ricans. The presence of U.S.-based sugar monopolies, they argued, drastically increased the disparities within local class structures. Focusing on this structural failure and Puerto Rico's geographic location, an editorial in the *Pittsburgh Courier* commented, "Our government does not want to turn Puerto Rico loose because of its strategic value and big investment of the sugar trust whose exactions have reduced the Puerto Ricans to abject poverty and disease."[38]

Brooks confirmed the devastating effects of the sugar industry in one of his earliest observations of the island: "There amidst the island's squalor poverty and disease where month-old babies die when half grown because emaciated mothers cannot nourish them properly; where greedy powerful sugar corporations gobbled up the richest, most fertile land, leaving 85 percent of the masses landless and destitute; where disease-ravaged cripples plaintively beg to eke out an existence, I learned this truth."[39] Not surprisingly, criticism of the sugar monopolies on the island and Puerto Rico's fragile economy constituted a major component of Brooks's analysis throughout the series.

In addition to incorporating critiques of U.S. and Puerto Rican sugar barons in his reports, Brooks dedicated his entire seventh dispatch to a discussion of Puerto Rico's economic dependence on sugar. In his August 21, 1943, article "Puerto Rican One-Crop System Needs Reform" Brooks aimed his journalistic wrath at the three largest sugar monopolies on the island: Central Aguirre, the South Porto Rico Sugar Company, and the Fajardo Company. "Cruel, arrogant despot, King sugar rules supreme," began Brooks, "All the people are his subject and none escape the tyranny of his reign. . . . Sugar is King of Puerto Rico."[40] Brooks's analysis of the U.S. sugar interests on the island strategically drew from the larger question of colonialism. In particular, Brooks revealed how the desires of U.S. racial capitalism crippled the Puerto Rican economy, especially during moments of social crisis such as World War II.

Highlighting this market vulnerability, Brooks detailed the risks faced by thousands of Puerto Ricans during the early war years. German U-boats continuously attacked large cargo ships carrying supplies into the region around the island, cutting off food shipments. At the same time, the majority of Puerto Rico's fertile lowlands were appropriated through taxation policies that favored corporate sugar interests. Aside from subsistence crops grown on small plots of land, the majority of Puerto Rico's food had to be imported from the United States. Brooks's investigation showed that during these early war years, Puerto Rico's *centrales* (mills) were stocked with tons of sugarcane. Meanwhile, thousands of Puerto Ricans starved while waiting for food supplies to get through the blockade of German U-boats. "There was plenty of sugar," remarked Brooks, "but no food."[41] In his own observations, Little related his surprise at the large amounts of sweets and sugarcane consumed on the island, likely due to the limited amounts of other foods available.[42]

In Little's analysis, the American economic interests that exposed Puerto Rico to market vulnerabilities were responsible for these perverse conditions. Sugar monopolization limited agricultural production for local consumption and markets. As such, extreme land concentration deprived Puerto Rico's proletariat, all of whom were U.S. citizens, of their basic means of subsistence and a balanced diet.[43] Describing a similar process Brooks wrote, "Year by year the companies gobbled more of the best land, squeezing out the small farmers who became landless. And because they were landless in a country which lives by the soil they become poorer, more illiterate, more diseased." Brooks further commented that more than 70 percent of Puerto Ricans lived in "indescribable poverty."[44]

The larger process of land concentration that left hundreds of thousands of Puerto Ricans landless helps to explain the explosion of Puerto Rico's proletariat. In order to make a living, most of these landless peasants were forced to work for the sugar monopolies on the same lands from which they had been expelled. Sociologist César Ayala observes that during a 1934 general strike "the stoppage affected 100,000 workers counting those employed in the sugar mills."[45] Brooks replicates these large numbers in his own research, stating that out of "an estimated 100,800 employed in the sugar industry, 92,000 are farm laborers falling within the group drawing the lowest salary."[46] According to Brooks, the average laborer in the sugar industry earned about $252 a year, or about seventy-eight cents a day. Consequently an average worker found it difficult to support a family in an area where "experts say it takes $800 per year for a family of five to live at a decent minimum standard."[47]

With poverty so widespread and highly visible on the island, Brooks and other journalists questioned the common assumption that Puerto Rico was doing well under the imperialist management of the United States. Citing Tugwell's own recently published report about the island, a 1943 editorial in the *Pittsburgh Courier* scornfully proclaimed, "Puerto Rico is no better off than it was when won from Spain in 1898, and [Tugwell] might have said with greater truth that Puerto Rico is actually worse off."[48] Another facet of the problem was that the sugar industry was at a crossroads. Because of the war, global demand for sugar was in steep decline and the industry had become heavily dependent on government subsidies to stay afloat.[49]

Within the context of sugar monoculture dominated by U.S. corporations, African American journalists easily linked Puerto Rico's economic model with that of the U.S. South. In the eyes of these journalists, Puerto Rican *agredados* and southern sharecroppers faced comparable challenges. "If Puerto Ricans have citizenship," asked Brooks, "why do they agitate, why aren't they satisfied? It's because they don't have full rights, their citizenship resembles in many respects that of the disenfranchised white and colored southern sharecroppers."[50] Brooks's personal knowledge and familiarity with the particularities of American citizenship, class, and race were important points from which he pivoted his larger critique of American democracy. Brooks understood that the economic disparity between differently positioned groups proved that citizenship did not always mean the same things for Puerto Ricans, African Americans, and poor southern whites as for their more privileged neighbors.

But Brooks also pointed to the ways in which race shaped how Puerto Ricans were positioned within the U.S. socioeconomic order. By making this connection, Brooks shed a light on the underlying racialized dimensions of Muñoz Marín's reforms and the opposition they faced. Accordingly, the PPD's economic and political reforms of this period became models from which Black journalists could talk about the convergence of land concentration, racism, and poverty.

Thus, Brooks continuously returned to critiques of the Bell Committee's report. Of the fourteen members of the committee, half were from southern states. Brooks directed his criticism of the committee squarely at these southern congressmen whom he viewed as symbols and protectors of Jim Crow segregation. It was in the interests of these congressmen, argued Brooks, to control Black labor and openly advocate for the economic interests of monocultural industries. In the case of the South, this meant protecting the traditional market economy from future challenges based on the reforms in Puerto Rico.

Rhetorically questioning the Bell Committee's opposition to the major land reforms in Puerto Rico, Brooks queried, "Why are Domengeaux and McGhee [sic] so concerned [about the new reforms]?" Mapping Puerto Rico as a model for critiquing the southern cotton aristocracy in the United States, Brooks reasoned, "They come from the south, and Puerto Rico's economy resembled that of the south: both are agricultural areas; both have one-crop economies, the south, cotton, Puerto Rico, sugar; and both viciously exploit their landless workers. We call them tenant farmers and sharecroppers in the south. In Puerto Rico they're *agredados*."[51] Certainly, Brooks's analogies were intended to make tangible connections for his readership, for whom a place like Puerto Rico must have seemed very far away. But his attachment of these analogies to southern opposition to land reform also brought into focus the racist undertones of congressional opposition to Puerto Rican reforms.

Members of the Black press corps believed southern members of Congress worried that if land and economic reforms could be passed in Puerto Rico, then the same might also occur in the U.S. South. Specifically, Brooks asked his readers to imagine what would happen in Dixie if similar land reforms were implemented. Brooks and members of the Bell Committee both realized that if similar land reforms were enacted in the South then "Negroes and poor whites" would become "respectable land owners."[52] All of these men, but especially Brooks, understood the role that land played in altering structural hierarchies and inequality. Recalling the use of Jim Crow provisions to block African Americans from voting, Brooks argued that land redistribution would help empower Blacks and poor whites in the South to vote. By voting they would, in turn, remove from office men like McGehee and Domengeaux who had consistently voted against "bill[s] like the anti-poll tax" and "anti-lynch or anti-strike legislation."[53] Connecting Puerto Rico's land reform program to these pieces of anti-segregationist legislation made Brooks's critique about U.S. racism explicit.

Other members of the Black press pushed Brooks's critique of southern racial politics even further. A column in the June 19, 1943, *Pittsburgh Courier* demanded that the U.S. government decide what it wanted to do with Puerto Rico. The column argued that the government remained conflicted between its political, economic, and social priorities for the island. On the one hand, the United States had no interest in seeing the island "turned loose" to the rest of the world because of its strategic military value and the lingering sugar lobby. And "the government does not want Puerto Rico admitted as a State, because that would give colored people too much of a voice in Congress, and four-fifths of the Puerto Ricans are colored, according to American anthropology."[54]

The short piece did not give a source for the anthropological claim, and it is unclear whether "colored" meant Black or simply nonwhite. Between the mid-nineteenth and mid-twentieth centuries, *colored* was understood as an inclusive term that covered people with any degree of Black ancestry.[55] In the 1940s context, the use of "colored" in the column most likely implied an understanding of Puerto Ricans as racially Black or, at a minimum, racially mixed. Journalists for the *Pittsburgh Courier* and *Chicago Defender* often thought of Puerto Rico as a Black nation, or at least mentioned it when discussing Black republics. For example, the Black press covered Puerto Rico's participation in the World Federation of

Trade Unions conference in Paris to end segregation in the workplace.[56] The *Defender*'s weekly quiz section even identified Puerto Rico as a possible answer to the question, "What is the only Negro Kingdom in the World?"[57] Other possible answers included Liberia, Ethiopia, and Haiti. Overall, then, the *Courier* column pointed to the reasons why the United States did not want to annex the island formally as a state because this could potentially destabilize the dominant white U.S. racial order.

Muñoz Marín's socioeconomic restructuring of the island threatened southern business and political elites hoping to avoid such reforms in their states. But, according to the Black press, the threat of a "colored" interracial alliance between African Americans and Puerto Ricans also loomed if the island were granted statehood. Brooks excitedly proclaimed that as landowners and citizens, Puerto Ricans and African Americans would vote together and "these cohorts of infamy would lose their power and their jobs as congressmen."[58]

The mention of a powerful political alliance between American Blacks and Puerto Ricans both affirms and challenges an overly idealized coalition between the two groups. Specifically, such a political coalition would entail Puerto Rico's incorporation into the American Union rather than its independence, though the latter was the overwhelming preference among the Black Left at the time.[59] John Badger implicitly pondered this political conundrum as he discussed the links between the enemies of African Americans and Puerto Ricans: "To Negro-Americans this means that the worst enemies of the Negro people—the poll taxers, Hooverite Republicans, and labor leaders who practice Jim Crow—are all in the same camp on the question of Puerto Rican freedom. Consequently, the fight for Puerto Rican freedom is part and parcel of Negro-America's struggle for first class citizenship."[60]

The connection between Puerto Rican freedom and the unfulfilled claims of citizenship for African Americans resists a romantic reading of the demands of both constituents. Instead, it shows the ways in which the dismantling of structures that allowed racism and exclusion to flourish were a necessary precondition for any truly radical project about freedom and justice.

## Questions of Color

The far-reaching uses of Puerto Rico by the Black Press were plagued with problems of analysis. Just as they had done with other international spaces, African American journalists tended to romanticize race relations in Puerto Rico. Part of this dynamic is directly linked to their comparisons of Puerto Rico and the United States. Essentializing both nations, Black journalists did not always assess the varied ways in which race operated in and across each place. Black journalists often misinterpreted racism as a phenomenon solely found in and caused by the imperialist endeavors of the United States. Americans visiting the island and the colonial priorities of the United States, argued the journalists, literally produced racial difference, and even the very idea of race, on the island.

Brooks and Little analyzed race relations on the island on several occasions in their series. Both men believed that race and the color line did not exist in Puerto Rico, or at least not to the degree they manifested in the United States. Brooks even devoted an entire article to a discussion about race on the island. In this report, Brooks distinguished between racism as institutionalized practice and everyday forms of racism. For Brooks, both types of racism existed in the United States but Puerto Ricans experienced only minor quotidian forms of racism. Somewhat reluctantly, Brooks conceded that "the question of color is bound to arise from time to time regardless of how much it is shoved into the background."[61] Along these lines, Brooks located racism as a problem found only along the coastal regions where most Black Puerto Ricans resided. By situating racism as something experienced only by those Black Puerto Ricans living along Puerto Rico's coasts, Brooks participated in what Puerto Rican anthropologist Isar Godreau terms "discursive distancing." This form of distancing situates Blackness as both premodern and as a social fact located within particular geographic spaces (the coast) and not others (the interior).[62]

"Race consciousness," in Brooks's opinion, was "more pronounced" as one moved up the economic ladder.[63] Brooks did not define what he meant by race consciousness. It is evident, however, that he believed race was not as significant for people on the lower end of the class spectrum. He also referred to the relationship between race and class in the article describing his time in Miami. While there, Brooks observed how "Brown" high-ranking Latin American military officers (because of their uniforms) gained access to social spaces "where ordinarily dark skinned people could not go."[64] Brooks did acknowledge the intersectionality of race and class and the striking absence of Black Puerto Ricans in the upper echelons of Puerto Rican class society. Nonetheless, he did not interpret this exclusion as the result of structural inequality.[65]

As Brooks talked to Black Puerto Ricans about their absence from high positions in government and business, he appeared confused when they claimed to be more unwilling to talk about racism than light-skinned or white Puerto Ricans were. This observation might have been an indicator of how elite or white Puerto Ricans typically framed discussions about race in ways that silenced Black Puerto Ricans. Brooks interpreted it instead as a "feeling that within the framework of the democratic concept that [sic] this subtle prejudice will work itself out."[66] Brooks's observation highlighted the faith and commitment he had in democracy and its ability to curtail racism. But it also revealed how he selectively ignored what he already knew about race and the promise of democracy from his experience in the United States.

Reiterating many of the same points about class, race, and democracy as Brooks, Little made more explicit connections between militarism, U.S. imperialism, and race in Puerto Rico. Discussing the growing presence of soldiers and military bases on the island Little remarked, "With the development of military and naval bases there has been quite the influx of peckerwoods by way of the armed forces and the civil services. These punks are distinguishable by their washed out appearance and their southern drawl and the general look of bewilderment. Bewilderment because they see all colors of people getting along together peaceably and congenially."[67] By emphasizing the "southern drawl" and "general bewilderment" of American military personnel (peckerwoods) stationed on the island, Little called attention to the racial conflict and violence to which they were accustomed in the United States. Little depicted Puerto Rico, by contrast, as a racial paradise where everyone got along. Little feared that American soldiers might disrupt the peaceful nature of the island's racial order and ultimately hamper the reforms being implemented by Muñoz Marín.

Interestingly, just as Brooks had done, Little briefly mentioned the existence of a "caste system" that "gives preference . . . to the 'white' natives"

PUERTO RICO WILL CHOOSE  Illustrated by HOLLOWAY

Figure 2.1. "Puerto Rico Will Choose," by Wilbert L. Holloway. June 16, 1945.
Reprinted by permission of the *New Pittsburgh Courier*. Pittsburgh Courier
Archives.

in the realm of work opportunities. He avoided discussing the caste system
he saw in action before his eyes, however. Had he done so he might have
been able to peel back the complex layers to reveal how racism worked
across the Puerto Rican class spectrum. Instead, he opted to emphasize
the "blood ties" that Puerto Ricans and African Americans shared. Little
concluded, "An effort should be made not only to establish unity within
our own group but also to develop a union with all of our people who are
bound to us by a common ancestry and by a common persecution."[68] Little
believed that both Puerto Rican and African American progress depended
on mutual aid and recognition of each other's struggles against racism.
This commitment outweighed his interest in a more nuanced examination
of Puerto Rico's caste system.

The Puerto Rican racial politics that Brooks and Little struggled with
are also observable in a June 16, 1945, *Pittsburgh Courier* editorial. The

editorial celebrated Maryland senator Millard Tydings's introduction of Senate Bill 1002, or the Tydings Bill, which called for an island-wide referendum allowing Puerto Ricans to choose among three options for the territory's future status. Favored by a wide segment of progressive groups, the options included independence, statehood, or dominion status (an "autonomous" territory under permanent control of the United States).

The editorial also emphasized that "at least half of the population are classed as Negroes" and that there is "no color line" in Puerto Rico. Aligning with the work of Little and Brooks, the editorial discussed the rights afforded to Puerto Ricans as citizens and the congressional barriers to decolonization. In the face of segregation, the editorial cited S.B. 1002 as a significant piece of legislation opposed by American reactionaries. "Never before has a great country like the United States even CONSIDERED allowing a subject land to decide what its future will be in a free election—especially not a COLORED land," observed the editorial.[69]

Accompanying the editorial was a political cartoon by longtime *Pittsburgh Courier* staff artist Wilbert L. Holloway. The cartoon depicted an aging Senator Tydings holding a serving tray with S.B. 1002's three options. In front of Tydings stands an apparently upper-class white Puerto Rican woman wearing traditional dress. She is also wearing a cross pendant—a symbolic reference to the island's predominantly Roman Catholic tradition. The woman smiles as she ponders the tray of political options. Tydings returns a downward colonial gaze toward the woman's body.

What is important about the cartoon is what the viewer misses in a cursory glance at it. Behind and to the left of the white Puerto Rican woman stands a Black Puerto Rican woman. The woman appears to be barefoot and carries a basket of fruit or similar goods—clear indicators of her class position. Unlike the woman in the foreground, the Black woman remains faceless and undefined.[70] Considered differently, the Black woman's minimal presence in the cartoon is highlighted by her striking absence in the frame.[71]

Tydings and the white Puerto Rican woman do not acknowledge the Black woman's presence in the scene. Her motionless posture indicates that she notices the figures before her. She stands at attention, leaning forward slightly, with her hands crossed and resting at her waist. She appears intrigued with the political happenings taking place before her. In many ways she is symbolic of the larger Black Puerto Rican population to which Brooks and Little alluded. More broadly, the cartoon and editorial present conflicting messages about Puerto Rican race relations. While at least half of Puerto Ricans are "classed as Negroes," they are excluded from the realm of politics. Instead, they are left to hope that a democratic system would somehow work out this racialized exclusion for them.

## Betrayal

At the start of World War II, poverty, misery, and uncertainty were widespread throughout Puerto Rico. Politically, the PPD achieved some crucial and surprising legislative victories aimed at drastically reforming the island's infrastructure. For a political party established only a few years earlier these successes were remarkable. As the war came to an end, however, not much had changed in terms of the material deprivations, including disease and unsafe living conditions, that continued to plague the majority of Puerto Ricans. The elections of 1944 marked an important moment that cemented the emergence of the PPD as a dominant political bloc. In 1944 the PPD almost doubled its share of the popular vote compared to only four years earlier, from 38 percent to 65 percent.[72] This referendum showed just how popular and powerful the PPD and its social reforms were on the island.

Luis Muñoz Marín's political thought had also evolved. Throughout much of his early political life, Muñoz Marín firmly self-identified as a believer in Puerto Rico's eventual independence. Even as he supported Roosevelt's New Deal policies, he objected on moral grounds to the island's colonial relationship with the United States because it denied Puerto Ricans a say in their political affairs and produced uneven economic development.[73] By the mid-1940s Muñoz Marín's position on both issues had gradually shifted. In economic terms, Muñoz Marín became convinced that only exclusive trading rights treaties with the United States and an influx of federal aid could support the amount of development that Puerto Rico required.[74]

Most interesting about this shift in perspective is that ultimately it required the PPD and Muñoz Marín to depend on the very forms of absentee capitalism that they had opposed in the sugar industry just a few years earlier.[75] Importantly, many of the populist land reforms introduced by the PPD did not dramatically alter landownership on the island. Sociologist Kelvin Santiago-Valles notes that the reforms were "aimed at those 500-acre plus 'latifundios' that were explicitly owned *by corporations*. Deliberately or not, this left untouched those corporate-owned 'latifundios' that were formally owned and/or registered *by individuals*."[76] In fact, between 1945 and 1950 Muñoz Marín moved away from his public criticisms of the sugar industry, shifting his attention to the island's large population and to internal fragmentations within the PPD.[77]

As late as 1945, Muñoz Marín still did not make his changing opinion on the question of the island's status public.[78] Instead, he preferred to continue to tout his economic program and push the political status question into the background. Recognizing the continued importance of the island as the Cold War began, President Harry Truman vetoed the Tydings Bill in 1946. Truman's veto effectively ended the possibility of a popular referendum where Puerto Ricans might decide the future status of their island. In order to offset his political shift on the colonial question, Muñoz Marín opted to take up the cause of Puerto Rican sovereignty in local political affairs. Using the same arguments about democracy he had used only a few years earlier to attack colonialism at an international level, Muñoz Marín advocated for full local self-government. This model of colonial self-government granted Puerto Ricans a level of sovereignty in matters of culture (that is, language and cultural institutions) and government (such as developing their own constitution and electing their own officials) even as they remained firmly under the control of the U.S. government.

Although Puerto Ricans at that time could elect politicians to represent them in the Senate they still could not vote for their own governor. This began to change in 1946 when Jesús Piñero became the first Puerto Rican to be appointed governor of the island. Piñero's rise within the PPD had come about through his election as the island's resident commissioner just two years earlier, in 1944. Muñoz Marín pushed Piñero's candidacy even as he struggled with the *independentista* and labor wings of the party, which had become disenchanted with his shifting political vision. Thereby, Muñoz Marín effectively neutralized the radical segments of the PPD. These party members either fell in line with the increasingly conservative movement within the party or were expelled and branded communists and fascists. Two years later Luis Muñoz Marín became the island's first elected governor, a position he held until 1964.

The political Left across the Americas did not look kindly upon Muñoz Marín's "betrayal," as it has come to be known. African American intellectuals, communists, and labor organizers counted themselves among those unhappy with Muñoz Marín. Muñoz Marín's rejection of independence as a viable political status and his political shift toward favoring capitalist development helped to account for Puerto Rico's disappearance as a subject of interest in the Black press after 1950.

The writings of Pettis Perry give just one example of the sense of betrayal felt by the Black Left at the time. The son of Alabama tenant farmers, Perry joined the CPUSA in 1932 and served as secretary of the party's Negro Commission. In this capacity, Perry worked to forge alliances among southern sharecroppers, farmers, and industrial workers across the United States. Perry did not count Muñoz Marín among these allies. In an unpublished paper from 1951, Perry criticized him as a "servant of Wall Street . . . following the path of his master," for his failure to fulfill his promises of reform.[79]

Perry marshaled a plethora of statistical data to show that the PPD failed to eradicate the poverty plaguing the island. In addition, he charged that the PPD promoted a colonial model of industrialization and accepted trade agreements with huge disparities between the total amount of exports and imports from the U.S. market. More simply, nothing had changed. The programs that caught the attention of the Black press in the United States in the early 1940s had failed. "Immediately after attaining the governorship," charged an angry Perry, Muñoz Marín "revealed in no unmistakable terms that he is the patron saint of United States imperialism, and all hitherto promises and declarations are shown to be made like a pie-crust—to break."[80] Perry continued by critiquing the PPD economic platform and U.S. colonial interests on the island. Much the same criticism was leveled by Brooks and Little. Unlike them, however, Perry looked at "Negro Liberation" and "colonial liberation" as similar but not inextricably linked social phenomena.[81]

The critical and multipronged critique of American racism vis-à-vis colonialism in Puerto Rico had lost its novelty by the 1950s. However, as chapter 5 shows, it did not disappear. It simply manifested in different ways and across other national spaces.

## Conclusion

Despite the momentary waning of Puerto Rico in the Black imagination, the colonial outpost remained an important locale for the Black radical tradition. The material points of imbrication between African American and Puerto Rican social life were difficult to ignore. From the nineteenth-century calls to purchase Puerto Rico in order to establish a Black republic on the island to the interracial political solidarities envisioned by the *Pittsburgh Courier* and the *Chicago Defender,* there is ample evidence of the overlapping histories between African Americans and Puerto Ricans.[82]

For Black journalists, the overlap between the island's economy and that of the U.S. South, the second-class nature of Puerto Rican citizenship, and the perception of Puerto Ricans as racially mixed or Black subjects were powerful links to their own interests. Using these areas of imbrication as key points of departure, they radically reimagined land tenure and property arrangements in the U.S. South. However, as this chapter has also shown, their interpretations of the connections between race and uneven capitalist development in both spaces also produced severely limited analyses of local conditions and social arrangements.

Nonetheless, for Brooks and Little, their writings helped them to make sense of their own subjugated position as Black subjects in the United States and to imagine new social and economic possibilities for their communities. Their support of Muñoz Marín's populism illustrated their hunger for economic development and social equity on the mainland United States. It also provided Blacks with a material model for how they might carry out such programs of reform in the United States. Thus, through the efforts of the Black press Puerto Rico provided an opportunity for marginalized groups to think about their relationship to racial capitalist development and how to labor against it. At the very least, it gave African Americans a temporary window to imagine possibilities for a different life.

# 3

# The Living Negro in Latin America

In his monumental 1944 study, *An American Dilemma*, Swedish sociologist Gunnar Myrdal lamented the embarrassing state of American race relations. "The Negro problem in America," noted Myrdal, "represents a moral lag in the development of the nation and a study of it must record nearly everything which is bad and wrong with America."[1] Commissioned by the Carnegie Corporation, the study sought to reconcile the stated principles of American equality with the actions of the American public in respect to the treatment of African Americans. The Carnegie Corporation's Frederick Keppel selected Myrdal, a "true liberal," to lead the study, in the belief that Myrdal's liberalism and Swedish ancestry made him a neutral researcher capable of investigating American racism objectively. But Keppel wanted more than just a scholar from outside the United States. Understanding the relationship between race and empire, Keppel specifically targeted a researcher from a non-imperialist nation "with no background of domination of one race over another." Keppel believed that hiring a scholar from an imperialist nation with tense race relations "might lessen the confidence of the Negroes" in the study.[2] Keppel encouraged Myrdal to spend time visiting the U.S. South before beginning his study, in order to gain a better understanding of the challenges that awaited him and his team of researchers. Myrdal returned from his travels "shocked and scared to the bones by all the evils [he] saw."[3]

Myrdal and his research team focused on the political challenges posed by southern conservatism and liberalism.[4] According to Myrdal, southern liberalism differed from other types of liberalism. Shaped by the unique racial history of the South and by inward-looking provincialism, southern liberalism, Myrdal contended, lacked any traces of radicalism. The cautious and callous ways in which southern liberals confronted the racial question mitigated progressive expressions of liberalism, especially with respect to labor.

*An American Dilemma* asserted that due to this provincialism southern liberalism had to *"get its power from outside the South."*[5] Myrdal claimed that southern liberals acted on the advice and influence of northerners who were more progressive than their southern counterparts. Southern society, suggested Myrdal, remained plagued by a larger culture of denial about its overt forms of racism. While his descriptions of the southern class and racial order were accurate, Myrdal incorrectly located the source of southern liberalism as exclusively rooted in the North. Even more importantly, he underestimated the imaginative capacities of southern liberals who were in search of models of racial progress.

Around the time Myrdal completed his study, part-time historian Tomás Blanco published his oft-cited essay *El prejuicio racial en Puerto Rico* (Racial Prejudice in Puerto Rico). Trained as a medical doctor at Georgetown University and a leading member of the literary *generación de los treinta*, Blanco argued that little if any racial prejudice existed in Puerto Rico. Like Myrdal, Blanco viewed racism as less a systemic phenomenon than the result of individual immorality. Even more than Myrdal, Blanco understood prejudice as a part of the individualized "complex terrain of psychology" and considered that its systemic manifestations were "difficult to measure" in Puerto Rico.[6]

Despite Blanco's assertion of the individualized nature of prejudice in Puerto Rico and the accompanying methodological challenges of this approach, he moved forward with his analysis. Blanco compared the behavior of the Puerto Rican middle class to the racism observed in the U.S. South.[7] Combining anecdotal evidence and the laws of Jim Crow America with an analysis of economic, religious, and "environmental characteristics" of prejudice in Puerto Rico, Blanco unsurprisingly concluded that the actions of Puerto Ricans were "less monstrous" than the racism of American southerners.

Although Blanco did not interview any Black Puerto Ricans and ignored class differences between the groups he studied, he boldly asserted that prejudice on the island had more to do with Puerto Rican *changueria* (tomfoolery and imitation) than with any deliberate acts of prejudice. An *independentista*, Blanco's paternalistic argument suggested that Puerto Rican prejudice was the direct result of behavior learned from the colonial metropole. Even then, according to him, the actions of Puerto Ricans did not rise to the level of racism and were just intrapersonal forms of prejudice. Aside from a few anecdotes from the United States, Blanco's essay lacks any significant evidence. We should take Blanco at his word when he concludes that, "in all or in parts, it could be that I am mistaken."[8]

His feeble disclaimer notwithstanding, Blanco claimed that even among the popular classes in Puerto Rico prejudice did not exist. More simply, prejudice was absent from Puerto Rico's *entire* class structure. With respect to difference, then, class disparity trumped any other social index. Puerto Ricans, claimed Blanco, did not "talk about the colored race, but rather the *kind* of color, or more simply of class."[9] Seduced by comparative difference, Blanco goes as far as to say that political affiliations and culture "cancel out prejudice . . . or cancel it out altogether" in Puerto Rico.[10]

As an *independentista*, Blanco desired a democratic, sovereign, and economically self-sufficient Puerto Rico, a mindset that explains much of his investment in discourses of racial liberalism. Puerto Ricans, claimed Blanco, needed to guard against culturally imperialist incursions that diluted the island's national culture and identity. In an earlier study, Blanco urged Puerto Ricans to "protect [their] difference, shaped by the tropics and the mixture of blood that connects [them] to the Hispanic community of nations."[11]

Blanco's narrative of Puerto Rican racial exceptionalism weakened his radical position on the national question. Driven by a political liberalism that homogenized Puerto Rican national identity, Blanco depicted an egalitarian nation. His endorsement of a nationalist politics that prioritized Puerto Rico's independence tacitly silenced debates about the state of race relations on the island. Ironically and unrecognized by Blanco, Puerto Rican liberalism and the southern liberalism Myrdal described converged along the axis of their denial of racism and class relations. Even more, they both garnered their power and rationalization from *outside* their national boundaries.

Analyzing southern journalist and anti-racism activist Harold Preece's writings on Puerto Rico, this chapter explores the process of racial imbrication evident in the uneven merging of U.S. southern and Puerto Rican liberalism. Between 1943 and 1946, Preece wrote two of the most extensive series on the American South and the Black diaspora in Latin America to appear in the Black press. Following a brief biographical sketch of Preece, I analyze his series "The Living South." In this series, Preece paid careful attention to the labor movement in the U.S. South and the kinds of organizing across racial lines it required to succeed. Significantly, Preece often based his news stories on the labor organizers and activists working on the ground in the South to make such a radical transformation within the labor movement possible. But these examples were not sufficient models to fully capture the type of world Preece imagined for the South.

In the second half of the chapter I shift my attention to Preece's incredible series "The Negro in Latin America." Driven by his research of and relationship with prominent Latin American race scholars, Preece's series about the Black diaspora in Latin America demonstrated his attempts to imbricate Latin American race relations, folk traditions, and labor movements with those of the U.S. South. Preece's reading of Latin American race and culture allowed him to imagine a broad transnational, multiracial, and class-based social movement. Plagued by limited source material and an uneven understanding of social relations in the Americas, the series succumbed to idealistic and homogenous readings of Black cultural and political life. Nonetheless, Preece's writings worked within and against the ways in which Liberalism in both spatial contexts garnered its legitimacy from beyond the boundaries prescribed by Myrdal and Blanco.

## Confessions of an Ex-Nordic

A Texan whose grandfather fought for the Union during the Civil War, Harold Preece explained his interest in Black political life and antiracism as a story of extraordinary personal transformation. As a child, he witnessed countless acts of violence against African Americans, including the stoning of Black children each day as they walked to school.[12] Years later in his correspondence with historian and fellow writer Tevis Clyde Smith, Preece admitted to "cheering wildly" in his adolescence after watching D. W. Griffith's white supremacist silent film *Birth of a Nation* several times.[13]

Somewhat paradoxically, Preece strongly supported Marcus Garvey's Black separatism. Preece viewed the immigration of African Americans to Africa as a practical solution to reduce the competition facing white laborers in post–World War I America. Garveyism appealed so much to him that he made a "plea for this gilded chimera" in a college sociology term paper.[14] Preece later wrote that his shift on the race question began during the Depression years after he realized that he shared the same economic fate as African Americans. While waiting together for work and food, "We drank unashamed from the same bottle, and I felt this was the rough communion of a better era yet unborn."[15]

Repeating the vulgar Marxism of other socialists, Preece understood racism as the product of larger class distinctions. Preece blamed his family's poverty on Southern pollcats who kept his father in wage slavery.[16] "White and Black no longer exist," argued Preece, "there are only oppressors and oppressed." From that point forward, Preece racially reclassified himself as an "ex-Nordic," with an "aversion to bourgeois Caucasians."[17]

Finding his calling in class struggle and antiracist activism, Preece began work as a news reporter and labor organizer for various unions in the South during the Depression. Preece identified politically with candidates from the CPUSA or the Socialist Party of America, most notably Norman Thomas.[18] By the mid-1930s Preece began writing full time for *The Crisis*, the official magazine of the National Association for the Advancement of Colored People (NAACP), founded by W.E.B. Du Bois in 1910.[19] His reports in *The Crisis* increased Preece's visibility in Black intellectual circles. With more prominence came more criticism of Preece's politics. He had several public disagreements with prominent Black anthropologists, including John Gibbs St. Clair Drake and Zora Neale Hurston, regarding their opinions about race, class, and culture.[20]

In spite of his emphasis on class relations and disagreements with these leading Black intellectuals, Preece remained committed to a broader antiracist politics. He asserted that racial capitalism hindered the development of Black cultural forms and social life. He also viewed culture as a valuable material form that had to be intimately connected with the actions of the folk rather than as some authentic expression of Black rural life. Preece affirmed the material connections between labor, race, and culture in the South in his most famous newspaper series, "The Living South."

## "The Living South"

As early as 1935, the *Chicago Defender* featured nationally syndicated excerpts of Preece's writing from other Black newspapers and magazines. "The Living South" appeared as a weekly column in the *Defender* between mid-1943 and early 1945. Editors at the *Defender* charged Preece with discussing the possibilities that a racially unified labor movement offered their readership. In the preamble to one of the first reports from "The Living South," editors introduced Preece as a "white Texas born . . . contributor to liberal magazines." Trusting Preece with a weekly feature, the editors gave readers "an inside view of progressive thinking by white liberals south of the Mason and Dixon line."[21]

Preece used his tokenization to full advantage. Stories of his own personal history and work in the South are sprinkled throughout "The Living South." Preece complemented these reports of personal transformation with stories of cooperation and exchanges between exceptional Black and white labor organizers. The discursive strategies Preece employed challenged traditional narratives that depicted a divided South full of mistrusting African Americans and violent white bigots. Instead, he showed readers in his column that race relations were progressing in a productive manner.

In a July 1943 report, for example, he contrasted the racial relations in Beaumont, Texas, with those in nearby Nashville, Tennessee. At the time, a jury in Beaumont had acquitted two white police officers of the shooting of a Black soldier. Making matters worse, the town's former sheriff, Tom Garner, had been exposed as a member of the local Ku Klux Klan. In contrast, Preece praised the leaders in Nashville who avoided having their city's name "added to the sorry roll" of cities in racial turmoil. Black and white leaders "sat down together at the same conference tables without any ideas . . . that anybody is inferior or that anybody is superior."[22] Significantly, Preece did not address the miscarriage of justice in the case of the soldier killed by white police officers. Furthermore, his framing of Black leadership implicitly suggested that local Black leaders' quest for equality was somehow comparable to the power enacted by white supremacy (that *anybody* is inferior or . . . superior).

Harry Koger and Clinton Clark appeared throughout the Living South series as examples of class collaborators across the color line. Koger worked as an organizer in Texas and Oklahoma for the Food, Tobacco, Agricultural and Allied Workers of America union. Preece admired Koger's willingness to publicize acts of racial discrimination against agricultural workers, including immigrants, in 1940s Texas. Koger also openly discussed racism during meetings as part of his efforts to bridge racial and ethnic divides within local unions. Open forums like these created a space where organizers chipped away at the large racial divide plaguing local unions in the South.

For his part, Clark headed the Louisiana Farmers' Union. Nicknamed the "Black Ghost of Louisiana," he earned a reputation for his ability to escape lynch mobs. Clark helped ensure that southern tenant farmers were properly compensated after they took their land out of production under the New Deal's Agricultural Adjustment Act.[23] Preece, who developed a lifelong friendship with Clark and helped him begin his autobiography, admired Clark's ability to lead diverse groups and stakeholders toward the same goals. Clark even continued to organize alongside members of the CPUSA during a period of rampant red baiting. During his labor organizing drives Clark drew extensively from the CPUSA network of grassroots organizers and unions, which could mobilize quickly. The dedication of the CPUSA and other Leftist groups to "organizing poor people to better their condition" most interested Clark.[24]

Not surprisingly, Clark counted himself as one of the biggest fans of Preece's series on the South. In a September 1943 letter to the editor, Clark enthused, "no other column gives me more thought than the one written by Harold Preece." Preece and Clark concurred that the way people in the South acted with respect to race could not change until the way they thought about how laborers of different racial groups interacted changed first. "I think this column is very important," concluded Clark, because it offers people a "new idea of the southern sharecroppers."[25]

As a number of letters to the editor indicate, the success of Preece's series in the *Defender* hinged on its focus on antiracist labor organizing in the South. A January 1944 article, for example, declared the upcoming year as the year of the "New South." Years earlier the old slave-owning aristocracy had embraced the same moniker as it sought to rebuild the southern racial order following Reconstruction. Reappropriating the term, Preece injected it with new meaning. Instead of a return to the racial hierarchy of the antebellum period, Preece advocated for a new liberalism that reimagined an "egalitarian" and "racially unified" South. "We're going to see decent people of all classes and both colors act drastically to remove the causes . . . of dangerous eruptions," proclaimed an optimistic Preece.[26]

The changing social conditions in the South at the time warranted some optimism. Nine years earlier, in 1935, labor leader John L. Lewis founded the Congress of Industrial Organizations (CIO).[27] Formed of a large alliance of various industrial unions, the CIO opposed craft unionism that left nonskilled workers with fewer rights and protections. The CIO also accepted rank and file members irrespective of race, sex, or age.[28] The CIO focused on outreach to African Americans during union membership drives as part of its effort to include communities of color. During the 1940s the CIO made significant strides in the South, where African Americans constituted the organization's most powerful base.[29] Preece sprinkled references to the CIO's productive efforts to unite labor across racial lines throughout his series on the South.[30]

The CIO's success impressed Preece so much that he hailed the organization as a key pillar in the "new abolition movement." In 1940, Preece joined the Abolish Peonage Committee and the International Labor Defense, and helped the latter organization publish the pamphlet *Peonage: 1940 Style Racism*. The informative pamphlet depicts the "solid South"— defined by Black disenfranchisement, wage slavery, and racial violence (lynching)—as points of departure for the new South he imagined in "The Living South."[31] The subjects of the new emerging southern order were "not wax figures out of fiction but flesh-and-blood people who [were] forging their deliverance out of their resentment and their will to live."[32]

Using the CIO as one example of Preece's vision of the new South, the series directed readers to embrace a culture of labor capable of *producing* the social transformation they sought. "The Living South" distanced itself from idealistic and static southern traditions and folklore. Instead, it emphasized a model of *movement* and social change demonstrated by local activists, the CIO, and even some intellectuals. One of the final installments of the series challenged readers to continue with these forms of dynamic activity: "Did you think that the South was old and paralyzed, past its period of birth and growth like an aged tree which can do nothing but suck nourishment from the fertile earth? Then, brother, you were mistaken for the South is sinking new roots and finding new causes."[33]

Preece might have been more forthcoming with his readers. As the next section shows, Preece had already begun to unearth the roots and "new causes" he had in mind. The abolitionist firmly fixed his gaze to the southernmost roots of his metaphorical tree and found the political nourishment he sought in Latin America. By turning his analysis to Latin America Preece hoped to reshape his readers' thinking about the transformative possibilities within race and labor relations. As the next section shows, Preece believed he had found the antidote to the South's decline and social paralysis in Latin America.

### "The Negro in Latin America," 1943–1946

Five months after he penned his first "Living South" column, Preece began writing another extensive weekly series. Between 1943 and 1946 he published the longest running column on Latin America in the Black press at the time.[34] Syndicated as a continental feature, "The Negro in Latin America" appeared in as many as fifty Black newspapers with a national circulation reaching, according to Preece, somewhere in the neighborhood of two million readers.[35]

Focusing on historical figures and events in different countries, the series detailed the presence and contributions of the Black diaspora in Latin America, broadly defined.[36] The data Preece compiled for the reports is one of the most striking elements of the series. Unlike other writers in the Black press, such as Robert Abbott, Deton Brooks, and George Little, Preece did not spend any significant time in the countries he featured in his series on Latin America.[37]

Preece admitted that his overreliance on secondary sources was problematic. Most of the texts he cited in his series had not been translated into English, making them inaccessible to most readers.[38] "The Negro in Latin America" extensively quoted a variety of prominent Latin American intellectuals who studied race. Tomás Blanco's *El prejuicio racial en Puerto Rico* served as one of Preece's key sources of data in the series, for example.

In addition to Blanco, the series frequently cited Fernando Ortiz's scholarship. A former Cuban politician and an anthropologist by training, Ortiz founded the Sociedad de Estudios Afro-Cubanos (Society of Afro-Cuban Studies) in 1937. There, Ortiz emerged as one of the leading intellectuals in the study and promotion of *antillanismo* and Black life in the Americas. Blanco and Ortiz shared an intellectual bond centered on the study of race in Cuba and Puerto Rico, respectively.[39]

Brazilian medical anthropologist Arthur Ramos's famous study *The Negro in Brazil* was another work that appeared throughout various reports in the series. Ramos hoped his 1939 study would be published in English and read by American race scholars. Transnational race historian Micol Seigel remarks that Ramos wanted to use his book as "fodder for comparison to other national units, especially the United States."[40] Happily taking the bait, Preece noted in his series that "the Negro in Brazil, is not only a part of the history of *our* people. It is part of the integrity of *our* people."[41]

In addition to their writing on race in Latin America, Blanco, Ramos, and Ortiz were connected through their relationship to American historian Richard Pattee. In 1936–37 Pattee helped W.E.B. Du Bois and historian Rayford Logan identify prominent Latin American race scholars as the pair worked on their massive *Encyclopedia of the Negro*.[42] In 1939 Pattee also published a short but significant essay on the Black diaspora in the Americas in the *Journal of Negro History*, edited by Black historian Carter G. Woodson. The essay originated from a lecture Pattee presented a year earlier at the Association for the Study of Negro Life and History (ASNLH) conference in New York. In his lecture Pattee encouraged attendees to "study the Negro as an integral element in the culture of these [Latin American] republics."[43]

In addition to recognizing the Black diaspora's significance in Latin America, Pattee's essay covered the research of Blanco, Ortiz, and Ramos on race in the Americas. In 1941 the Schomburg Collection at the New York Public Library commissioned Pattee to translate Ramos's book on race in Brazil.[44] Pattee's study characterized Ramos as the "most outstanding contributor to the scientific study of the Negro" in the Americas.[45]

Pattee also worked closely with Ortiz. Both men presented at the ASNLH meetings in New York. Just as he did with Ramos, Pattee showered Ortiz and his race work with the highest praise. Pattee was especially impressed with Ortiz's Sociedad de Estudios Afro-Cubanos. "Dr. Fernando Ortiz," observed Pattee, "has probably done more than any other single Cuban for Africanist studies."[46]

In the same lecture, Pattee briefly mentioned Puerto Rico but did not refer to Blanco's scholarship. Both he and Blanco had worked at the

University of Puerto Rico (UPR) for ten years before Pattee left to work at the Catholic University of America and as a cultural liaison with the State Department. As historians in Puerto Rico interested in the relationship between race and national identity, the men undoubtedly knew one another. In fact, while he was at the UPR Pattee favorably reviewed Blanco's first book, *Prontuario histórico de Puerto Rico* (1935).[47]

Sometime after moving back to the continental United States in 1941 or 1942, Pattee met Preece. In his series Preece described Pattee as a friend with whom he celebrated the publication of Pattee's translation of *The Negro in Brazil*.[48] Through their friendship, Preece secured a number of crucial secondary sources he referenced throughout his string of reports.

More striking, however, is the reason Preece believed Ramos, Ortiz, and Blanco to be significant resources for his series. Preece went out of his way to mention that all three Latin American intellectuals, like Preece himself, were white. White scholars writing about Blackness, argued Preece, were "important as an omen of that appreciation for the black man's achievements which will be a cornerstone of that new civilization, combining the genius of all races, which we will build here in the Americas."[49] Extolling Ortiz, Ramos, and Blanco's whiteness and scholarship, Preece symbolically linked his own writing and antiracist politics for the American South with the work of prominent white Latin American race scholars. However, Preece's writing about Blackness and its achievements (as well as the writings of Blanco, Ortiz, and Ramos) are predicated on Blackness being assigned value by whites rather than being allowed to stand on its own merits. The documentation of Black life in the Americas by all four men, in fact, tells us very little about a "new civilization" or even about Blackness. Instead, it tells us a lot more about the tenuous position of whiteness, labor, and the larger nationalist (or regional) projects each man was a part of in his respective context.

In addition to consulting secondary sources from Latin American scholars, Preece collected interviews and anecdotes of his interactions with Black Latinas/os living in the United States. "You see this column is not just something that I turn out each week from the mass of material covering one big section of my library, which I've accumulated on the Negro in Latin America," admitted Preece. "All of you have helped me give [my series] its present form."[50] In his first report about Brazil, for example, Preece recounted the "romantic story" of the Black presence in Brazil as told to him by a "Brazilian, who had the blood of all three races as [they] talked in a Harlem café just off Lenox Avenue."[51]

Another June 1945 column, "Latin American Negroes Make Good Citizens," focused on the presence of Latin American diasporic Blacks in Brooklyn and the benefits of extending U.S. citizenship to them. The primary informants in the report were army private Melbourne Smith, a young Panamanian, and his Trinidadian colleague Franklyn Emanuel Long. The column detailed the experiences of both Black Latin American soldiers as they underwent the naturalization process to become American citizens. Preece recounted that a Department of Justice official conducted the ceremony in "Old Mother African." The article's emphases on soldiers from two Latin American countries with large concentrations of Afro-descendants and on the language used in the ceremony are especially telling. Predicated on militarized and masculine constructions of citizenship that fetishize Blackness, the article highlighted the limited conditions under which inclusion within the U.S. nation-state could be attained.

In addition to the two Black Latin American soldiers, the "thousands of Spanish-speaking Latin American Negroes from Puerto Rico" living in Harlem at the time also made a cameo appearance in the June 1945 column. Preece emphasized the spatial and racial integration of Puerto Ricans in New York. Beginning in the 1920s, driven by a precipitous decline in agricultural work on the island, large numbers of Puerto Ricans migrated to and settled in parts of Harlem and Brooklyn. In fact, by 1920, 62 percent of all Puerto Ricans living in the United States lived in New York.[52] The column declared that Black Puerto Ricans "occupy and attend the same schools with white Puerto Ricans and you wont [sic] find one Uncle Tom among a thousand of them."[53]

The article's implication of Puerto Rican racial democracy in the American ghettoes where Puerto Ricans resided is significant for two reasons. First, Preece's "Uncle Tom" reference discursively separated Puerto Ricans from white America and simultaneously racialized them as nonwhite and part of the larger Black diaspora. Second, the article posits racial democracy as a practice found among diasporic Puerto Ricans. Perhaps most importantly, the article implicitly frames white Puerto Ricans as racially tolerant.

In doing so, the column ignores how Puerto Ricans, regardless of how they self-identified, had little say in the ways in which they were racialized as they migrated to urban centers throughout the United States. Equally troubling is that Preece makes this assertion without considering the possibility of the lure of whiteness to some Puerto Ricans who wished to disassociate themselves from the stigma of Blackness attached to their African American neighbors in New York.[54] Preece's dependence on secondary sources from some of Latin America's biggest proponents of racial democracy resulted in a series that reproduced this intellectual strand of Latin American liberalism and further extended its apparent legitimacy. Even more important, Preece latched on to these secondary sources because they modeled the types of race relations he imagined for the American South.

## Empire and the Folk

Preece's overreliance on secondary source material and lack of familiarity with Latin America limited the number of personal stories and relationships of racial progress in his series on Latin America. The series compensated for these gaps by including biographies and stories of little-known and deceased popular Black Latin American leaders. Black Latin American figures appeared alongside iconic American figures such as George Washington, Thomas Jefferson, Abraham Lincoln, Frederick Douglass, and Booker T. Washington. Through nationalist heroes and race scholars from across the Americas, readers were given strategic points of reference that allowed them to better appreciate the accomplishments of figures from the Black diaspora.

"Puerto Rico Faces Revolution," for instance, tells the story of nineteenth-century Puerto Rican abolitionist and *independentista* Ramón Emeterio Betances.[55] Preece describes Betances as Puerto Rico's "Black Washington." Betances's father came from a prominent family in the Dominican Republic while his mother's family hailed from France. Upon completing his medical studies in Paris, Betances established a successful practice in Puerto Rico. In late 1867, while based in Saint Thomas, Betances composed *Ten Commandments of Free Men,* principles on which Puerto Rico was to seek its sovereignty from Spain. The abolition of slavery, the right to vote on taxation, free trade, and the right to assembly were among the most prominent commandments in Betances's edict.[56]

In the article Preece does not focus on Betances's work as a mulatto abolitionist but rather on questions of empire: "If you lived in Puerto Rico, you might think that the American flag was pretty and that George Washington, the white Virginian whom you had learned about in the American controlled schools was a great man. But maybe you might be wondering when your country's flag, the captive flag of a captive people would take its place among the banners of the world's free nations."[57]

The article's symbolic use of Washington is twofold. It highlights the uneven colonial relationship between Puerto Rico and the United States, specifically the imposition of American schools on the island as a form of benevolent colonialism. According to historian Solsiree del Moral, the U.S. racial regime used public education to train students and teachers whom they hoped would ultimately serve as colonial administrators. More importantly, education became the central state apparatus to "expand the reach of the government into rural areas, to manage urban populations, and to consolidate the authority of the central state."[58]

At another level, the article marries the revolutionary work of Betances against Spain with that of Washington against Britain. This strategy couples the two national leaders' quests for sovereignty in the minds of readers and equates them as similarly marginalized in their struggles against empire. Nonetheless, conflating Washington and Betances in a series premised on the connections among the Black diaspora also conceals how both men belonged to the dominant land- and slave-owning classes of their era and prioritizes politics that correspond to their social positions in society.

In 1868 Betances penned Puerto Rico's first "decree of the revolution." The first article of this decree called for the permanent abolition of slavery in Puerto Rico. Article 2 indemnified slave owners, paying them the value of their slaves so long as they agreed to participate in the larger anticolonial revolutionary project.[59] Such indemnification maintained class and racial inequality on several structural levels. The policy rewarded property owners, provided slaves with no forms of reparation, and left the emerging state economically vulnerable, given the amount of money required to pay compensation of this magnitude.[60] Betances's decree illustrated how his abolitionist and larger antiracist politics remained contingent on the island's independence. Preece might have overlooked or purposefully remained silent on these issues in his accounts of Blackness in Latin

America because they troubled the transformative potential he saw in Latin American race relations.

In addition to discussing political figures, "The Negro in Latin America" also documented Black cultural traditions throughout the Americas. In key parts of the series, music, folk festivals, and religion (voodoo) dominated what readers learned about the Black diaspora in Latin America. These accounts relied heavily on folk and romantic readings of the practices of the Black diaspora. Describing El Salvador's Black diaspora, for example, an idealistic Preece ventured that "the Negro must have left something distinctive in the soul of El Salvador, something which responds with a deep ancestral longing towards the spirituals whose tunes were sung long ago in Daloney and Ghana."[61]

Preece's turn to the folk is surprising given his earlier critiques of anthropologist Zora Neale Hurston's classic study of Black folk life, *Mules and Men* (1935). Even though Preece himself spent a great deal of time collecting Texan folklore with acclaimed folklorist John A. Lomax, he objected to what he saw as colonialist anthropological depictions and uses of the folk in his earlier writings.[62] Preece accused African Americans like Hurston of seeking acceptance from white Americans who "cleverly exploited and distorted" Black folk culture. Hurston, claimed Preece, ignored the political and economic reasons behind the poverty experienced by the Black folk.[63]

Preece critiqued more than Hurston's reading of Black folk traditions. He believed that Hurston and other folklorists like her were opportunists "concerned with their pocketbooks," intent on making their names off the backs of poor Blacks. "When a Negro author describes her race with such servile terms as 'Mules and Men,'" accused Preece, "critical members of the race must necessarily evaluate the author as literary climber."[64] Although he cautioned readers against the self-promotion of the Black folk in these early writings, "The Negro in Latin America" made Preece's position on the folk more ambiguous.

## Race and Labor in Latin America

"The Living South" and "The Negro in Latin America" appeared at the same time and share significant points of overlap. While "The Living South" focused on labor movements, discussions of working-class culture and its connection to the material conditions of Latin American political economy are scattered throughout "The Negro in Latin America." Given the range of countries covered in the latter series, descriptions of the working classes are often underdeveloped. Attempting to work through these difficulties, Preece detailed the organizational activities of the Confederation of Latin American Workers (Confederación de Trabajadores de América Latina, or CTAL). Founded in 1938 by Mexican union leader Vicente Lombardo Toledano, CTAL came to prominence as the largest umbrella organization for trade unions in Latin America, with a total membership of about four million workers.[65]

A committed Marxist, Lombardo and CTAL envisioned a hemispheric labor movement in the Americas that would simultaneously seek political emancipation from dominant colonial powers. During his lengthy leadership, Lombardo remained committed to working alongside U.S. labor unions. Lombardo distinguished himself from other Latin American Leftists whom he claimed suffered from "fatal sectarianism," or the unwillingness to build alliances with workers in imperialist countries. He often urged CTAL and its leadership to discard this limiting isolationism from its organizational politics. The "fight against imperialism," Lombardo reminded workers in 1945, "requires that we in Latin America greatly strengthen our friendship with the working class and the greater masses of the United States and Canada."[66] Despite CTAL's efforts to reach out to American labor during its inaugural meetings in Mexico City, American Federation of Labor (AFL) president William Green "condemned the congress as an attempt to spread communist doctrine among the labor movements in Latin America."[67]

Green's comments reflect the AFL's allegiance to racial capitalism and American empire. The AFL promoted and endorsed labor practices that eliminated competition between skilled white and Black laborers and failed to offer equal representation to all of its constituents.[68] As labor historian Bill Fletcher emphasizes, the AFL sutured itself to whiteness in its belief that the "union's role should be exclusive to the workplace, focusing on wages, hours, and working conditions." Built on the premise of unifying labor, this insular approach ultimately ignored racism in unions and how racism fomented capitalism and empire beyond the realm of labor.[69]

Preece appreciated the CTAL's efforts in transnational and multiracial organizing. "The Negro in Latin America" criticized the AFL for rejecting an alliance with their Latin American counterparts. Preece accused the AFL of being "disturbed by the upsurge of colored workers in Latin America" and consequently trying to "Aryanize" the region. More importantly, the AFL, argued Preece, remained suspicious of the effects that CTAL's broad model of multiracial labor organizing would have on labor groups in the United States.

> I am not saying that President William Green of the American Federation of Labor is consciously helping Hitler, even if their . . . pro-racist policies in this country are prolonging the war because those policies keep Negroes from war jobs that need to be done. But I am asking why leaders of the [AFL], which excludes most American Negro workers, have been sounding out Latin America's bloodiest dictators, offering to set-up rival organizations to the Confederation of Latin American Workers with its huge majority of Negroes and Indians.[70]

Indeed, Toledano suspected members of the AFL of trying to infiltrate his organization. He also believed that the AFL wished to prop up Bernardo Ibáñez, leader of CTAL's Chilean delegation, and help Ibáñez establish a rival labor confederation.

Preece admonished Ibáñez for "some funny business that bodes no good for colored people" during his January 1944 visit to Washington, D.C. Part of the story tracked Ibáñez's movements in Washington, including meetings with then Assistant Secretary of State for Latin America Adolf Berle and members of the AFL leadership.[71] Preece cautioned that Ibáñez's meeting with Berle tied him to Wall Street bankers and pro-capitalist economists. "They liked Ibáñez," suspected Preece, "because they could talk business with him." Toledano and Preece's misgivings were confirmed in 1948 when Ibáñez became chairman of the anti-communist Inter-American Confederation of Workers (CIT). The CIT mobilized as an umbrella labor union counter to the CTAL and ultimately undermined the hemispheric labor movement that Preece and Lombardo sought.[72]

"The Negro in Latin America" also promoted the work of Puerto Rico's Confederación General de Trabajadores (CGT). The CGT developed in 1940 as a coalition of more than thirty unions and political groups, including the Puerto Rican Communist Party, which opposed the Federación Libre de Trabajadores (FLT). Muñoz Marín strategically aligned the PPD with the CGT, creating a coalition that played a key role in the party's rise in elections throughout the first half of the 1940s. By the mid-1940s the confederation swelled to well more than three hundred unions. Despite its heavily politicized wings, the CGT's platform focused on protecting the rights of all workers regardless of party affiliation. In this respect, the CGT framed its politics exclusively around class struggle. At the same time, the CGT perceived Puerto Rico's class struggle as inherently anti-imperialist. This served as a key point of departure from the fledgling FLT, which aligned itself to large sugar monopolies. Additionally, the FLT supported the unfavorable labor concessions agreed to in the Sugar Act, including a drastic reduction in workers' wages.[73]

Just like Preece's column on the CTAL, his column on the CGT characterized the AFL as a "lily white" organization. Given the strong faction of *independentistas*, communists, and presumably, the number of Black Puerto Ricans found among the CGT's ranks, Preece also described the CGT as an emergent multiracial labor union and as the more radical organization. In sum, the CGT was, for Preece, "Puerto Rico's Negro and White fighters for freedom."[74] The emphasis in "The Negro in Latin America" on the region's inclusive and radical labor movement served as a concrete model of what Preece imagined for his native South.

Preece even urged African Americans to migrate to parts of Latin America, including Brazil and Puerto Rico. Merging Preece's earlier Garveyist tendencies with a quasi-imperialist vision of Latin America, the column depicted the Southern Hemisphere in economically opportunistic terms: "Booming Latin America will welcome American Negroes who are qualified on the same basis as American white workers."[75] To prepare Black workers to migrate farther south, the series encouraged them to learn Spanish and provided useful information on where they could obtain the documentation required for migration.[76]

Puerto Rico's unresolved status also allowed Preece to illustrate the contradictions between American diplomacy and labor relations. Between 1898 and 1920, U.S. military forces entered the territory of a sovereign country in the Caribbean on at least twenty different occasions.[77] Thereafter the Great Depression brought the economic limits of costly imperialist military incursions into sharper focus.

In response, President Roosevelt implemented a model of soft power, known as the Good Neighbor Policy. The Good Neighbor Policy changed the official U.S. position throughout the region from one of active military involvement to one of nonintervention and noninterference. This new diplomatic stance permitted some levels of resource nationalization and some economic and social programs not previously fathomable in Latin America. The Roosevelt administration refused to provide the same type of assistance that had previously been given to American corporations during economic disputes with local governments and regulators.[78]

Newspaper columns addressing the Black Latin American diaspora approached the diplomatic tensions of the Good Neighbor Policy in inconsistent and contradictory ways. On a practical level, Puerto Rico's continued colonial status belied the Good Neighbor Policy's stated intention of nonintervention in the Americas. Nonetheless, Preece argued that the policy provided a unique opportunity to rethink the ways in which the United States interacted socially and economically with people of color throughout the hemisphere. "You can't do business with colored people in Latin America on the old gun and whip basis," begins Preece's March 3, 1944, column, "anymore than you can keep on doing business with the colored people of the United States by handing them ropes and fatback for wages."[79]

Preece believed that Roosevelt's new policy opened avenues to provide non-conditional aid to Latin America and to bring together colored populations, especially workers, across the hemisphere. The article noted "many of the benefits of that [Good Neighbor] policy are going to countries where Negroes have played great and heroic parts or where they constitute big percentages of the population." The remainder of the article focused on the results of these diplomatic interventions in Puerto Rico; specifically, the creation of decent-paying jobs on U.S.-sponsored projects. "That means saving the lives of a lot of Puerto Rican Negro children who had been starving to death before President Roosevelt appointed the wise and humane Rexford Tugwell as governor of the island."[80]

The article touted the economic and land reforms of Tugwell and the PPD as means to decrease the high infant mortality rate on the island, which averaged about 105 deaths per 1,000 live births between 1940 and 1944.[81] Preece considered the establishment of vocational schools on the island as fulfilling the dream of Puerto Rico's pioneer Negro educator Rafael Cordero to "teach Negro boys and girls to do other jobs besides swinging machetes on the sugar plantations."[82]

Preece's support of the Good Neighbor Policy had its limits. For one, he considered such forms of diplomacy as productive only insofar as they also assisted African Americans in the United States and created links between Black workers across the diaspora. An April 1944 feature, for example, began: "What's good news for Negroes in King Sugar's colonies of Louisiana and Florida is also good news for Negroes in King Sugar's colony of Puerto Rico." Preece then reprinted a letter he had received in Tennessee from an unnamed "Negro friend in Puerto Rico." The letter applauded the recent U.S. Supreme Court ruling in *Smith v. Allwright,* which found white primaries in the South to be unconstitutional. Preece's colleague in Puerto Rico hoped that the ruling supporting African Americans' right to the franchise would lead to "[American] Negroes . . . stand[ing] by Negroes" on the island. Unlike traditional racial narratives about Puerto Rico, the reprinted letter offers significant evidence that Puerto Ricans on the island self-identified as Negro and aligned their struggles with those of African Americans.[83]

In a February 1945 column on the Office of Price Administration (OPA), Preece explored how federal protections offered to Puerto Ricans also benefited African Americans. Another agency of Roosevelt's New Deal, the OPA rationed food supplies and froze prices on consumer goods. These actions prevented inflation and protected consumers from merchants hoping to exploit wartime shortages to hike up food prices.[84] OPA's presence on the island provided significant protection guarding Puerto Rican workers from food speculators who worked for the large sugar trusts.

Citing an OPA report from the Office of War Information, Preece's article briefly mentions the price gouging experienced by four Puerto Rican laborers. For example, one worker paid "two weeks [sic] earnings for a quart of oil, half a pound of pork fatback, half a pound of blue laundry soap, half a pound of coffee, and half a pound of codfish before I [an OPA official] sued for treble damages." Following the OPA's intervention, merchants compensated workers and organizations in Puerto Rico more than $2,000. More importantly, Preece connected the exploitation behind price gouging to a system of global capitalism that extended beyond Puerto Rico and that thrived locally in the South. "Suppose that the OPA started instituting treble damage suits against the whip-histing [sic] gentlemen who run the plantation commissaries down in Georgia and Arkansas," asked Preece. "Wouldn't it be a pretty good sign that Old King Cotton was on the way out in Dixie?"[85]

Even as the United States offered economic support and federal programs on the island, Puerto Rican self-determination remained an elusive goal. "Puerto Ricans, like the Americans, concluded an August 1945 entry, "want simply the right of every people to live under a government of their own choosing and their own making."[86] Preece went so far as to warn his predominantly Black readership that "the time may come very soon when Negro boys from Harlem and Arkansas may be conscripted to shoot down Negro boys in Ponce and San Juan."[87]

While his focus on Puerto Rico's sovereignty, race, and labor remained constant, Preece's favorable views of Governor Tugwell evolved by the time the series came to a close. In "Puerto Rico Faces Revolution," Preece became one of the first voices in the Black press to take on Tugwell's shifts on the island's colonial status, key labor issues, and his liberalism more broadly: "Imperialism had to make vague promises and a few liberal concessions to win the support of the colored peoples for World War II. But now imperialism, represented in Puerto Rico by Governor Tugwell, sheds its new silk gloves and takes up the old familiar whip as the colored peoples demand that the promises be kept and concessions broadened."[88] Understanding both the limits and possibilities of empire, Preece often walked a very delicate tightrope in his column with respect to Puerto Rico's colonial status. More specifically, he simultaneously saw the potential utility in exploiting imperialism to forge unforeseen alliances among workers and people of color across the Americas while maintaining that this strategy could succeed only so long as workers of color—not colonial administrators—remained the true agents of social change in any anticolonial project.

By early 1945, Tugwell convinced Muñoz Marín that independence would ruin Puerto Rico's economy and bring an end to any support from the metropolis. Tugwell also grew increasingly frustrated with Muñoz-Marín's continuous pandering to the CGT and Puerto Rican workers, whom he characterized as "noisy, disorderly, and perhaps violent."[89] On May 8, 1945, Tugwell signed into law the Puerto Rico Labor Relations Act (PRLRA). Modeled after the National Labor Relations Act, its federal predecessor, the PRLRA curbed the ability of sugar workers to strike against the sugar trusts. Perhaps more importantly, the PRLRA did not grant any of the major CGT demands, such as an eight-hour workday and overtime pay.[90] In his column, Preece cited the CGT's response to the PRLRA, describing the legislation as "an instrument to serve the interests of capitalists and a negation to all the rights and all the conquests achieved by the workers of Puerto Rico during the past 26 years."[91]

Preece coupled the denial of the CGT's demand for overtime pay with the denial of similar concessions to southern agricultural workers. "Lack of overtime pay," he noted, "has been one of the sore spots in Puerto Rico where the sugar workers, like the cotton workers of Mississippi, toil from sun up till sun down for wages which, before the war, averaged less than 50 cents a day."[92] In 1938 Mississippi's delegation to Congress from both political parties attempted to block the Fair Labor Standards Act of 1938, which granted workers overtime wages and a limited workweek. Although they failed to block the legislation, they did succeed in excluding domestic workers and agricultural workers (who were predominantly Black and Latina/o) from the final bill.[93]

As the CGT ramped up its radical union activities and the PPD moved away from its original pro-independence stance, Tugwell encouraged Muñoz Marín to bring the CGT into line. Through political nepotism, Muñoz-Marín forced the CGT to abandon its neutral position on political affiliations. As he pushed some CGT leaders to claim loyalty to the PPD Muñoz-Marín also successfully expelled others and branded them as communists. By the summer of 1945 the CGT's strong coalition of more than three hundred local unions began to break into two separate camps: the CGT Gubernamental and the CGT Auténtica. Historian Juan Angel Silén describes this split within the CGT as between the "populist tendency that sought to transform the labor movement into a dependency of the PPD (*gubernamental*), and the struggle to maintain an independent labor movement (*auténtica*)."[94]

Not entirely satisfied with these results, Tugwell actively courted the CIO in the hope that it could absorb the CGT's radical elements in much the same way that the AFL defused the FLT's militants. The CIO's incorporation of the CGT a few years later is especially surprising given that the CIO ignored the CGT's requests to affiliate with the American labor movement during the first half of the decade. Unbeknownst to Preece and many other members of the CGT, Tugwell himself made the request for affiliation between the CGT and CIO.[95] The CIO granted Tugwell's request in 1949 but immediately ran into problems due to the CIO representatives' unfamiliarity with the Puerto Rican labor movement and local conditions. Even worse, CIO representatives often racially abused and berated Puerto Rican workers. Labor historian Dionicio Nodín Valdés documents xenophobic treatment of Puerto Rican laborers by Alex Summers, director of the CIO's Sugar Division of the Packinghouse. During a meeting with Puerto Rican organizers Summers charged, "You seem to forget that I am the boss here in Puerto Rico, because I represent the International. How in the hell can you speak in that damn language [Spanish] when all of you understand and speak English?"[96]

Not yet aware of these future outcomes, Preece imbricated "The Living South" and the "The Negro in Latin America," constantly pointing out the connections and overlaps between large numbers of workers across the Americas and in the Black diaspora. "The Negro in Latin America" used Latin America as a model for what the South might become. In the final year of the series, an optimistic Preece concluded, "Someday I hope we'll have here in Dixie the same friendship and respect and equality between the races that humanity has already established in Latin America."[97]

## Conclusion

By the end of 1946 Preece had completed what were arguably his two most influential journalistic series. Even after being chased out of Tennessee by the Ku Klux Klan in 1946, he continued to write from Texas about labor, antiracism, and politics through the end of the decade.[98] In the latter half of the 1940s fewer of Preece's writings appeared in the Black press. In the 1950s he returned to his southwestern roots and began to write about the West and western outlaws.[99] Up until his death in 1992, Preece remained a committed socialist.[100] Accordingly, his diminished presence in the Black press cannot be attributed to a drastic political shift on his part. More likely, the Communist purge of the late 1940s and early 1950s heavily curtailed Preece's radical commitments. In 1945, Mississippi senator John Rankin lobbied to make the House Committee on Un-American Activities (HUAC), which had been slated for elimination, a permanent standing committee.[101] A segregationist and anti-Semite, Rankin ushered in an era of fervent anticommunist hysteria often based on unlawful and baseless innuendo or rumor.

After he returned to his home state of Texas Preece took on HUAC's persecution of communists and socialists. There, he began working as a correspondent for a small cluster of Black newspapers, including the *Houston Informer* in 1947. Owned by African American lawyer Carter Wesley, the *Informer* carried a statewide circulation of nearly 45,000 readers.[102] Sometime in the early months of 1947 Preece and Wesley had a falling-out over Preece's public opposition to the Rankin Committee. Fearing the damage that the HUAC might do to him or his newspaper, Wesley terminated Preece's contract with his group of newspapers.

Concerned about his dismissal, Preece wrote to W.E.B. Du Bois on August 3, 1947, appealing for his help and guidance. "For some time," wrote Preece, "there has been a growing rift between Mr. Wesley and myself over his present course which I believe is inimical to the progress of both the great mass of Negroes and the great mass of poor whites in the South." Preece vowed to continue publishing in small presses and to resume his antiracist activism regardless of the outcome of his dispute with Wesley. "I hate white supremacy so implacably—as my people, Southern white fighters for the Union hated slavery, that I am ready to go to work as a common laborer to keep the column going if my readers say so."[103]

Du Bois responded nine days later with a frank and straightforward letter. In it he described the difficult and often contradictory bind that faced Leftists like Preece: "Liberal and Radical white Southerners and liberal and radical Negroes are having a pretty tough time these days; especially the white southerner who talks a liberal creed with one side of his mouth and contradicts it with the other and does nothing with his hands."[104] Always attuned to the relationship between race and capitalism, Du Bois reasoned that Wesley just wanted to sell newspapers and avoid racial violence or censorship. In the end, Du Bois offered only a small but heartfelt apology: "He [Wesley] probably is figuring that he can make more money by dropping your column than gain prestige by printing it. I am sorry."[105]

A newspaper editor once characterized Preece as "the country's leading authority on the Negro in Latin America."[106] Three presses considered publishing the "Negro in Latin America" series in book form. Two rejected the proposal outright while the third, remarked Preece, "wanted [the book] to be an Uncle Tom piece of work with nothing about the part being played by the modern Latin American labor movement and its fine young Negro leaders."[107] As a result, Preece's writings on Latin America in the Black press fell into obscurity.

Yet through his series, Preece crafted a vision of his native South that coalesced around his limited understandings of race and labor relations in Latin America. By relying on other sources, he committed himself to the faulty premise that the Latin American scholars he studied and drew upon for his data, such as Tomás Blanco, fully understood the Puerto Rican racial dynamics they wrote about. Nonetheless, "The Negro in Latin America" demonstrates how Latin American epistemologies about race offered possibilities and resources that southern liberalism needed in order to reinvent itself. These possibilities engendered a revisionist history of the contributions made by key historical black figures whom Preece considered "the common denominator of the Americas." Through a consideration of multiracial unions in Latin America, such as CTAL and CGT, the column mapped opportunities and challenges the American labor movement faced in attempting to replicate cross-racial alliances in the South.

Importantly, Preece's understandings about race in the Americas came with an inaccurate and incomplete depiction of Black Latin American history. The conflation of nationalist icons across nations, for example, concealed unequal class, racial, and gendered arrangements in the service of anticolonial critiques. Because of his limited use of primary sources, Preece's series too easily succumbed to idealistic and homogenous readings of Black cultural and political life in the Americas through a folk lens.

In the end, Preece's "The Living South" and "The Negro in Latin America" produced contradictory readings of race in both Puerto Rico and the United States. He affirmed Myrdal's assertion in An American Dilemma that southern liberalism gained its power from beyond the U.S. South. Yet by limiting his discussion of racism to the United States, Preece simultaneously affirmed Tomás Blanco's racial liberalism, which gained its strength from homogenous understandings of racism as existing outside of Puerto Rico. Blanco and Myrdal never imagined that powerful possibilities for racial liberalism in the Americas endured in the imaginative mind of a little-known "ex-Nordic" journalist.

# 4

# The Republic of the Penniless

"I must have looked damned queer to the people of the district when I first moved in," states Emil Bluemelein in one of the opening scenes of Edwin Rosskam's 1964 novel *The Alien*. Set in the 1950s, the novel tells the story of Bluemelein's journey to El Fanguito (The Little Mud), a squatter slum just outside of San Juan, Puerto Rico. Bluemelein understands that, as a former colonial bureaucrat, his presence raises suspicions in a shantytown among Puerto Rico's poorest population. "They were afraid of me, no doubt about that. Some thought me a treasury agent looking for numbers runners. Other conceived the idea that I was a detective, different kinds of detective depending on who was talking." But the residents of El Fanguito are not simply afraid of Bluemelein. His presence in El Fanguito suggests a default on the promise of upward mobility in the United States. They demand an explanation.[1]

Rosskam tackles this glaring problem by likening his lead protagonist to the residents of the slum. "At least I have just about nothing to lose," explains Bluemelein, "since I gave up my standing as a non-Negro, non-Caribbean resident of impeccable Continental origins and said the hell with that and moved to the muddy edge of the city where nobody has much of anything except the marvelous final security of being on the bottom."[2] Bluemelein at once claims an entirely new class identity, renounces his status as an American, and more importantly, renounces what George Lipsitz terms his "possessive investment in whiteness."[3] Even more brazenly, Bluemelein's estrangement from the (white) American colonial project is likened to the poverty and violence that El Fanguito's residents experience. Rosskam's depiction of a 1950s post-racial (white) subject, however, was symptomatic of a larger move away from race among U.S. *and* Puerto Rican academics and the larger American political Left.

In this chapter I argue that Puerto Rico served as an ideal space to promote class-based typologies that overlooked or entirely ignored racial difference. Beginning in the mid-1940s, the University of Puerto Rico (UPR) developed into an important research arm of the PPD modernization efforts and of U.S. models of governance. The research at UPR earned the praise of American colonial bureaucrats who used Puerto Rico as a model for capitalist development against the looming threat of socialist expansion after World War II. In contrast, Rosskam and American social scientists challenged the positive depictions of the PPD modernization efforts.

American social scientists and activists within the U.S. political Left, including Rosskam, critiqued the forms of social and economic disorganization produced by capitalist expansion. Both groups weighed the adverse effects of capitalist-oriented industrialization on rural populations. Studying the massive displacement in the rural countryside, U.S. social scientists documented how uneven colonial development and dispossession increased alienation and fractured homogenous understandings of Puerto Rican national identity and culture.

Using Rosskam's novel as a sociological resource, I discuss in the second half of this chapter how Rosskam's career as a Farm Security Administration photographer and editor of several significant photo-books trained him to think about the racialized, capitalist-induced crisis in the countryside. However, Rosskam disregarded the ways in which capitalist practices shaped race relations on the island. By deploying sociological interpretative mechanisms Rosskam also sidestepped deeper questions about the contours of racial capitalism on the island. Using sociological typologies meant to explain social and cultural disorganization, Rosskam portrayed estrangement as a race-neutral and universal condition. Rosskam's false class equivalencies ignored the outcomes of racial capitalism and ultimately reinscribed categories of racial difference through his discussions of the Puerto Rican diaspora.

## The Puerto Rican Research Laboratory

On June 5, 1950, President Truman approved the creation of the Point Four Program as part of the Act for International Development. The Department of the Interior launched the Point Four Program as a means to provide U.S. aid and technological training to elite and professional classes in more than thirty-two countries in the Global South. The program's goals emerged as direct responses to the growing sphere of influence of the Soviet Union. Communism, claimed the Department of the Interior, could not be stopped by brute force alone. Securing American hegemony required an economic strategy to "maintain freedom and offset the appeal of Communism to the hungry, poverty-stricken, and distressed."[4] The Department of the Interior utilized all of the methods of scientific inquiry to approach these problems while promoting capitalist development.

The roots of the Point Four Program reached back years earlier in Puerto Rico, to when the Truman and Muñoz Marín administrations agreed to use the island as a training ground for initiatives to be implemented later throughout the rest of the world.[5] Given incursions of radicalized socialism into other parts of the Americas after the end of World War II, American policy analysts visualized Puerto Rico as *the* antisocialist model for countries in transition from the clutches of traditional colonial domination. Puerto Rico's colonial status, high rate of poverty, health and sanitation problems, and growing population made the island an appealing site for U.S. government researchers. Numerous prominent social scientists from U.S. institutions, foremost among them the University of Chicago and Columbia University, began arriving at UPR in the early 1940s. They used UPR as a research base to launch a massive modernization program based on capitalist-driven industrialization. U.S. government officials charged academics in Puerto Rico with raising the island's standard of living and governance using strategies they could extend to other countries without appearing to infringe upon national cultures or sovereignty.[6] By 1964 the number of people receiving training in Puerto Rico as part of the Point Four program ballooned to more than 23,000 foreign government officials from 137 different countries in the Global South.[7]

Within UPR, the Centro de Investigaciones Sociales (CIS; Social Science Research Center) "provide[d] the public university with a means of investigating the country's fundamental problems."[8] A large number of the research projects and reports originating from the CIS supported the mission of the colonial government, including the PPD, which had begun to secure its standing as the ruling hegemonic political bloc. The *Annals of the American Academy of Political and Social Science*, for example, devoted a special issue to the research being done at the CIS and the changes in Puerto Rico under the PPD. CIS director Millard Hansen and Yale professor Henry Wells presented Puerto Rico's success and symbolic importance in the foreword: "Puerto Rico's achievements are significant because they are at once common and grave. They are to be encountered in many parts of the troubled globe, and nowhere are they being attacked so confidently or so successfully that lessons cannot be drawn from the Puerto Rican experience."[9] American policy analysts and researchers who assisted the PPD or served as members of the PPD administration filled the remainder of the special issue with articles touting Puerto Rico's progress.

Not all CIS scholarship, however, supported the PPD's agenda or the desires of the State Department. Among the better known studies and publications to emerge from the CIS is *The People of Puerto Rico*. Originally proposed by Clarence Senior and directed by Columbia University anthropologist Julian Steward, the project utilized modern social science techniques to address the social and economic problems of Puerto Rico.[10] Scholars have critiqued CIS projects like this one as "colonialist enterprises" but this characterization does not fully capture the complicated political relationship that Puerto Rican and U.S. researchers had with the island.[11] Whereas some researchers certainly wished to keep Puerto Rico in a subjugated colonial position, others viewed their work as a part of Puerto Rico's larger decolonization project.[12]

The People of Puerto Rico project studied two significant strands of inquiry. To begin, it considered how changes in the modes of production increased class polarization and affected cultural practices. More specifically, the project measured the impact of technological transformations in different regions dependent on monocultural production of coffee, tobacco, and sugar as the national economy moved to industrial manufacturing. As the island's agricultural economy collapsed, new industrial factories emerged in the cities of Ponce and San Juan. However, the limited number of factories that opened on the island did not provide a sufficient number of jobs for the migrants from the rural countryside.[13]

Secondly, the project's interdisciplinary approach presented a more

Figure 4.1. "Do not let the dollar emigrate from your country," 1938. Photo by Edwin Rosskam. FSA Office of War Information Photograph Collection, Library of Congress.

nuanced account of subcultural variation within national populations than Puerto Rican government accounts did. Specifically, the research team examined the ways in which class, racial, and gender differences rooted in local modes of production fractured presumed nationalist affinities. Somewhat ironically, however, at the same time technological innovations such as radio and increased access to transportation expedited cultural exchange.[14]

The project's emphasis on the relationship between capitalist development and class polarization of society pointed the team toward a Marxist analysis of social relations on the island. Given the strength of external pressure from the PPD to produce a pro-capitalist development study, anthropologist Antonio Lauria-Perricelli argues that the project disguised its Marxist orientation in the final published book.[15] More plainly stated, the project did not present the favorable view of the transition to capitalist industrialization or the romantic nationalist narrative about culture and sovereignty that the PPD and Truman wanted to hear.

In order to give Truman and the PPD what they wanted, the team would have had to deliberately overlook the poverty they encountered in Puerto Rico. In 1948 more than one-third of the land owned or leased by the government remained committed to sugar production.[16] Furthermore, more than 88 percent of Puerto Ricans lived below the poverty line as late as 1953.[17] The migration of unemployed rural workers into urban

Figure 4.2. Child in workers' quarter of Puerto de Tierra, San Juan, Puerto Rico, 1938. Photo by Edwin Rosskam. FSA, Office of War Information Photograph Collection, Library of Congress.

Figure 4.3. Water supply in the workers' quarter of Puerto de Tierra, 1938. Photo by Edwin Rosskam. FSA, Office of War Information Photograph Collection, Library of Congress.

centers illustrated the shortcomings of the PPD's land reform initiatives. According to a 1943 Puerto Rico Office of Information report, more than a quarter million families in Puerto Rico lived in substandard, small, and poorly built housing. American academics, politicians, and journalists zeroed in on Puerto Rico's shantytowns.

The social and economic conditions of Puerto Rico's slums fed liberal critiques of the American racial and colonial regime. Urban slums like El Fanguito, built on swamplands outside of San Juan, absorbed displaced workers from the rural countryside. During the first half of the 1940s alone, Puerto Rico's urban population ballooned at a rate of more than 30,000 people per year.[18] In 1943, close to 6,800 families resettled in El Fanguito. The number of families moving to the slum continued to climb throughout the remainder of the decade.[19] The March 8, 1943, issue of *Life* magazine referred to El Fanguito as one of the world's "slimier slums" and a "shocking disgrace." In the ultimate show of colonial paternalism, the article questioned the United States' ability to solve the island's problems and bring "order out of the chaos in the rest of the world."[20]

El Fanguito's denizens consisted of displaced poor, rural, and uneducated workers. The shacks were constructed of discarded pieces of wood and zinc, and were elevated above the swampland on large wooden stilts, making them highly susceptible to natural disasters such as hurricanes. An intricate and unstable web of wooden planks connected many of the homes. The lack of basic public utilities including running water, trash disposal, and electricity left families—especially children—vulnerable to intestinal diseases such as hookworm, tuberculosis, and malaria. In 1939, the death rate from tuberculosis stood at 258 deaths per 100,000 persons on the island; by comparison, the death rate in the United States was only 47.2 people per 100,000. Intestinal diseases such as diarrhea and enteritis killed even more Puerto Ricans than tuberculosis did.[21]

William Foster, national chairman of the CPUSA, left El Fanguito deeply disturbed following his 1948 visit to the slum. One month after his trip, Foster drafted a letter to President Truman in which he described the inhumane conditions he witnessed and the U.S. failure to address them. Referencing Truman's own February 1948 trip to the island, Foster emphasized the burden of colonial responsibility:

> Mr. President, although you as the head of the great imperialist country which holds Puerto Rico as a colony, coldly ignored the grave slum problem of the Puerto Rican people by callously riding past El Fanguito, I, as an American citizen conscious of our nation's heavy responsibility to this oppressed people did not ride past. I went into this most wretched of slums with its immense population and talked to many of its miserable inhabitants. And I saw sights and heard stories of extreme poverty that will stay with me until my dying day. I burned with shame that such outrageous conditions exist on Puerto Rico and are caused by us. . . . A modern Dante, seeking to write a new *Inferno*, need go no further than El Fanguito.[22]

Foster visited with numerous families during his time in the slum, speaking with single-parent families and with orphans who "lived by picking up whatever food they could find among their impoverished neighbors."[23]

The leading figure in the Puerto Rican Communist Party, César Andreu Iglesias, invited Foster to Puerto Rico to meet with local party officials and talk to more than two thousand workers at the Teatro Puerto Rico in San Juan. In his speech (a version of the letter he sent Truman) Foster demanded that the United States respect Puerto Rican sovereignty. He also called on Truman to acknowledge the responsibility of American sugar companies and capitalist practices for fomenting the massive exodus from the countryside that produced the immense poverty he witnessed.

Foster also lamented the segregation experienced by racially mixed Puerto Rican soldiers. The "democratic fraternal ties between Black and White Puerto Ricans (i.e., *mestizaje*)," believed Foster, "were sufficient to defeat this racist attack."[24] Foster informed his audience that the bonds among Puerto Rico's racially mixed working class would be impossible to replicate under American racial capitalism. Capitalism, he claimed, did not respect any nation or people that did not have an "Anglo-Saxon historical and cultural tradition." Foster even labeled organized labor and progressives in the United States as not "up to par in their solidarity efforts with the struggles of the oppressed people of Puerto Rico."[25] Taken together, Foster's analysis pointed to the ways in which he understood Puerto Rican labor as an ideal model for American workers because of its class composition and ability to work through racial difference.

The CPUSA party leadership believed that addressing the race question could broaden the labor movement domestically and internationally. Journalist James Allen, who published what is arguably the most complete analysis of the party's position on the "Negro Question," reiterated the necessity of a "central Negro people's front," arguing that "other groups and forces [would] gravitate towards it as towards a magnet." Allen's optimism about a multiracial labor movement remained problematically linked to the idea that racism was a product of the "economic super-exploitation of the Negro," overlooking how race also shaped the very terms of exploitative labor and living conditions.[26]

Allen structured his class analysis in starkly black-and-white terms, conceptualizing the race question within a Black Nationalist frame. In spite of this, his study hinted at how the CPUSA viewed other racialized and colonized countries such as Puerto Rico. "The Negro question in the United States," argued Allen, "is essentially the same as that of retarded and oppressed peoples . . . in the colonies. Like these peoples the American

Negro has been retarded in their social development under American imperialism."[27] Like the African American journalists discussed in chapters 1 and 2, Allen used the colonies as a point of departure to analyze the colonial relations and corresponding racialization that American imperialism produced domestically.

Foster drew on the CPUSA's position on race in his 1948 letter to Truman. Puerto Ricans, he maintained, "hate us for compelling them to teach their children in English instead of Spanish; they hate our attempts to force the infamous Jim Crow system upon their people. In a word they are demanding their national independence."[28] Connecting Jim Crow segregation, Puerto Rican sovereignty, and the impoverished Puerto Ricans he encountered on his visit to the island, Foster tacitly characterized Puerto Rico's dispossessed population as a racially tolerant and unified class of workers.

It is instructive at this point to return to the People of Puerto Rico project and its attention to race and class. Different members of the research team analyzed race relations in the various regions they studied. Supporting Foster's position, three of the ethnographic chapters on regional and subcultural variation observed racial differences between classes but not within a class group. Elena Padilla, for example, concluded that in the government-owned sugar plantation "members of this [lower] class are very conscious of racial characteristics, especially skin color, to which they frequently refer. But within their class, color differences do not usually form the basis for discrimination."[29]

Padilla's conclusion is instructive because it demonstrates that race remained a crucial index of social and economic difference across class groups. The lower-class workers described by Padilla were not detached from ideas about race, especially the ways in which presumed biological markers positioned individuals within the prevailing class strata. Despite this hyperawareness, Padilla quickly moves past "color difference" and minimizes its prevalence within a given class group. Padilla states only that race "usually" does not lead to discrimination. As such, the reader is left to wonder when race is a significant variable in experiences of discrimination and what is significant about the racial consciousness she describes.

Contrary to Foster's and Padilla's findings, Eric Wolf's and Sidney Mintz's regional studies documented racial difference within class groups

Figure 4.4. Negro workers in front of their homes near Ponce, Puerto Rico, 1938. Photo by Edwin Rosskam. FSA, Office of War Information Photograph Collection, Library of Congress.

and across regional spaces. Wolf described the racialized fears that coffee plantation workers had about moving to work in the sugar fields along the coast. In particular, they feared the "Negroes who live on the coast" whom they believed to be "witches" that would poison and kill them.[30] Mintz similarly observed that workers from the highlands dreaded Puerto Rico's coastal regions because of the large concentrations of Blacks there, whom they too considered to be witches. Mintz did mention that these intraclass racial tensions dissipated somewhat once workers labored side by side on the coastal sugar plantations. Nonetheless, Mintz maintained that whiteness remained the ideal among Puerto Rico's rural proletariat.[31]

The relationship between race and space outlined the limits of a co-hesive and racially integrated class of workers in Puerto Rico. The racial composition of Puerto Rico's slums appeared to support these claims. In her brief 1949 study about race and prejudice in Puerto Rico, the American sociologist Maxine Gordon observed that major slum areas on the island housed "predominantly . . . large numbers of low paid colored workers." Echoing Wolf's and Mintz's critiques of the presumed absence of racism among Puerto Rico's proletariat, Gordon scrutinized the methodology of an unnamed project that aspired to prove racism did not exist on the is-land. Given her observations of Puerto Rico's slums, Gordon ruled out an economic approach for the study since it "[robbed] the project of its original purpose: to demonstrate that Negro and white Puerto Rican [sic] have the same way of life."[32] Importantly then, Puerto Rico's proletariat was not in fact a racially tolerant and unified class, as Foster and others claimed. Instead, informal segregation and cultural assumptions about racial difference thrived within Puerto Rico's proletariat throughout the 1940s.

Wolf's, Mintz's, and Gordon's investigations stand out as exceptions among the plethora of studies completed at the UPR during the 1940s and 1950s. Their work countered prevailing nationalist narratives about Puerto Rico, especially the myth that racism did not exist in Puerto Ri-can working-class communities and within labor groups. But there should have been more accounts and critiques that delved deeper into these pre-liminary findings about intra-class race relations on the island. Using Ed-win Rosskam as an example, in the sections that follow I consider how and why American liberals did not take more critical approaches to race rela-tions in Puerto Rico. Despite his career as a photographer of various racial and ethnic groups, Rosskam eschewed discussions about race in Puerto Rico through his use of sociological mechanisms and typologies common at the time.

## Photographing Race

Detachment and alienation defined much of Edwin Rosskam's personal biography. Born in 1903 to American parents, Rosskam lived the first fifteen years of his life in Germany. On returning to the United States,

Rosskam completed high school and enrolled in Haverford College, only to transfer to the Philadelphia Academy of Fine Arts. Ultimately, Rosskam took an avid interest in photojournalism and landed a job with the liberal newspaper the *Philadelphia Record*. In 1936 Rosskam married his second wife, Louise Rosenbaum Rosskam, who traveled and worked alongside Edwin as a photographer.[33]

Like other liberals of their day, the Rosskams displayed a profound sensibility to class conflict and to inequality more generally. Art historian Laura Katzman wrote that Edwin appeared to have been "well versed in theories of class struggle." For her part, Louise sympathized with "the pressing problems of the day: unemployment, poverty, hunger, disease, racial and class inequality and the threats to democracy posed by the war and fascism raging abroad."[34]

In 1937 Edwin Rosskam's friend and longtime editor for *Life* magazine, Roger Butterfield, helped Rosskam land a job with *Life*. The editors at *Life* sent Rosskam to Puerto Rico to cover the Ponce Massacre of March 21, 1937. On that day members of the Puerto Rican Nationalist Party assembled a peaceful demonstration in the city of Ponce to commemorate the abolition of slavery and protest the jailing of nationalist leaders. On the orders of Blanton Winship, the appointed American governor, local police callously gunned down fourteen nationalists and five bystanders. The *Life* editors wanted Rosskam to produce a photo essay about the *independentistas* on the island.[35] Rosskam's lifelong fixation with Puerto Rico began during this brief stint with *Life* early in his career.[36]

The conservative editors at *Life* considered Rosskam's account of the massacre politically unsuitable for their readership. They especially disapproved of Rosskam's support for Senator Muñoz Marín, who at that point had begun to distinguish himself in the Puerto Rican Senate. The editors supported another, unnamed local politician and condemned the article's "critical evaluation" of Puerto Rico's colonial status.[37] Rosskam's article about Puerto Rico was never published, but during this trip he met Muñoz Marín in an apartment above a local newspaper's office, and the two became lifelong friends.[38]

The FSA soon hired the Rosskams to work as photographers and editors of their massive photo file. FSA director Rexford Tugwell tapped his former student at Columbia University, Roy Stryker, to lead the agency's Historical Section. The Historical Section used photography to document and promote the resettlement of displaced rural families onto land provided by federally approved loans.[39] Most importantly, the FSA file gave the American public a class-based vision of America defined by rural displacement and urban poverty.

At times, the FSA file did not accurately reflect the face of American poverty because it strategically limited the number of projects that focused on nonwhite racial and ethnic groups. FSA historian Nicholas Natanson reports that Stryker carefully managed the race question so as not to antagonize southern congressmen who opposed funding large segments of the New Deal state apparatus. In all, 10 percent of the file's total collection of photographs depicted African Americans. This percentage is surprising given that there was no formal directive for FSA photographers to focus on African Americans. The coverage of African Americans appears instead to have arisen organically from the political interests of the FSA photographers, who chose to avoid such a gap in their work.[40]

Rosskam and fellow photographer Jack Delano (who later joined the Rosskams in Puerto Rico with his wife, Irene), for example, proposed a photographic study of Black urban life to Stryker in 1941. "We have pictures of farmer's meetings . . . and town meetings, but we are almost completely lacking in the urban counterpart," stated Rosskam and Delano.[41] Rosskam also desired to publish photo-books about every U.S. minority group.[42] Though Stryker did not respond to the memo from Rosskam and Delano, Rosskam finally got the opportunity to carry out an FSA collaborative project on Black urban life in 1941 when he took the photographs for the renowned Black writer Richard Wright's 12 Million Black Voices.

Prior to the publication of 12 Million Black Voices, Rosskam edited Oliver La Farge's 1940 book of photographs by Helen Post, As Long as the Grass Shall Grow. Read alongside each other, the two photo-books underscore the limitations of American racial liberalism. By focusing on the racialized outcomes of modernization and industrialization, they illustrated that the status of subjugated groups within the American racial regime remained precarious at best. At worst, marginalized communities within the American racial regime experienced segregated housing, cultural genocide, and social dispossession.

La Farge and Post's photographic study focused on the difficult position of Native American tribes facing continual incursions into their land and sovereignty. The captions for the final seven photographs in the book, most likely written by Rosskam, read: "We shall learn all of these devices the white man has, we shall handle his tools for ourselves. We shall master his machinery. His inventions. His planning. And still be Indians."[43] The captions provide insight into Rosskam's thinking about Native American acculturation and the threat to Native cultural practices and identity posed by modernization efforts. Rosskam linked Native Americans' agency to their ability to adapt to modern technology rather than completely rejecting assimilation to dominant modes of American life.

*12 Million Black Voices* continued this intellectual thread through its attention to the plight of African Americans during the Great Migration to urban centers throughout the North and Midwest. Rosskam's partnership with Wright trained him to think about photographing race through a sociological lens. In the acknowledgments, Rosskam thanked Stryker as well as University of Chicago sociologist Horace Cayton. Cayton, who went on to coauthor *Black Metropolis* with John Gibbs St. Clair Drake, introduced Rosskam and Wright to the methods and theories about urbanization, assimilation, and alienation that were central features of the Chicago School of Sociology. Rosskam pulled many details for his photo captions from Cayton's 1940 study, *Negro Housing in Chicago*.

Wright's familiarity with Chicago enhanced Rosskam's understanding of the structural challenges faced by African Americans moving to urban centers. Wright, observed Rosskam years later, "knew where everybody was, and he knew everybody in the Negro world of Chicago. And I don't know if many white men had the opportunity to see it the way we saw it."[44] Given his perhaps unprecedented access, Rosskam critically reflected on how subjects of Wright and Rosskam's joint venture perceived him as a white outsider. "The challenge for Ed, working in the ghetto," observed Louise Rosskam, "was not fear. . . . What he tried to avoid, at all costs, was condescension toward 'poor' subjects. What he liked to do . . . was to try and melt into the background, photographing the world as it went by."[45] Louise's comments point to the sociological deliberations about race that emerged in Edwin's work and were facilitated by his relationship with Wright.

In 1945 Tugwell, who had assumed the governorship of Puerto Rico, recruited the Rosskams to work in the Office of Information for Puerto Rico (OIPR). The OIPR mirrored the FSA's mission in that it disseminated information about Puerto Rico's problems to the larger American public.

Figure 4.5. Portrait of Edwin and Louise Rosskam, full length, posed with cameras sitting on a wall by the sea, Puerto Rico. Photo by Charles Rotkin. Library of Congress.

It organized traveling photo exhibits documenting the suffering on the island, which Tugwell used to secure additional federal funding for future projects in Puerto Rico.

Frustrated that the OIPR focused solely on the island's difficulties, Rosskam proposed to Senator Muñoz Marín and Governor Tugwell that a new agency be created.[46] Following his election as governor in 1949, Muñoz Marín signed Law 372, which established the División de Educación de la Comunidad (DIVEDCO). With Rosskam as its director, DIVEDCO combatted the island's most pressing problems through public education campaigns that used informative booklets and traveling photo exhibits and films.[47]

These films and photos captured the attention of the Puerto Rican police. Local police disapproved of the Rosskams' work as photographers and remained suspicious of how they intended to use their photos, given their political sensibilities.[48] A series of confidential letters forwarded directly to Governor Muñoz Marín from Chief of Police Salvador Roig identified the Rosskams as intimate associates of Charles Rotkin and the Delanos. In addition to Rotkin being a member of the CPUSA, his wife, Adele Diamond Rotkin, was secretary of the Heights Unity Club, a communist political group.[49]

The Rosskams' political affinities with the American Left annoyed Muñoz Marín, whose political outlook had become increasingly conservative over time. A 1950 news brief, for example, remarked that the governor appeared to "leave unsatisfied" after viewing DIVEDCO's film *Vecinos*. "From what we have been told," commented longtime *El Mundo* reporter Eliseo Combas Guerra, "the film had some scenes and dialogue resembling communist propaganda and others that had an intense colonial flavor."[50]

The police never charged the Rosskams with any crime, and there is no mention in the archive of a public falling-out between Muñoz Marín and Edwin over his photos and films. Nonetheless, the Rosskams left the island in 1952 after the local Catholic church accused them of being communists. According to photography critics Laura Katzman and Beverly Brannan, the allegations surfaced in the midst of an election year, so the Rosskams decided to leave Puerto Rico in order to avoid embroiling Muñoz Marín in a political scandal.[51]

Back in the United States, the Rosskams settled in Roosevelt, New Jersey. A New Deal–era township, Roosevelt had quickly gained a reputation as a "left-wing enclave." New Jersey experienced the same racial tensions and upheavals as the rest of the country. For example, urban rebellions in Elizabeth, Patterson, and Newark, New Jersey, challenged state practices of exclusion and violence around the time that Rosskam was completing his novel, *The Alien*.[52] In Newark, the unwarranted arrest and beating of Black taxi driver John Smith led to violent protests that resulted in twenty-six deaths and more than fifteen hundred arrests.[53]

The social unrest surrounding Roosevelt prevented a smooth transition to the mainland for the Rosskams. Even though the couple felt welcomed in Roosevelt, Edwin missed the political connections and impact of his work in Puerto Rico.[54] Rosskam opened up to Muñoz Marín and his wife, Inés Mendoza, in several letters that chronicled his estrangement from Puerto Rico. In a November 1960 missive he confessed that he and Louise were "dying of nostalgia" for Puerto Rico.[55] One month later Rosskam disclosed more feelings of nostalgia: "Frankly, Don Luis, I find it difficult to think of my future divorced from the island, the people, and the movement which have given meaning to the last dozen years of my life."[56]

Louise Rosskam recounted that Edwin fell into a "real decline" in their first year in Roosevelt because "he could not adjust to leaving Puerto Rico . . . it was very serious." A family friend and psychiatrist attended to Rosskam and recommended that he work through his yearning for Puerto Rico by writing. This prescription motivated Rosskam to immerse himself in writing and led to the publication of his little known novel *The Alien*.[57]

### The Emergent Post-Racial Subject

*The Alien* tells the story of Emil Bluemelein's journey from rural Montana to El Fanguito. The novel shares striking similarities with Rosskam's own biography, including his feelings of displacement and his work with the FSA and the OIPR. Given these parallels, the novel's preface cautions readers that the story is simply "an image in the mind, not a document." The novel, he continues, "pursues personal truths and fancies, not facts" as well as characters that "have never existed."[58] The distinction between autobiography and fiction is, however, blurred. Years later Rosskam confessed that the documentary detail in the novel is "starkingly [sic] complete . . . because I have photographs of it. No memory can do this for itself."[59]

Bluemelein is the son of a German immigrant and former watch repairman who sells his business in Philadelphia and moves the family to Montana to become a homesteader. Against his father's wishes, Bluemelein spurns working the family homestead and opts to become a government bureaucrat in Washington. He ultimately lands a job with the State Department's Division of Territories and Island Possessions. This decision is significant because it is the first of several moments in the novel where he detaches himself from the symbolic and material importance attached to the acquisition of property within the American imaginary.

Bluemelein's rejection of landownership and life in rural America is strategically meant to evoke parallels between him and the denizens of El Fanguito. As mentioned, large segments of El Fanguito's population were dispossessed workers forced to move to urban centers in search of work as the island transformed its market-dependent economy based on agricultural monocultures. The characters in the novel have all unwillingly relocated from towns throughout the island, such as Peñuelas, and from interior mountainous regions such as Orocovis and Adjuntas. They are all either themselves displaced sugar, coffee, or tobacco workers or the children of displaced workers. It is important, however, to note that, unlike everyone else in El Fanguito, Bluemelein *voluntarily* relocates to the slum. This significant detail speaks to the underlying disconnect that the Puerto Rican residents of El Fanguito can see but Bluemelein is blind to.

Following CPUSA chairman William Foster, Rosskam criticized the role of U.S. colonial policy in creating a class of displaced workers. Rosskam's portrayal of Puerto Rico's landless proletariat did not just repeat the then-accepted truths about Puerto Rican poverty. Rather, like the People of Puerto Rico Project, the descriptions of poverty that saturate the novel point at uneven colonial development as the structure undergirding the economic and racial marginalization being experienced by Puerto Rican workers. "Were there ever under the Stars and Stripes such beggars?" asks Bluemelein after being reassigned to Puerto Rico from the Washington office. "The ragged women with eroded faces carrying babies too sickly to be true," provide a grisly picture of the extreme poverty on the island more than half a century after the U.S. occupation of the island began.[60]

Despite the overwhelming presence of poor, displaced workers, Rosskam recognized that alleviation of poverty remained a distant second priority behind the promotion of capitalist development on the island. "Not that beggars matter. . . . The cane fields and cane mills matter, the tobacco slopes, the coffee plantations in the western mountains, the docks, the warehouses, the banks."[61] Foreign capital invested in agriculture depended heavily on a large class of migrant workers to perform the work required in different growing and harvest seasons. Positioning capitalist priorities against the paupers in the streets of urban slums, Rosskam accurately critiqued the outcomes of U.S. economic colonial policy. In short, the novel was first and foremost an indictment of colonialism in Puerto Rico. But Rosskam's depictions of Puerto Rico's economic crisis centered on class difference and, through Bluemelein, framed race through an exclusively white lens.

Bluemelein abandons his post as a colonial bureaucrat and opts to settle in El Fanguito after witnessing the Ponce Massacre. This "displacement" from the American colonial project is married in the novel to the displacement of the workers in El Fanguito. Even more, it explains why

Figure 4.6. Sugar worker taking a drink of water on a plantation, 1938. Photo by Edwin Rosskam. FSA, Office of War Information Photograph Collection, Library of Congress.

someone like him lives and is accepted in the multiracial slum. The relationship between the two imbricates sociological typologies that conflate Bluemelein's estrangement with class-based disorganization. Unexamined beneath these overlapping phenomena, however, is the articulation of an emergent white class subjectivity. Specifically, the contrast between Bluemelein's displacement from the United States and the material dispossession of workers of color in El Fanguito impels Rosskam to construct Bluemelein as a post-racial subject who "gave up [his] standing as a non-Negro, non-Caribbean resident of impeccable Continental origins."[62]

Bluemelein's estrangement from the U.S. rural countryside is most evident during the funeral of his younger brother, Charley, who dies by being sucked headfirst into a baler. Bluemelein interprets burial as an act of being "forsaken and imprisoned forever in the earth." Even more significantly, the land "had meaning for the older men who settled this country, but not for me and now certainly not for [Charley]."[63] As Bluemelein grieves his brother's passing and his own separation from the land, he gets his very "first and pretty desperate glimpse of island." The trope of island, or the ways one is materially and symbolically disaffected within a space one inhabits, runs through the entire novel. Puerto Rican intellectuals also used (cultural and political) insularity resulting from national shifts in economic priorities as a popular trope for understanding Puerto Rico's colonial predicament. In the next section I consider the ways in which these uses of Puerto Rican insularity overlapped with sociological typologies—including "the marginal man" and "the mulatto"—which were meant to describe the alienation resulting from contact between different groups.

## Insularity and the Marginal Man

Antonio Pedreira's canonical text, *Insularismo: ensayos de interpretación puertorriqueña* (1934), weighed the effects of colonialism and the contact between different national and racial groups on Puerto Rican national culture. Unapologetically Eurocentric and patriarchal, Pedreira's study callously dismissed the contributions of women and of Puerto Rico's early native and African populations. Distinguishing between the desirable traits of European blood and the undesirable traits of African blood, Pedreira proposed whiteness as a corrective to Puerto Rican cultural lag.[64]

   Key thinkers who shaped Pedreira's thinking included his professor at Columbia University, Spanish Hispanophile Federico de Onís, and Oswald Spengler in his *Decline of the West*. Onís argued that, as the frontier of Spanish civilization, the Americas maintained the vitality and legacy of the former Spanish Empire. Onís's view of the colonial frontier as a regenerative space influenced Pedreira's thoughts about the relationship between Puerto Rico's limited geographical space and its ability to stimulate national culture.[65] In Spengler's *Decline of the West*, Pedreira admired the distinction between civilization, where economic considerations and efficiency take precedence, and the spirit of national culture. According to Pedreira, the nexus between capitalist economic development, urbanization, and the need for cultural protectionism constituted the central tension of

Puerto Rican insularity. In short, Puerto Rico's limited territory—exacerbated by the selling of public land under capitalist development—hampered the possibilities for cultural regeneration. "Only yesterday we took the land to heart and embraced it," lamented Pedreira, "today it is slipping out of our hands in a seesaw of sales, changing its patriotic value for an exclusively economic one."[66]

The monopolization of land by absentee U.S. corporations and Puerto Rico's dual colonial history left a displaced, culturally marginalized, and racially hybrid (mulatto) subject in the urban shantytowns. *Insularismo* traced the history of the mulatto back to the moment of contact of Puerto Rico's indigenous population with Spanish colonizers and subsequently with African slaves. Pedreira argued that the Spanish (especially the lowest classes) gave in to "overindulgences" (that is, sexual violence) through which they "fused" with African slaves and became "con-fused mulattoes."[67]

Pedreira's description of Puerto Rican biracialism and mestizaje reads like a battle between racial strands: "The mulatto . . . not one thing or the other, is at bottom undefined and wavering, in conflict, maintaining both racial dispositions without ever defining himself socially. . . . He is prudent but indecisive, like a man who finds himself caught in the fire between two warring camps." To resolve this racialized schism Pedreira suggested that mulattos decide which racial camp they wished to belong to. The choice to side with Europe is facilitated by Pedreira's portrayal of Blacks as culturally impotent and irrational. Despite his supposedly nationalist sentiments, Pedreira's articulation of the Puerto Rican mulatto shares striking similarities with the ways in which American social scientists wrote about racial mixture.

In the same year as Pedreira published *Insularismo*, sociologist Edward B. Reuter released his edited volume *Race and Culture Contacts*. A southerner from Missouri, Reuter studied how modernization and urban migration created physical, sexual, and cultural exchanges that opened up possibilities for individual freedom and thereby enabled the advancement of society as a whole. But because the new freedoms that came with modernization challenged and destabilized established norms, they also produced feelings of estrangement and social disorganization, especially in urban centers.[68]

Reuter's advisor at the University of Chicago, Robert Park, evoked the sociological concept of the "marginal man" to explain the social disorganization resulting from migration and cultural contact. Based on German sociologist Georg Simmel's "stranger" and citing Spengler extensively, Park defined the marginal subject as torn between the "cultural life and traditions of two distinct peoples, never quite willing to break . . . with his past traditions, and not quite accepted, because of racial prejudice, in the new society."[69] The Chicago School sociologists (like Simmel) often cited the Jew as the ideal of the "marginal man," but they also believed that the mulatto exemplified the in-betweenness they described.

Similar conceptualizations of the mulatto conjoin Pedreira's, Reuter's, and Park's scholarship on race. Despite Park's and Reuter's best efforts to distance themselves from biological explanations of group achievement, their notes on the mulatto at times resorted to making weak correlations between biology, culture, and group outcomes—results not supported by data.[70] Park, echoing Pedreira's own description, depicted the mulatto as someone who "feels the conflict of warring ancestry in his veins. The conflict of color is embodied, so to speak, in his person. His mind is the melting pot in which the lower and higher cultures meet and fuse."[71] Reuter, who spent a year at the UPR as a visiting professor, extended his pseudo-biological observations on cultural achievements to Latin America and the Caribbean. "The half-breeds," wrote Reuter, "form a more or less distinct and separate class somewhat inferior to the whites and distinctly superior to the pure blood natives."[72]

Reuter considered Puerto Rico a prime example of cultural contact between traditionalism and modernity. Focusing on the tension between mechanization and culture on the island, Reuter deployed hybridity as a racialized trope to make sense of this material and cultural dissonance: "Puerto Rico is neither Spanish nor American; it is a mixture of both. . . . The [Puerto Rican's] state of mind is one of painful confusion. The Puerto Rican is often divided between his sentiments and his interests; economically he turns to the United States; sentimentally he turns to Spain and Latin America."[73] Using a history of racial contact equivalent to that given by Pedreira, Reuter characterized Puerto Rico as a socially and culturally disorganized mulatto nation.[74] According to all three thinkers, Puerto Rico's urban proletariat constituted a racially and socially marginalized class.

Interestingly, in 1934 Park eliminated racial discrimination as a characteristic of the marginal subject. He claimed that the alienation experienced by marginalized groups of color could just as easily apply to poor whites in Appalachia. He confirmed this shift when speaking about the mulatto and the marginal man in American race relations. "Race conflicts in the modern world . . . will be more and more in the future confused with, and eventually superseded by, the conflict of classes."[75] In other words, if Park believed the mulatto to be an example of the alienated person in a violent, racially segregated, and capitalist-driven urban context he also considered the mulatto as the harbinger of an equally racially tolerant world. More than expanding the parameters of the marginal subject, Park's reformulation points to the ways in which sociological typologies ignored race even as they were meant to highlight the social disorganization and estrangement triggered by racial capitalism.

In *The Alien* Rosskam asked readers to view the estrangement resulting from economic crisis as a condition of uneven class relations at best and as a universal condition at worst. But throughout the novel there are traces of structural advantages that facilitate Bluemelein's arrival in El Fanguito. Importantly, these traces are informative because they problematize the parallels Rosskam hoped to draw between Bluemelein and the Puerto Ricans in El Fanguito. For example, following the death of his father Bluemelein inherits half of one of the largest wheat and barley homesteads in Montana. Yet Rosskam does not reveal how Bluemelein's father acquired this homestead. Readers are led to believe that the family simply moved west and worked hard as farmers.

Government homesteading policy, however, was steeped in exclusionary and discriminatory practices. Beginning with the passage of the original 1862 Homestead Act, white Americans benefited exponentially more than Black Americans from the distribution of 246 million acres of federal lands at no or very little cost. The procurement of these lands provided the base for significant future wealth accumulation. As social policy analyst Trina Williams shows, the current beneficiaries of these asset-building policies are almost entirely white because many homestead policies carried restrictions that prohibited African Americans and other racial and ethnic groups from participating until 1930.[76]

Bluemelein sells his portion of the inheritance to his brother-in-law for an undisclosed sum. Using the land as a transformative asset, Bluemelein decides to quit his job with the Department of the Interior and purchases a home in Puerto Rico.[77] Even his decision to settle in El Fanguito is dependent on his capacity to mobilize his assets to find a residence. Following the Ponce Massacre, Bluemelein purchases a trash and bottle business from a local resident in exchange for a one-way plane ticket to New York. Once in El Fanguito, Bluemelein is one of the few unemployed residents able to participate in the local informal economy.

Ignoring the lessons about the racialized outcomes of displacement he learned in his earlier work on African Americans and indigenous groups, Rosskam subscribed to a liberal misreading of alienation that attempted to conceal the material benefits of his own whiteness. He conflated Bluemelein's estrangement with that of El Fanguito's proletariat and thereby diminished his novel's criticism of white supremacy and colonial development. His desire to approach alienation as a post-racial typology led Rosskam to overlook the ways in which the residents of El Fanguito were already racialized within the national imaginary. As I argue in the next section, Rosskam mobilized racialized understandings of the Puerto Rican diaspora in order to further the parallels he drew between Bluemelein and El Fanguito's poor denizens.

## Criminalizing the Diaspora

Between 1950 and 1965 almost 530,000 Puerto Ricans migrated to the United States as part of Operation Bootstrap, a government-facilitated economic strategy meant to attract foreign industrial capital and alleviate unemployment on the island.[78] C. Wright Mills, Clarence Senior, and Rose Kohn Goldsen's 1950 book, *The Puerto Rican Journey*, surveyed Puerto Rican migration to New York and compared how Puerto Ricans fared relative to their counterparts on the island and to other U.S. ethnic and racial groups. As he did for Pedreira and the Chicago School sociologists, the mulatto proved a useful typology for analysis. The authors thought Puerto Ricans to be worth studying because, as mulattoes, they were at "once Negro and foreign." The racial difference of Puerto Ricans, claimed the authors, told the story of contact and conflict between Latin American migrants and North American groups.[79] They argued that these tensions were resolved through Puerto Ricans' ability to become "functioning" and "inconspicuous" strangers, or more simply, "conventional members of society."

Rosskam did not believe in the redemptive possibilities of the diaspora. His depiction of El Fanguito as a post-racial space of social disorganization is heavily dependent on his treatment of racism as a social phenomenon found only in the continental United States. Accordingly, Bluemelein's tenuous inclusion in El Fanguito stands in contrast to the racialized exclusion of the Puerto Rican diaspora living in the United States.

Rosskam, for example, strategically begins his novel with *two* strangers: Bluemelein and a government bureaucrat investigating someone who listed Bluemelein as a job reference. "I know why you're here," Bluemelein interrupts as the stranger approaches. "I'm an embarrassment and this is no way for my kind to live."[80] The reader is given only a physical description of the anonymous twenty-eight-year-old bureaucrat, a man with a "mouse of a dark mustache and big dark rimmed spectacles"—in other words, an academic.[81] The bureaucrat admits later that he attended university at Fordham. This confession links him to the large cadre of American social scientists conducting research on the island at the time.

Readers learn that the young bureaucrat's parents are "New York Puerto Ricans" after he passes out from the stench in the slum. For the young émigré, Puerto Rico is not as his parents described it. His disappointment suggests his middle- to upper-class sensibility and upbringing. Bluemelein is particularly surprised to find out that this is the man's "first visit to what could be called his country of origin."[82] The *americano*'s presumed association with a detached trans-local Puerto Rican elite racializes him as an outsider on the island.

The denial of a Puerto Rican diasporic subjectivity also scaffolds the novel's ending. In the novel's final scene, Bluemelein is happy to be alive after nearly being shot by Gaspar, a scrawny typist and local resident. Gaspar goes into a rage after his common-law wife, Modesta, leaves him for Eloy. Described as a "Negro" with the "face of an easily hurt boy," Eloy is the novel's most physically imposing figure, with hands that signal others to "keep out of trouble with him." Later Bluemelein saves Eloy and Modesta's home from being burned to the ground by Gaspar, earning the praise of the people of El Fanguito. His near-death experience and bravery bring his desire for inclusion in El Fanguito despite being a former colonial bureaucrat into sharper focus.[83]

As Bluemelein receives the acceptance he longed for, the diaspora re-emerges to challenge his tenuous sense of belonging. Overwhelmed by his recognition, Bluemelein stumbles and Eloy catches him to prevent him from falling. A "city colored adolescent" with a "pinkish-purple satiny zipper jacket" laughs like a "horse [with] all teeth and heehaw and no mirth."[84] Turning toward the menacing adolescent, Bluemelein stumbles again and this time slips into the mud. Eloy pushes the young man away, sparing Bluemelein further humiliation. As the young man runs away Bluemelein notices the name *Viscounts* written in English on the back of his jacket. Rosskam's description of the young "city colored adolescent" and his affiliation with a street gang (the Viscounts) racializes the diaspora as a criminal class.

Eloy's response when Bluemelein questions him about the young man's identity is even more telling. "Who knows? Could be one of the gang that hangs out near the cathedral. Big shots. Because they've been to New York. Great men they think they are."[85] Eloy's words echo those of local urban planners who linked housing issues with criminality. "Bad housing," commented the OIPR in 1943 (the government agency Rosskam worked for years earlier), "also represents a social problem . . . the everpresent [sic] overcrowding results in family instability and moral laxity . . . lack of community facilities and opportunities for wholesome recreation contribute to juvenile delinquency and crime."[86] Urban sociologist Zaire Dinzey-Flores details that these concerns about non-normativity pushed government officials to create public housing on the island as a preliminary and temporary step ("staircase to housing") meant to promote upward class mobility.[87]

The racialization of youth in the novel is not linked to San Juan specifically but to the urban spaces inhabited by the diaspora. Revealing his new sense of belonging in the community, Bluemelein responds to Eloy: "I remember the place. Three foot high inscriptions of a gang name smeared sloppily over the ancient Spanish walls. Imported defiance, as though we didn't have enough of *our own*; the displaced, the corrupted feckless young shipped back where they came from with little to their names except very special greetings from the side walks of New York. The unofficial Peace Corps."[88] Yet even as Bluemelein characterizes the diaspora as a criminal class, Rosskam maintains his implicit critique of colonial policy.

Colonialism had not ameliorated local poverty, and the return migration of Puerto Ricans from the U.S. mainland speaks to their having experienced similar forms of dispossession there.

The troubled adolescent returns later in the evening with the rest of the "screaming Saracens from the East Side, West Side and all other color ghettoes" to beat Bluemelein and vandalize his garden. As they roll Bluemelein around in the mud, one of the attackers mocks the older American's transformation into a "brown . . . cigar."[89] Thus, the novel begins with Bluemelein renouncing his whiteness and concludes with his simulated racialization through the Viscounts' assault.

Rosskam's unpublished work reflected similar suspicions of the Puerto Rican diaspora. In the late 1950s, he helped Puerto Rican secretary of labor Fernando Sierra Berdecia to complete a series of educational films for Puerto Ricans who planned to migrate to New York. Feeling that a series of films to educate New Yorkers about Puerto Ricans was also needed, Rosskam wrote a preliminary script for a "major film for use in theatres, on T.V. and with interested groups."[90]

His script, "But This Family I Know," tells the family drama of Magdalena Cruz de Burgos. Cruz de Burgos's husband, Pepe, migrates to New York. He is offered a job as a sewing machine operator. Offended by this offer to do "women's work," he sends for Magdalena so that she can take the job. Unable to accept the fact that his wife makes more money than he does, Pepe abandons Magdalena and their four children shortly after their arrival in New York.

The center of the plot is the search for Magdalena and Pepe's oldest son, Pepito, who has gone missing. Pepito struggles to adjust to life in New York as a neighborhood gang harasses him. The gang eventually accepts Pepito and he begins acting out before he disappears. Eventually finding a badly beaten Pepito in the territory of a rival gang, Magdalena learns the pain experienced by "all mothers whose children have been trapped in the incomprehensible forces of the city." Rosskam positions Puerto Rico as a "counterpoint to the tensions and the clash of big New York; a residual image of a smaller place where the ways of the fathers still manage to survive, however precariously, the flood of imported American food and goods."[91]

Pairing this portion of the script with Bluemelein's final conversation with Eloy in *The Alien* ("the great men they think they are") demonstrates how gender relations also shaped the marginalization of the diaspora from the Puerto Rican nation. The racialized masculinity of returnees to the island and, more implicitly, their feminization, is directly correlated to New York's urban space. The simultaneous feminization and masculinization of the diaspora is an example of what Puerto Rican studies cultural critic Frances Negrón-Muntaner has described as the blurring of traditional gendered binaries between imperial arrangements and colonial subjectivities.[92]

In the plot of "But This Family I Know," Pepe's inability to adapt to his loss of status as the primary wage earner symbolizes the disintegration of the Puerto Rican nuclear family throughout the diaspora. American studies scholar Roderick Ferguson explains that modernity's underside promotes various forms of social disorganization, including sexual transgressions, that are at once racialized and disciplined. Bluemelein benefits the most from the struggle between Eloy and the diaspora, since his own whiteness and masculinity remain unexamined and unchallenged. Concerned about the threats posed by American colonial modernity to Puerto Rico's presumed patriarchal traditionalism, Rosskam reinscribed the dominant ways in which both U.S. social scientists and Puerto Rican writers like Pedreira understood the adverse effects of modernity and urbanization on traditional family structures, gender, and different racial groups.

## Conclusion

At around 3 a.m. on October 26, 1974, a series of bombs exploded at five banks in Manhattan. The bombs caused significant structural damage to the banks but did not injure anyone. Members of the Fuerzas Armadas de Liberación Nacional (FALN, Armed Forces for National Liberation), a militant Puerto Rican anticolonial group, claimed responsibility for the bombings. FALN released a statement demanding the release of five Puerto Rican political prisoners and the immediate independence of Puerto Rico.[93]

Despite the *New York Times* labeling the bombings as acts of terrorism, more than twenty thousand people packed Madison Square Garden two days later at a rally calling for Puerto Rico's independence. Well-known attendees included Black radical Angela Davis; actress and activist Jane Fonda; and Juan Mari Brás, the secretary general of the Puerto Rican Socialist Party. Mari Brás refused to condemn the bombings, declaring defiantly, "There is a diversity of forms and means by which the people of Puerto Rico are striving for independence."[94]

A week later an angry Rosskam wrote to Luis Muñoz Marín and his wife, Inés Mendoza, to discuss his feelings about the bombings. He characterized FALN as a "band of lunatics" and dismissed their actions as not "remarkable" given the recent "fashionable" nature of bombings. Juan Mari Brás's speech angered Rosskam more. "Of course I have no knowledge how Juan Mari Bras' manoeuvres are being received in Puerto Rico," admitted Rosskam. But "in New York and California he seems to be attracting considerable attention and . . . support."[95]

True to form, Rosskam's letter conveyed a deeper anxiety about his continued separation from Puerto Rico and Muñoz Marín's political project. "Even though you are no longer in a position of power, you still represent the legitimacy of the Commonwealth, and this remains the chief target of the nationalist fanatics. Please be careful," he warned. Rosskam closed his letter with a hopeful postscript alerting them that he and Louise planned to visit Puerto Rico soon.[96]

In the opening line of *The Alien*, Bluemelein says of the Puerto Rican émigré: "I knew about him long before he reached me. The community of the Little Mud is suspicious of outsiders."[97] Rosskam's haunting words are symbolic of the perversions he believed Puerto Ricans brought back to the island after living in New York. But they are also emblematic of the ways in which ideas about Puerto Ricans were literally created and disseminated by American liberals. Aided by American sociology, these narratives prioritized class-based typologies that ignored or minimized racial difference on the island. Rosskam imagined Puerto Rico's slums as spaces that were both color-blind and socially disorganized. A colonial bureaucrat to the end, Rosskam romanticized El Fanguito, the space that most represented the devastating effects of racial capitalism.

Both Rosskam and Mari Brás criticized the uneven capitalist development that ravaged Puerto Rico. They both also believed in the political possibilities for a better and sovereign Puerto Rico. But Mari Brás's internationalism and openness to alliances with American radicals differed drastically from Rosskam's exclusive, class-based insularity. As I show in the next chapter, however, Mari Brás and the broader Puerto Rican Left to which he belonged were not immune to complicated and often contradictory understandings of race. The unknown history of race and the fracturing of the Puerto Rican Left is the story that follows.

# 5

# You Are Here to Listen

"The Third World was not a place," affirms historian Vijay Prashad in his dynamic treatise on the Global South's response to empire. "It was a project."[1] Prashad conceives of the Third World not as a static place on a map but as a multifaceted and contradictory project buoyed by millions of people of color imagining a future not constrained by colonialism and racial capitalism. In this way, the Third World consisted not of one project but numerous *projects*. These projects aimed to achieve and secure national liberation and a future separate from the economic and political control of traditional ruling colonial powers.

This final chapter uncovers one such project. Focusing on Puerto Rican doctor Ana Livia Cordero's Proyecto Piloto para Trabajo con el Pueblo (Pilot Project for Work with the Nation), this chapter reveals the ways in which the project imbricated two significant strands of radicalism. The Movimiento Pro-Independencia (MPI), a Leftist *independentista* organization, established Proyecto Piloto in 1967. Proyecto Piloto continued beyond and departed from the MPI's anticolonial struggle through its outreach into various communities where Puerto Rico's racialized proletariat resided. As I discuss in the first section of this chapter, Proyecto Piloto separated from the MPI due to the larger organization's inability to fully embrace the work on race being done by the project and by Cordero as its leader.

Given this shortfall within the MPI, Black radical internationalism and Black Power more broadly buttressed Proyecto Piloto's anticolonial politic. At an organizational level, Proyecto Piloto shared a variety of overlapping ideological and methodological similarities with the young corps of African American activists on the Student Nonviolent Coordinating

Figure 5.1. Members of Proyecto Piloto. Ana Livia Cordero is second from left. Photo by Mandín Rodríguez, *El Mundo*, February 29, 1968. Colección El Mundo, UPR, Recinto de Río Piedras.

Committee (SNCC). As I argue in the second half of the chapter, Cordero's extensive work and activism in Ghana and the United States with African diplomats and African American expatriates gave her a keen understanding of the significance of race and racism in anticolonial struggle, knowledge she applied to Proyecto Piloto.

Predating José Luis González's canonical scholarship on race, Proyecto Piloto developed into one of the few radical groups on the island to analyze the relationships among race, colonialism, and capitalism. Cordero and her colleagues actively worked to educate the Puerto Rican proletariat about the history of racism on the island and the ways in which racial difference scaffolded the American colonial project. Using a variety of grassroots cultural and educational approaches, Proyecto Piloto empowered the proletariat to make broader connections between race and empire across the globe. The project's vanguard racial politics redefined Blackness as a dynamic political project but in some instances also succumbed to essentialist reductionism. U.S. and Puerto Rican historiography has paid significant attention to the Leftist strands of Black radicalism and Puerto Rican anticolonial social movements. What follows is an exploration of the points of convergence between these two ideological strands of radicalism and the hidden history of Ana Livia Cordero's Proyecto Piloto.

## The Puerto Rican Left: From San Juan to Cairo

Cordero's project emerged from a strong but fragmented Puerto Rican political Left that worked for decades to internationalize the commonwealth's independence struggle. The years between 1930 and 1955 were the height of anticolonial struggle in Puerto Rico. At the same time, this era came to be defined as one of the most politically repressive moments in twentieth-century Puerto Rico. In 1930 the Puerto Rican Partido Nacionalista elected Harvard graduate Pedro Albizu Campos as its leader. Historians César Ayala and Rafael Bernabé note that the Partido Nacionalista distinguished itself from other parties through its strong belief that the Puerto Rican people needed to capture their independence rather than wait for it to be granted to them through colonial patronage.[2] The *nacionalistas* favored state ownership of public services and strongly supported labor unions but remained opposed to socialism as a political and economic doctrine. Because of its deep loyalty to conservative Catholicism, the Partido Nacionalista also promoted "traditional" family roles, ignoring the contributions of women to the struggle for independence and making white patriarchy and heteronormativity key features of its anticolonial platform.[3]

The UPR became a central hub of anticolonial activism for the Nationalist Party during the 1940s. When Albizu Campos returned to Puerto Rico on his release from a federal prison in Atlanta in 1948, UPR suspended five students, including Juan Mari Brás, for raising the Puerto Rican flag in honor of his arrival. To protest these suspensions and the university's refusal to let Albizu Campos speak on campus, students declared a general strike and demanded that Chancellor Jaime Benítez reinstate the suspended students.[4]

Not long after the student strike, the Puerto Rican Senate approved Law 53, popularly referred to as the *ley de la mordaza* (gag law). Modeled after the Smith Act in the United States, Law 53 made it illegal to speak out against the U.S. government, display the Puerto Rican flag, or even to discuss Puerto Rican independence in public. The PPD enforced this draconian law to curb growing dissent among *independentistas* and communists as it secured the island's colonial relationship with the United States in 1952 via the establishment of commonwealth status. The *ley de la mordaza* proved especially useful during the 1950 nationalist uprising, when *independentistas* attacked several police stations and attempted to assassinate President Truman while he resided at Blair House.[5]

In 1954 four nationalists—Lolita Lebrón, Rafael Cancel Miranda, Irving Flores, and Andrés Figueroa Cordero—entered the U.S. House of Representatives and opened fire as they demanded Puerto Rico's independence. As part of its overall response, the Puerto Rican police raided Albizu Campos's residence five days later and arrested him and four other nationalists who were in the home trying to protect their aging leader.[6]

The Partido Independentista Puertorriqueño (PIP, Puerto Rican Independence Party) developed into the other significant Leftist party of the era, though it shared some of the Partido Nacionalista's conservative tendencies. Following Muñoz Marín's moderate turn away from independence in 1946, a significant number of independentistas defected from the PPD and helped establish the PIP. In 1952 the culturally conservative PIP garnered close to 173,000 votes, the second strongest showing after the PPD. The PIP's voter base plummeted in the following election in 1956, however, when they received slightly more than half of the votes (86,552) they garnered four years earlier. This downward trend continued for the remainder of the decade.[7]

The electoral decline in popularity of the Puerto Rican Left in the 1950s cannot be understood as resulting solely from ineffective political tactics or the declining influence of political nationalism on the island. In fact, the need for repressive legislation, severe police repression, and banishment actually hint at the effectiveness of anticolonial struggles during the 1950s. However one chooses to interpret the temporary lull in the Puerto Rican nationalist movement, by the end of the decade the Puerto Rican Left needed to offer new approaches to decolonization in order to remain a legitimate political force.

Continuing the anticolonial struggles of an earlier generation, students at UPR founded FUPI in 1956. Members of FUPI used direct confrontation and violence as part of their political strategy to attain national liberation. FUPI became a pivotal feeder organization for the MPI, following the latter's establishment in 1959. Members of the newly formed MPI accused the PIP of abandoning its commitment to militancy and falling victim to co-optation by the PPD. The MPI looked internationally for models of anticolonial struggle, most especially to the 1959 Cuban Revolution.[8]

Established by defectors from the PIP, including Juan Mari Brás, the

MPI organized students, women, and workers. Mari Brás described the MPI as the patriotic and revolutionary vanguard of the Puerto Rican Left. The MPI incorporated various threads of earlier local and internationalist radicalism, including Marxist socialism, electoral boycotts, and strategic violent confrontations. This ideological flexibility helped the party consolidate its membership, unite the deteriorating Puerto Rican Left, and create a more concerted nationalist front.[9]

The MPI used the United Nations (UN) as one venue to advance its cause through international diplomacy. Progress via the UN remained slow and fraught with tension, however, given the extensive voting power and influence of the United States and Puerto Rico's ambiguous standing within the international body.[10] While the case of Puerto Rico fit squarely within the provisions of Chapter XI, Article 73, of the UN founding charter, the establishment of the island as a commonwealth in 1952 clouded the issue of colonialism for international bodies and countries.

Less than one year after Puerto Rico gained commonwealth status the Eighth UN General Assembly passed Resolution 748. The resolution stated that, because of the island's new status, "the people of Puerto Rico have been invested with attributes of political sovereignty which clearly identify the status of self-government attained by the Puerto Rican people as that of an autonomous political entity."[11] Accordingly, Resolution 748 exempted the United States from Article 73 and the duty to report the island's political status to the UN. This provision made it extremely difficult for nationalists to bring motions or debates about the island's colonial status to the floor of the General Assembly. This changed in late 1960 when—due to the larger anticolonial movements taking shape across the globe—the General Assembly approved Resolution 1514, which called for "the end of colonialism in all of its manifestations."[12] This provision opened a political window for the MPI to take its case to the UN.[13]

Concurrently, the Non-Aligned Movement (NAM) held its first conference in Belgrade, Yugoslavia, in 1961. NAM had materialized a few years earlier as countries emerging from colonialism sought political alternatives to the dominant U.S. or Soviet cold war spheres of influence. As Prashad explains, NAM pushed an agenda of "peaceful co-existence" through the democratization of the UN so as to give the people of the Global South a place at the table of international governance.[14]

Given this focus, the MPI viewed NAM meetings as a vital political space to advocate for Puerto Rican independence. Their efforts failed miserably at NAM's inaugural conference in Belgrade, however. MPI international relations officer Gabriel Vicente Maura's trip ended abruptly when Yugoslavian police detained him at the airport shortly after his arrival and literally placed him under "house arrest," taking Maura home with them.[15] Maura's arrest is evidence of the continuing U.S. influence within NAM. In particular, during the organization's infancy key NAM nations consistently tabled discussions about Puerto Rico's status so as not to agitate the United States. As part of its policy NAM also did not permit anyone to participate in or attend its proceedings unless they were part of a recognized national delegation residing in the hotel where the meetings were held. Shut out of the Belgrade conference, the MPI used some political ingenuity to make sure they made it to the following NAM conference in Cairo in 1964. The Puerto Rican militants paved their path to Cairo through Accra.

Six years earlier, in 1958, the Pan-Africanist Ghanaian prime minister Kwame Nkrumah presided over his country's transition from British colonial control to national independence. Nkrumah promoted a vision for Ghana in which the peoples of the African diaspora would incorporate Leninist and Marxist socialism to achieve their emancipation.[16] During his time as a student in the United States in the 1930s, Nkrumah had recruited hundreds of Leftist African American professionals, intellectuals, and artists to work alongside him in Ghana in an effort to create a socialist-oriented Pan-Africanist movement. Among this cluster of African American expatriates was W.E.B. Du Bois, Maya Angelou, John Gibbs St. Clair and Elizabeth Drake, and Julian Mayfield.[17]

Mayfield moved to Ghana with his wife, Ana Livia Cordero, a white Puerto Rican physician and MPI militant.[18] Given her strongly anticolonial political worldview and Mayfield's position as a speechwriter for Nkrumah, Cordero enjoyed significant access to Nkrumah's administration and to African American expatriates in Ghana.[19] Du Bois and Cordero frequently traveled throughout Accra and the Ghanaian countryside in a Russian Chaika given to Du Bois by Soviet premier Nikita Khrushchev. Together Cordero and Du Bois debated colonialism, Pan-Africanism, and even Du Bois's unease with Nkrumah's political shortcomings. As Du Bois biographer David Levering Lewis recounts, Cordero stood out as one of the few people whom Du Bois trusted and confided in during his final years in Ghana. She was one of the last doctors to attend to him before his death in 1963.[20]

Cordero displayed her tenacity and brilliance as a political tactician at the NAM's second conference in Cairo. In observation of the NAM's strict conference protocol, Cordero accompanied Nkrumah's Ghanaian delegation to the conference. This move allowed her to be admitted to the conference hotel as part of an official national delegation. According to Mari Brás, once she was in the conference, the Cuban delegation requested that Cordero and two other members of the MPI be seated as observers. Egypt strongly opposed this request but removing Cordero from the conference would require that she also be expelled from the conference hotel, which would risk alienating the larger Ghanaian delegation. Arab diplomats, asserted Mari Brás, also considered such a drastic action "highly improper" due to their "sense of chivalry."[21]

The NAM leadership relented and agreed to seat Cordero and the Puerto Rican delegation. As a result of Cordero's activism, the NAM's final conference report of its meeting in Cairo included a paragraph calling on the UN to reconsider Puerto Rico's colonial status based on Resolution 1514. Cordero's clever maneuvers opened a space at the Cairo conference that led to Puerto Rico being placed back on the list of countries under review by the UN Special Committee on Decolonization and ultimately culminated in Puerto Rico's first nonbinding plebiscite on the island's political status in 1967.[22]

Cordero continued her international diplomacy in 1966 at the Tricontinental Conference in Havana, Cuba. She served as part of the Puerto Rican delegation chaired by ranking MPI member Norman Pietri Castellón.[23] The Tricontinental Conference provided a space for anticolonial activists and intellectuals from Africa, Asia, and Latin America to organize and decide how to challenge imperialism and the war in Vietnam. Cordero's notes summarizing the conference detail the efforts she, Pietri Castellón, and the other MPI delegates made to put Puerto Rico's colonial status at the forefront of the conference agenda.[24]

More importantly, Cordero also made note of discussions about the racial tensions existing in Latin America. "It was known," commented Cordero, "that the majority of the political leadership [in Latin America] is petite bourgeoisie and white and that in Latin America there is discrimination and racial prejudice among the whites."[25] Cordero's observations about race and conference attendees' focus on opposition to the war in Vietnam became important themes that developed in Cordero's later work with Proyecto Piloto. Cordero would have to carry out much of her increasingly militant agenda apart from the MPI, however.

### "We Will Not Let Anyone Destroy It"

The MPI at first rewarded Cordero's diplomacy and activism in Ghana and Cairo. To honor "one of the MPI's biggest diplomatic victories, if not possibly the greatest achievement [in the struggle] for Puerto Rican independence," the MPI recognized Cordero as one of its "militants of the year" in 1965.[26] By the end of 1965, Cordero and Mayfield began living separately as Mayfield took a leave of absence from Ghana and resettled in Ibiza.[27] Not long thereafter, while Nkrumah was visiting Chinese prime minister Chou En-Lai in February 1966, Ghana's National Liberation Council (NLC) staged a coup in Accra.[28] The revolutionaries temporarily detained the newly single Cordero and her two sons, then deported them from Ghana back to Puerto Rico for "security reasons."[29]

Cordero's internationalism in Ghana and Cuba on behalf of the MPI allowed her to reintegrate herself effortlessly back into Puerto Rican political life. In late 1966 and early 1967, she labored diligently as an organizer and spokeswoman for the MPI. In one of her first public appearances following her return, Cordero and Pietri Castellón discussed their time at the Havana Tricontinental.[30] Similarly, Cordero worked on other pressing political issues, including the 1967 plebiscite that the MPI ultimately decided to boycott as part of its "zero colonial plebiscite" campaign.[31]

It is not coincidental that the MPI's interest in the struggles of African Americans in the United States and racism more generally coincided with Cordero's return from Ghana. While the *independentista* Puerto Rican Left traditionally ignored race in its discussions of colonialism, under Cordero's influence the MPI explored the possibilities of nurturing alliances with African Americans. On July 25, 1967, for example, Stokely Carmichael began a three-day tour of Puerto Rico as a special guest of MPI and FUPI. Carmichael also gave a lecture at UPR, at which Cordero introduced him to the audience.[32] Carmichael's talk linked the "relationship between the struggle for Black Power and the struggle of Puerto Rican independence."[33] Encouraged by Carmichael's visit, throughout 1967–68

Mari Brás focused a notable number of articles in the pages of his newspaper, *Claridad,* on Black Power and racial violence in the American South.[34]

As president of SNCC, Carmichael echoed Cordero's call for an internationalist project centered on race and colonialism. When asked about the parallels between SNCC and "the struggle of the Puerto Rican people for their independence" during an interview in Havana, Carmichael asserted,

> Now, brother Malcolm taught us that we must internationalize our struggle. In an effort to follow some of his teachings, we started with Puerto Rico; we started with Puerto Rico for many reasons. No. 1, it is very close to the United States in terms of its geographic position. No. 2, it is a colony of the United States in every sense. And thirdly, a large number of people who live inside the ghettoes of the United States with us are Puerto Ricans.[35]

Carmichael's acknowledgment of Puerto Rico's significance in shaping the SNCC's internationalist politics speaks to the continued role of the island as a pathway for African American activists to a broader internationalism and an anticolonial politic. Following Carmichael's visit to the island in January the SNCC published a report about Puerto Rico and colonialism in May of that year.[36]

Cordero befriended not only Carmichael but also SNCC executive secretary James Forman. Cordero likely met Forman in the summer of 1961 when he and other Black activists were headed to Monroe, North Carolina, to meet with Robert Williams, the local chairman of the NAACP. Williams opposed nonviolence as a civil rights political strategy and argued that violence against Blacks should be met with armed self-defense.

In response to the NAACP's suspension of Williams for his non-pacifist views, Mayfield, Cordero, and other Black writers worked to establish the Coordinating Committee for Southern Relief. This committee aided Williams and the community in Monroe by sending clothes, food, and even guns.[37] Led by Forman, members of the SNCC and the Freedom Riders traveled to Monroe to defend the value of nonviolence as a strategy.[38] In Monroe an angry mob of white protesters overwhelmed and violently beat the group of nonviolent demonstrators. Williams and Mayfield (and probably Cordero) quickly came to the defense of Forman and the other pacifist demonstrators and rescued them from the attackers, who did not expect to be met by African Americans with guns.[39]

Cordero and Forman remained close friends following Forman's brush with death in Monroe. Years later Forman completed the majority of his autobiography, *The Making of Black Revolutionaries*, in Puerto Rico as Cordero's guest. In his acknowledgments, Forman recognized the "tremendous impact" that Cordero had on his life and thanked her for teaching him "always [to] affirm the Blackness of Puerto Ricans and to understand that they suffer the same general oppression as Black people in the United States."[40]

In the summer of 1967 Cordero founded the Proyecto Piloto para Trabajo con el Pueblo with MPI sponsorship. The new project shared striking similarities with the SNCC. Like the SNCC, Proyecto Piloto began as a grassroots venture designed to better understand the "effects of colonialism on Puerto Rico's lower classes." Members of Proyecto Piloto "mix[ed] with [communities] to gain firsthand knowledge of their problems."[41] Using a Marxist lens, community-based activism, and social scientific research models, Proyecto Piloto studied conflict in order to "organize the community around this conflict, and confront the power structure with conflict."[42]

Just like in the SNCC, a small cluster of former or current university students filled the ranks of Proyecto Piloto. The majority of the students in both organizations hailed from working poor families whose parents were employed in factories, domestic labor, or service industries.[43] The overwhelmingly young cadre of the SNCC and Proyecto Piloto activists consciously separated themselves from older generations of political activists whom they considered to be estranged from the lived realities of their respective communities. The SNCC attributed the generational break to "overly cautious elders" who had achieved a level of upward social mobility and were more familiar with the potential racial violence that awaited the young SNCC members.[44]

All was not well within the MPI by the summer of 1967. As Cordero continued working with the MPI following her return from Ghana, she and a cadre of young activists within FUPI as well as the Juventud del Movimiento Pro-Independencia (JMPI; Youth of the Pro-Independence Movement) grew increasingly impatient with the MPI leadership. The MPI relied heavily on the grassroots activism of FUPI and JMPI in order to accomplish its political projects, and especially to build its membership. Generational, gendered, and racial divides among the increasingly older

MPI leadership and FUPI bred discontent between members of the different camps. A small faction of FUPI and JMPI accused the MPI leadership
of being overly defined by a white and middle-class sensibility and of being political reactionaries. As Cordero's notes show, she considered the
"process of rebellion [to be] sharper in [the] younger generation" because
the "general feeling of impotence in solving the basic issues is not fully
internalized by the youth in conflict with the colonial establishment."[45]

The MPI countered these claims by accusing its young members of being despondent and lacking proper discipline.[46] The internal dissension
came to a head in the late summer of 1967 when the MPI's governing committee expelled the secretary of JMPI from the party. This move catalyzed
a small exodus of FUPI and JMPI members.[47]

It is debatable whether the MPI expelled the group of young radicalized *independentistas* or they voluntarily left the organization. On October 12, 1967, in the town of Naranjito, the Bayamón section of the JMPI,
along with a select group of members from other municipalities, approved
a statement explaining their departure from the MPI. They criticized
Juan Mari Brás, calling him a patriarchal authoritarian figure. "The role
of leader," charged the group, "should be one of assistance, capacity, to
teach the militants; not to be an authoritarian father." Leadership, the
statement continued, "is not something that is permanently obtained like
when one earns a diploma. Rather it is maintained consistently through
the exercise of the real traits of leader."[48]

The small splinter group of JMPI youth indicted the MPI leadership
for lacking a clear and inclusive strategy for carrying out its goals among
Puerto Rico's racially diverse proletariat. They further critiqued the MPI's
unwillingness to embrace a research program that would better identify
the needs of Puerto Rico's proletariat. The dissatisfied members ultimately
declined a hearing with the MPI's governing committee, concluding, "it is
not possible within the MPI to properly develop the alternative work that
we propose to complete and as such it is *our decision to resign from the
movement and dedicate ourselves to the work we consider more appropriate.*"[49]

The day after the meeting in Naranjito, Juan Mari Brás published a
letter to the MPI membership in his weekly column in the *Carta Semanal.*
Titled "Hay un plan maestro para romper el Movimiento Pro Independencia" (There Is a Master Plan to Destroy the Pro-Independence Movement), the column accused Cordero of being an undercover CIA agent sent

to create internal discord within the MPI. Accordingly, he suspended her from the MPI. Cordero's standing within the MPI had fallen dramatically from its height following her heroic arrival from Ghana and Havana a little more than a year earlier.

> [Conspiratorial work] has been happening in the MPI for some time now. [Ana Livia] Cordero's criticism [of the MPI] has given way to anarchism while advancing her ideas, not through open discussion in forums and meetings, but in divisive meetings outside the organization. . . . One can aspire to change the direction of an organization. But in the meantime you must work within the [organization's] direction and accept its legitimate exercise of authority. Not to do so is organized chaos. And it is this chaos that our comrade Cordero wants to bring to us.[50]

Cordero's position as a high-ranking woman within the MPI should not go unnoticed here. Her leadership style and unwillingness to compromise led the predominantly white and male party leadership to ostracize her.

Despite the participation of women such as Luisa Capetillo, Blanca Canales, and Lolita Lebrón in key labor and anticolonial struggles, women have persistently been excluded from leadership roles within the Puerto Rican Left. The patriarchal nationalism promoted by the likes of Pedro Albizu Campos, instructs historian Laura Briggs, "identified women with motherhood, which in turn became 'the insides of nationhood'—mothers made citizens, reproducing both bodies and culture."[51] According to former Proyecto Piloto member Miguel Rodríguez López, Cordero challenged these limits as a very "independent woman who had her own critiques and stimulated the participation of other women but of men as well."[52] "There was a level of pride," adds the former early group member Lydia Milagros González García, and she "initially looked down upon the whole [independence] movement. She rejected it . . . and never wanted to give them [independence leaders] any recognition."[53]

The MPI leadership's decision to expel a high-ranking and well-respected female member raised red flags within the organization. Rubén Sánchez, another former Proyecto Piloto member, noted that "it was politically more expedient for [the MPI leadership] to say that she left versus saying that they [Proyecto Piloto members] left."[54] By its actions the MPI effectively treated a larger ideological and organizational critique of its gender and race politics as the rogue workings of one member whom they accused of being a CIA spy. A bristling Mari Brás concluded his letter to the MPI membership by reminding everyone that he remained firmly entrenched as head of the MPI and that "we are not going to allow anyone to destroy it."[55] Mari Brás terminated Proyecto Piloto following Cordero's expulsion and prohibited MPI members from aiding the group. In spite of these efforts to end the project, Cordero and her young cadre of activists continued their work in local communities.

### Researching Race and Conflict

Under Cordero's leadership Proyecto Piloto aimed to methodically study the problems of Puerto Rico's proletariat through rigorous sociological survey and research. The use of scientific inquiry, claimed the group, would better equip them to "understand institutions . . . and how they affected individuals and their communities."[56] Although formally trained as a physician, Cordero also had extensive experience as a researcher. For example, she organized a sociological study on access to medical care in the rural community of Comerio during her time in Puerto Rico in the late 1950s.

Cordero's Comerio study sought to determine what constituted an adequate and economically feasible level of medical care in developing nations. Her work shows the influence of one of her former teachers, the eminent medical sociologist Jack Elinson.[57] The resultant journal article criticized standards of care among colonial powers. These standards, claimed Cordero, came to be defined as "the optimal utilisation of the existing scientific knowledge in the diagnosis and treatment of the total morbidity of the patient, *as agreed upon by the consensus of authoritative opinion*."[58] American institutional knowledge ignored local community needs, which served to make "these standards . . . so clearly unattainable that they could not be used to control or improve the existing quality of care." Cordero charged colonial powers and academic institutions with "artificially impos[ing]" standards of care and with "interfer[ing] with a realistic appraisal of [public health] and with the most efficient use of limited resources" in developing nations (former colonies).[59]

As discussed in the previous chapter, the UPR became one of the central state institutions charged with alleviating Puerto Rico's socioeconomic problems during the 1940s. As their original research proposal documents, Proyecto Piloto did not view the changes at the UPR as rooted in a genuine moral desire of the U.S. government to help the island and its citizens. They emphasized "that the heads of government and university social science research institutions are generally Americans who support the existing government structure, and that aside from more serious social scientists Puerto Rico has become a paradise for previously unheard-of social scientists."[60] The U.S. government and the ruling PPD, argued Proyecto Piloto, opportunistically used the UPR as a research arm to curtail radical alternatives developing in the Global South.

Even as Proyecto Piloto critiqued the PPD and American social scientists, the group invested heavily in the legitimacy of social scientific research. Accordingly, they had a much more critical appreciation of the work at the UPR than other Puerto Rican Leftists at the time. For example, Cordero and members of Proyecto Piloto praised the People of Puerto Rico project (see chapter 4) as an excellent model of social scientific research. In a rare moment of congratulating research conducted by mostly American social scientists, Proyecto Piloto characterized the People of Puerto Rico as among the few "excellent studies of community structure and function utilizing anthropological techniques . . . available."[61]

Using the same Marxist lens as the People of Puerto Rico project, Proyecto Piloto considered Puerto Rico's proletariat as agents of change rather than as powerless colonial subjects who needed policies to be dictated to them. As longtime Proyecto Piloto member Efraín Negrón mentioned in his brief account of the group, "the proletariat [were] the real protagonists for transforming society."[62] Given the troubled history of the UPR's research endeavors in local communities, Proyecto Piloto members remained critically mindful of their role as outsiders entering communities they were not a part of. As González García explains, Proyecto Piloto members understood that local conditions in each respective community were "distinct from the ones many of us knew from the popular sectors. They had their own vision of the world [and] their own cultural forms which we had to respect . . . but in solidarity with the community, not as outsiders."[63]

Proyecto Piloto applied a four-pronged approach to understanding the lives of Puerto Rico's working masses. This approach included assessing social conflict within communities, hypothesizing about possible social actions, conducting experimental community projects, and evaluating the results of the research.[64] The group used an action-oriented research approach that more accurately captured the needs and social conditions of the Puerto Rican proletariat. Unlike the UPR projects, Proyecto Piloto hoped to use its research to better understand the preconditions required to destabilize Puerto Rico's colonial and class order.

Proyecto Piloto tasked all of its members to immerse themselves in the everyday life of the community as a part of this research agenda. The group required that the members work with and for their respective communities, rather than simply observing or directing them. One former member recalled that Cordero told him, "you are here to listen."[65] Listening entailed carrying out extensive surveys on family life, religious beliefs, politics, culture, and labor.

The research team used the surveys to determine the projects that would most effectively generate the social transformation they sought. Miguel Rodríguez López, a Proyecto Piloto member who later became an accomplished anthropologist, described the project members' work as extending beyond a simple academic exercise: "We talked about political struggle but more about social struggle. . . . We talked about the housing problem in Puerto Rico, which was a very serious problem and which we understood as a political problem not just a social problem. . . . We didn't really talk about independence. We talked more about national liberation."[66] Rodríguez Lopez's words point out that Proyecto Piloto and the MPI continued to share an aversion to the electoral process even after their separation. Rather than simply emphasizing the need for independence, Proyecto Piloto viewed national liberation as a more profound project defined by rights to housing and safety. Unlike the MPI, however, the project's emphasis on national liberation also centered on race, poverty, and the voices of local communities rather than traditional party leaders.

In 1970 about 65 percent of Puerto Ricans remained in poverty. Proyecto Piloto focused on the racialized dimensions of that poverty, not captured in official statistics.[67] The group believed that the Puerto Rican Left and its predominantly white leadership failed to adequately address the island's troubled racial history. Cordero described Puerto Rico as first and foremost a Black nation. Rodríguez López remembered these lessons well when he acknowledged in an interview with me that the members of Proyecto Piloto considered themselves to be part of a Latin American and

Black nation.[68] Fellow project member Efraín Negrón elaborated further: "[Puerto Rico is] a Caribbean nation. From the northern edge of South America to the southern United States the Caribbean is Black . . . we are not white."[69]

Proyecto Piloto framed its analysis of race in contradictory and inconsistent ways. As the group's rich archive of documents and cultural texts demonstrates, the project reduced race to phenotypical characteristics on some occasions. In others, Proyecto Piloto extended meanings of race to account for political and cultural dimensions of national identity that were not dependent on race as a biological determinant. This conflicting approach shaped the group's cultural production and how it studied race in each community.

Cordero and Proyecto Piloto's understandings of Blackness in Puerto Rico predate José Luis González's essay "El país de cuatro pisos" by more than a decade. In this canonical essay, González used a Marxist analysis to portray Puerto Rico as a racially tiered country with Blackness constituting the foundational component of Puerto Rican national identity. Like Cordero, González critiqued the traditional Puerto Rican Left for its *hispanofilia*, or the ways it romanticized Spanish imperialism. González argued that to celebrate Puerto Rico's Spanish colonial heritage also implicitly meant to exalt Spain and ignore that country's complicity in the transatlantic slave trade. Such romanticizing also overlooked the ways in which African slaves materially advanced Puerto Rico's economic and consequently social development.[70]

Proyecto Piloto located its first research headquarters in Barrio Tortugo in Río Piedras. Like the People of Puerto Rico project, which studied select subcultural and geographical communities, Proyecto Piloto assigned its researchers to what it considered to be the prevailing types of communities in Puerto Rico at the time: "the urban slums; the urban housing projects; the urban lower middle class; the small town; the peasant community of the highlands; the coastal sugarcane plantation; and the highway hamlets."[71]

In a rare 1968 interview appearing in the San Juan Star, members claimed that Barrio Tortugo was selected in part as a "representative example" of a highway hamlet (*comunidad de carretera*).[72] Highway hamlets in Puerto Rico were established rural communities that were later bisected by major highways built during the modernization of the island's

Figure 5.2. Proyecto Piloto members at a news conference in Barrio Tortugo following their arrest. Photo by Ivonne Rosso. *El Mundo*, March 1, 1968. Colección El Mundo, UPR, Recinto de Río Piedras.

transportation infrastructure. The structural transformations resulting from these modernization efforts negatively affected communities where poor and working-class families lived. Barrio Tortugo was an ideal location for Cordero's team to trace the island's transformation in order to "learn or see the history of the nation as it is reflected in the history of the community."[73]

According to Proyecto Piloto's initial survey of the community, "mostly . . . low-salaried wage earners" lived there. More than 68 percent of Barrio Tortugo's residents were under the age of twenty-five, and 65 percent were classified as "trigueño" (mixed race).[74] Chemical and clothing factories arrived in Barrio Tortugo shortly after the new highway was completed. Aside from constructing their plants, these firms did not invest capital within the local community, and they did not create sufficient employment to significantly alter the socioeconomic situation of the highway hamlet.[75]

Proyecto Piloto's only historical survey of Barrio Tortugo offers an example of the group's Marxist understanding of the relationship among race, capitalism, and national identity in Puerto Rico. Through collecting oral histories from community members, Proyecto Piloto developed a rough sketch of the history of Barrio Tortugo. Seventy-three-year-old Don Martín Rivas and eighty-four-year-old Don Timoteo de Jesús are the two figures who appear most often in the study.

Rivas settled in Tortugo around 1936 after bartering land he owned in the coastal town of Naguabo for a plot in Tortugo. He moved his family to Tortugo in order to be closer to the UPR so that his children could attend college. A lifelong socialist, Rivas demonstrated a profound understanding of Barrio Tortugo's economic and labor history. Having been a worker in a coastal region, he lost much of his capital with the collapse of Puerto Rico's sugar market—an economic disaster that likely shaped his politics.

Born and raised in Tortugo, de Jesús was popularly known as the "cacique del barrio" (neighborhood chief). De Jesús's economic upward mobility and connections with local police contributed to his high standing in the community. He earned a living in the underground economy, particularly selling contraband liquor and gambling. He invested in local plots of land as they came available. At times de Jesús also "advised poor people who saved money" on the best way to invest their savings. The report implies that de Jesús purchased counterfeit land titles with some of the money entrusted to him and pocketed the rest. The report further called de Jesús's character into question by citing his arrest for murder on at least two occasions.[76]

Proyecto Piloto framed its historical survey of Barrio Tortugo by positioning these two community leaders against each other. Whereas Rivas was deeply involved in the local socialist and labor movements, de Jesús was described as a "republicano" aligned with the PNP, the statehood party. The relationship between Rivas and de Jesús appeared tenuous at best, and each man seemed deeply suspicious of the other. The two men even engaged in at least one verbal confrontation, and on one occasion de Jesús had to apologize to Rivas for publicly insulting him.[77]

Although the two men's different socioeconomic positions merit attention, their racial identities, as defined in the Proyecto Piloto study, are equally important. The classification of Tortugo's two most respected elders as "negro" underlines the centrality of Blackness within the local community. Accordingly, the historical study illustrates how Black subjectivity undergirds the economic and social history of the community. Yet the community's racial history remains fragmented in the narrative as it attempts to reconcile Rivas's and de Jesús's divergent life paths.

A socialist and former sharecropper, Rivas struggled through an agricultural recession. Unfavorable colonial policies, including the island's economic reliance on sugar production, limited his employment opportunities.[78] Yet despite this background Rivas was what de Jesús was not: honorable, respectful, and hardworking: "Don Timoteo [de Jesús] referred to them [community members whose money he "invested"] as stupid, as incapable of managing [their money], crooks, bandits. [If] they asked him for money he insulted them before giving it to them. One day Don Martín [Rivas] told him: 'If you want to be my friend you need to treat me with respect and with fairness.'" De Jesús's callous treatment of community members was linked to his involvement in the underground economy and his shady land dealings. But de Jesús's political and colonial loyalties (he was a PNP member, after all) also frame how readers should interpret his actions. Both Rivas and de Jesús exemplify the detrimental effects of colonialism. But de Jesús's propensity for violence, his exploitation and manipulation of workers, and his colonial allegiances place him on the side of imperialism. Imbricated alongside Rivas, de Jesús is an example of what happens when Black political consciousness is corrupted.

Proyecto Piloto did not content itself with a class-based vision of Puerto Rican society centered on dynamic forms of Blackness. Members of Proyecto Piloto understood that Puerto Rico's long colonial history under Spain and the United States marginalized Blackness and privileged Eurocentric constructions of Puerto Rican identity. Specifically, Cordero and her team opposed the ways in which Puerto Ricans regarded whiteness as "intellectually, physically, and culturally superior" to Blackness.[79] The group undertook cultural work in order to ameliorate the negative connotations associated with Blackness in Puerto Rican history and culture.

### Race, Diaspora, and Comics

As indicated, Proyecto Piloto's multifaceted work on race and national identity often operated from varied and contradictory meanings. At times the group referred to Puerto Rico as a "mulatto nation" in an effort to acknowledge the island's indigenous population and Puerto Rico's colonial relationship with Spain. Acknowledging Spain helped Proyecto Piloto locate the roots of racism on the island. Specifically, the group considered racism to be a European myth created to "justify the enslavement of Africans."[80] In "The Importance of Being Black," a 1974 Proyecto Piloto study, *mulato* and *negro* were used interchangeably and in opposition to white (*blanco*).

Proyecto Piloto also argued that Puerto Ricans in the diaspora developed a new valorization of Blackness as a result of their proximity to African Americans. Countering arguments that Puerto Ricans in the United States disassociated themselves from African Americans in order to avoid the racism perpetrated against Black people, Proyecto Piloto argued that such interactions allowed Puerto Ricans to challenge the ways that people on the island privileged whiteness:

> The power that racial identification has on national identification explains in part the extraordinary resistance against cultural assimilation that 40% of our workers who have migrated over the last three generations to the United States have. Racism in U.S. society has forced us to confront our own racial reality and the "Black Pride" movement has taught us to begin affirming our national identity.[81]

Proyecto Piloto's attention to the relational histories and experiences shared by African Americans and Puerto Ricans in American ghettoes opened up avenues to reconsider the island's racial history. Instead of seeing the racialization process as a negative imposition from the metropolis, Proyecto Piloto contended that the proximity between African Americans and Puerto Ricans facilitated the revalorization of Blackness and shared solidarities in ways not previously possible.

As discussed in chapter 4, Puerto Rican agricultural and industrial workers in the United States have often been stereotyped on the island as passive and inauthentic national subjects contaminated by the colonial metropole. This line of thinking further insists that it is in the United States where members of the diaspora are first racialized as Black and experience racism.[82] In one Proyecto Piloto brochure, the group unsettled these traditional narratives about race and re-centered the importance of the diaspora within Puerto Rican national identity:

To be Puerto Rican is to have to migrate away from the land to the slums of San Juan in search of work. It is to spend three months of the year picking tomatoes in New Jersey and the rest of the year working the family's two acres of tobacco and plantains. To be Puerto Rican *is* to be Black *and* to have lived in Harlem, the Bronx, or Newark—the victim of racial, economic, and cultural discrimination—and to return to live in a small wooden house built on stilts over the mud of an urban slum in San Juan.[83]

By referring to urban centers and boroughs in the Northeast, the brochure links the fates of Puerto Ricans and African Americans who constitute a majority of slum dwellers. Nonetheless, these spaces and relationships are not what racialize Puerto Ricans as Black. "To be Puerto Rican is to be Black and to have lived" in these urban spaces, but having lived in these slums does not make one Black. In other words, racialization is not solely within the institutional authority of the colonial metropolis. That said, it is notable that the definition of Puerto Ricanness in this instance remains selective. Even as the brochure acknowledges the trauma and agency of the diaspora, it does so at the expense of those migrants who do not return to the island whether by choice or circumstance.

Proyecto Piloto's inclusive racial politics also incorporated critical conversations about racism within Puerto Rico. One strategy entailed the creation of short comic books (*paquines*). Each easily reproduced and distributed comic conveyed a brief political story. "Remember that the people who we were working with," explained Efraín Negrón, "didn't read books like this" (pointing to a large book on his desk). Recognizing the practical and pedagogical limitations of traditional printed material, Proyecto Piloto opted to use comics to illustrate the relationships among race, colonialism, and history in Puerto Rico.[84]

Proyecto Piloto also used public performances (*sociodramas*) that featured community leaders as actors. The stated objectives of the performances were to motivate individuals to learn and participate in community action, to empower individuals through affirmative images of the individual and the community, to develop basic understandings of economic and social conflicts and structures, and to become proficient in democratic practices and the use of the scientific method.[85] In addition

Figure 5.3. "Época del saqueo: máquina del tiempo," by David Pagan. Proyecto Piloto comic. Ana Livia Cordero Personal Papers. Courtesy of Rafael Mayfield.

to challenging Puerto Rican racial history, both pedagogical tools offered specific solutions and plans that local communities could use to guide collective and democratic action.

The war in Vietnam and the consequent military draft garnered the lion's share of attention in Proyecto Piloto's comics and performances. Years earlier, in the midst of World War I, President Woodrow Wilson signed the Jones-Shafroth Act, which unilaterally imposed U.S. citizenship on all Puerto Ricans born on the island. In accordance with this colonial imposition, the act required Puerto Ricans to register for compulsory military service.[86] Puerto Ricans considered the military draft an added blood tax levied on them even as they lacked congressional representation and the right to vote in federal elections.

Opposition to the Vietnam War reached a fever pitch on the island at the same time as Proyecto Piloto began to develop its research agenda and cultural work. Between 1960 and 1971 alone, more than a dozen skirmishes occurred at the UPR between students opposing the war and students serving in the U.S. Army's Reserve Officer Training Corps (ROTC). These clashes at the UPR left at least two students dead along with a taxi driver killed while searching for his daughter during a protest on the UPR campus.[87]

Proyecto Piloto's comics and performances focused on the colonizing and detrimental effects of the military draft on Puerto Ricans' family and other social relationships. The community meeting—a common setting in all of Proyecto Piloto's cultural texts—served as a key locale for deeper analysis of the ways in which race and class informed militarization in Puerto Rico. In some instances, discussions about race even superseded the military draft and war as the central motif in these works.

In the comic "The Age of Plunder: The Time Machine" (Época del saqueo: máquina del tiempo), for example, David Pagan rethought the island's racial history through the lens of the military draft. Set in a small community meeting, the single-frame comic depicts women and men gathered to discuss the Vietnam War:

Community Member 1: Did you all hear that the Vietnam War ended and that the Vietnamese won?
Community Member 2: I never understood that war and why we Puerto Ricans had to fight in it.

Community Member 3: Not just any Puerto Ricans. You mean the Black and poor Puerto Ricans.

Community Member 4 (Jacinto): I know some white Puerto Ricans who fought in the war.

Community Member 5: Look, Jacinto, no one in Puerto Rico is white. We are all Black with different skin colors.[88]

The diverse voices quickly shift a conversation about the Vietnam War into a reconsideration of Puerto Rican national and racial identity. The third community member's assertion points to the inequitable deployment to Vietnam of Puerto Rico's racialized poor relative to their elite and lighter-skinned counterparts on the island.

But Jacinto's comment and the response from the final community member also resist racial binaries based on rules of hypodescent. Indeed, the rearticulation of Blackness in the comic as an ideological and political category simultaneously challenges both phenotypical characteristics and narratives of *blanqueamiento* in Puerto Rico associated with upward class mobility. Instead, Puerto Ricans across the class spectrum are classified as Black and only distinguished by "different skin colors."

"Manela," the first comic ever produced by Proyecto Piloto, grappled with the effects of the military draft on the Puerto Rican family. But the comic's treatment of the normative Puerto Rican family also contained a message of racial affirmation.[89] An eighteen-year-old Black Puerto Rican woman, Manela struggles with her partner Manuel's pending deployment to Vietnam. Manela resides in a "barrio of Black people" where the sugar mill shut down leaving a large portion of the community unemployed.

In one scene, Manela and Manuel prepare to go out dancing on Manuel's last night in Puerto Rico before his deployment. Manela straightens her hair because people refer to it as "bad hair," reflecting the negative and racialized connotations associated with curly hair (*pelo malo*) in Puerto Rico. Manela's apprehension about her hair helps to contextualize the poem "Soy yo" (I am myself). Expressing a powerful "Black is beautiful" message, the poem appears at the beginning of the comic. Accompanying the poem is an image of a Black Puerto Rican woman with an Afro wearing a dress, necklace, amulet, and large earrings and standing before a slum.

Significantly, "Soy yo" does not focus exclusively on Black aesthetics within a social milieu hostile to such positive assertions. Instead, the

Figure 5.4. "Manela," by David Pagan. Proyecto Piloto comic. Ana Livia Cordero Personal Papers. Courtesy of Rafael Mayfield.

poem brings Proyecto Piloto's understandings about race full circle as it moves seamlessly between Black aesthetics (phenotype) and the socio-economic relationship between race, empire, and nation. The poem identifies Blackness as a foundational component of Puerto Rican economic development. The poem's fourth stanza proclaims that Puerto Rico is the "Borinquen of Caribbean Sea; Nation of Sugar and slaves; Coast and slum. . . . Foundation that now Harlem; Sees you with your head held high; Shouting Black Power! ¡Poder Negro!" Through the utilization of the indigenous name for the island (Borinquen), the poem locates the island as part of the nations of the Antillean archipelago "forged in blood" alongside other Black nations including Haiti, Trinidad, and Cuba.[90] Project members also believed that Puerto Rico's unwillingness to deal with its history of Blackness prevented it from creating bonds of solidarity with these Black republics and with African Americans.[91] As such, we might also read the poem and accompanying comic as cultural texts situating Puerto Rico within a larger Black internationalist moment that often excluded the island and its potential role in securing Black freedom.

The poem's identification of the material and human commodities (sugar and slaves) of Puerto Rico connect the island to the larger history of western racial capitalism in the Caribbean. The association between coast and slum in the poem reveals the ways in which the group ascribes Blackness to certain geographical spaces on the island. Puerto Rico's coastal sugar-harvesting regions had long been associated with Blackness, given the island's participation in the transatlantic slave trade. Proyecto Piloto did not consider the prevalence of mulattoes and Blacks in Puerto Rico's slums to be an incidental feature of the island's social landscape. Instead, the group linked the de facto segregation found in Puerto Rico's slums to its longer racial history of slavery and violence. As with the aforementioned brochure, the poem extends the parameters of the nation to include the diaspora, or the "foundation" that relocated to Harlem. "Soy yo" refuses to think of Harlem's multiracial and multiethnic populations and neighborhoods as just a space of despair and economic marginalization. The poem imbricates Harlem and Puerto Rico to rework Harlem within the Puerto Rican imaginary as a regenerative space for racial pride.

On the other hand, Proyecto Piloto's racialized conceptualizations of Puerto Rico lacked consistency. *Federico*, a play written by a "group of proletariat youth from Barrio Tortugo," tells the story of Federico Ortiz as he struggles to decide whether or not to report for military service after being drafted. Federico is eighteen years old and "Black and beautiful like an African Prince." Federico searches for guidance in his barrio of San Antón. Located in the southwestern urban center of Ponce, San Antón is widely recognized as the birthplace of the Afro–Puerto Rican folk traditions of *bomba* and *plena*. Following a dream where he envisions dealing with a racist commanding officer and then dying in battle, Federico opts not to report for duty. Community members and his family support his objection to the draft and hide him from FBI agents.[92]

Like other Proyecto Piloto productions, *Federico* has a minimal cast and focuses on opposition to the Vietnam War within a racial and class analysis. One of Federico's friends, referred to as Obrero (Worker), is dressed in "jeans, an unbuttoned shirt and a hat made of a paper bag." His other friend, Blanquito (Whitey), wears a "blazer and tie as he holds a stack of books underneath his arm." The fact that Blanquito is scripted as standing and talking down to Obrero, who is seated, accentuates the class and racial differences between the two men.[93]

The name Blanquito represents a racial category but also suggests an upper-class sensibility typically reserved for members of the island's elite. The racial and class positions of the two men predictably shape how they advise Federico. During a tense exchange, Obrero challenges Blanquito to acknowledge that his privilege exempts him from the very military service he is advising Federico to report for. "Since you are a university student and white you get to stay [in Puerto Rico] in the National Guard. They only want to screw those of us workers who are Black. We who are from the barrios."[94]

Even as Obrero challenges the advantages that exempt Blanquito from fighting on the front lines, Blanquito views the military as an opportunity to achieve upward class mobility. As such, the script simultaneously questions whether military conscription truly offers upward mobility and the ways in which colonialism feminizes Puerto Ricans. Proyecto Piloto's critique, however, holds that there are other ways of being masculine, such as through anticolonial struggle rooted in a form of Black nationalism. In this way, the group's anticolonial work hinged on normative and patriarchal understandings of the nation and resistance common at the time. The conflict remains unresolved as the scene ends, and Federico turns to his family for help.

Proyecto Piloto's claims about Puerto Rican racial and national identity also reflected the larger ambivalence with which outsiders viewed their work. The ways in which Cordero—a member of Puerto Rico's white elite—embodied the group's ideology of race jarred opponents and even members of the group. Miguel Rodríguez described being mesmerized by Cordero the first time he met her. Cordero's traditional African attire impressed him so much that he remembered thinking of her as "la gran jefa africana" (the great African chief).[95]

Rubén Sánchez inferred that the MPI male leadership's discomfort and annoyance with Cordero stemmed in part from her style of dress. According to Sánchez, members of the MPI disparaged Cordero in hushed whispers asking, "What is that white woman doing dressed as an African or Black woman?"[96] Sánchez acknowledged that the group's approach to race had nothing to do with being either politically correct or inclusive. Instead, their confrontational and community-based approach challenged the racism found within everyday Puerto Rican life and made race a constitutive component of the language and terms of anticolonial struggle on the island and in the diaspora.

## Conclusion

Trouble plagued Proyecto Piloto from the moment the group launched its community-based research and projects throughout the island in 1968. Not only did their falling-out with the MPI leave them isolated and ostracized from the larger political left, they also had to deal with increased police surveillance and repression. In late 1968 Puerto Rican police major Luis Maldonado Trinidad testified before the Congressional Subcommittee to Investigate the Administration of the Internal Security Act about the increased presence of communism in the Caribbean. Maldonado Trinidad joined the police force after he graduated from high school. Then, in the 1960s he received advanced surveillance training at the FBI police academy and eventually served briefly as police superintendent before being forced to resign amid evidence of corruption.[97]

Maldonado Trinidad's testimony before Congress revealed the police department's extensive surveillance file on Proyecto Piloto. The file included records detailing early police infiltration of the group and listed early meeting locations, the names of all the members, and even meeting notes. Maldonado Trinidad's testimony described the group's goal as to get in "contact with the poor people living in slums, so they can live together with them. They are there to observe the problems of these people and . . . indoctrinate these poor people with revolutionary ideas."[98] Aside from making vague references to communism, Maldonado Trinidad did not describe the group's revolutionary ideas, and the Congressional Record makes even less mention of the problems faced by Puerto Rico's poor.

By February 1968 local police were keeping all Proyecto Piloto members under twenty-four-hour surveillance. "The vigilance and persecution," confessed Miguel Rodríguez, "were very strong. [The police] would follow us. They talked to the neighbors about us. They would say bad things about us in the communities."[99] With tensions at an all-time high following another violent confrontation at the UPR, police raided Proyecto Piloto's headquarters in Barrio Tortugo on February 28, 1968, without a search warrant.[100] They arrested twenty-two group members, including Cordero, and charged them with assault, theft, and battery. Most of these charges stemmed from the violent confrontation that took place after the unlawful police entry into the group's headquarters.

Even though the media implied a connection between the arrest of the group and a string of recent bombings, police were never able to find any corroborating evidence and the charges against the group were dropped. Members of another radical Leftist group, Comandos Armados de Liberación, later claimed responsibility for the bombings. In fact, the majority of the police surveillance against Proyecto Piloto only detailed the group's ongoing meetings, surveys, and community improvement projects (even the construction of speed bumps on neighborhood roads merited a mention in the police file).[101] But local police continued to intensify their harassment of the group, culminating in a second arrest of Cordero and four other members in May 1968 on charges of obstruction and aggression against police. These charges were later dropped as well.

In spite of police repression, Proyecto Piloto and other Leftist groups continued to organize against the military draft and the Vietnam War. Confrontations between the ROTC, students, and activists became common occurrences at the UPR. On March 4, 1970, UPR chancellor Jaime Benítez called in riot police to arrest protestors after they set fire to the

ROTC building. During the violence that spilled out onto the streets of the local Río Piedras neighborhood, police shot and killed university student Antonia Martínez Lagares who was watching the events from a balcony of her home.

Two police officers and one ROTC cadet were also killed a little more than a year later in one of the most violent confrontations at the UPR. Massive police reprisals followed the deaths of the police officers. Police beat and arrested students, raided the homes of *independentista* leaders, and occupied the UPR campus for more than a month. As part of this state terror, police also stormed and burned down the Proyecto Piloto head-quarters in Barrio Tortugo.[102] Cordero argued that police used the death of an officer as an excuse to burn Proyecto Piloto's home in order to attack "those people who [police] considered to be the key players [in creating] unity and strength in the barrio."[103] With few exceptions, former members of Proyecto Piloto with whom I spoke considered the 1971 fire as one of the main catalysts of the group's eventual dissolution.

As it did with other social movements of the era, police repression gradually began to wear on the group and foment internal discord. As the group understandably grew increasingly suspicious of outsiders and each other's actions, they began to lose sight of their original organizational goals and mission. One former member noted "we fell into the trap of the very thing we critiqued that other *independentista* groups were doing at the time. We became a *grupusculo* [isolated group] that only talked to itself because we thought we were right."[104] Moreover, others in the group grew increasingly concerned that their "political analysis was wrong." In an ef-fort to reach beyond narrow racial and nationalist frameworks, the group lost sight of local conditions. As another former member lamented, "the political struggle in Puerto Rico was obviously not the one in Africa and it also wasn't like the one in the United States. Racial conflicts exist here but we also have to understand them in our own way within a colonial situation."[105] Ironically, the group's effort against the longstanding history of racial neglect in Puerto Rico alienated them from the very people they sought to work with.

By the mid-1970s the initial Proyecto Piloto team had turned over. Some members returned to university to begin what would become fairly prominent careers as Puerto Rican intellectuals. Others left after end-ing romantic relationships with partners who remained as members of the group.[106] Still others simply disappeared and were never heard from again. A core group of Cordero loyalists continued their community and anticolonial work on the island. Cordero even served as one of the medical doctors that investigated and produced a scathing report of the police murder and cover-up of two *independentistas* at Cerro Maravilla in 1978.[107] The remaining members of Proyecto Piloto also spent time in Nicaragua with the Sandinistas and assisted Haitian asylum seekers sent to Puerto Rico after being transferred from Florida.

Proyecto Piloto officially ended with Cordero's unexpected death in 1992 of respiratory complications. Her passing along with the traumatic history of the group made it easy to forget the significance of Proyecto Piloto's work. Accordingly, the stories of Juan Mari Brás and groups such as the MPI and FUPI have dominated accounts of the 1960s Puerto Rican political vanguard. Thanks to Cordero's extensive recordkeeping, however, there remains an extensive archive of the group's important reconceptualization of race and national identity on the island. Cordero's archive and life work with Proyecto Piloto is a rare moment that shows traces of what can happen when political leaders on the island step back from the pulpit of traditional politics and listen to and work alongside the people who have entrusted their futures to them.

# Conclusion

*Seams of Empire* has traced the imbricative encounters between Puerto Rican and U.S. racial regimes during the mid-twentieth century. Racial imbrication describes the points of overlap regarding race, empire, gender, and politics in the work of journalists, writers, and activists in Puerto Rico and the United States. The concept of imbrication allows us to think about the ways in which these little-known cultural and political workers imagined sociopolitical futures hinged on racial affinities that at times were saturated with contradictory meanings. In an era of radical transformation, writers and activists in both national contexts reimagined their sociopolitical futures through the practice of racial imbrication.

The extensive New Deal–like economic and social reforms that the emerging PPD promulgated in Puerto Rico shaped African American journalists' writing about economic and political reforms in the post-Reconstruction American South. Similarly, the radicalization and perceived racial progress of Latin American labor movements contributed to the future that Harold Preece envisioned in his writings for the Black press. Assumptions about race and class relations in Puerto Rico also influenced the ways in which Edwin Rosskam depicted the island as an ideal location where progressive white liberals could relocate to escape their own estrangement from the American colonial and racial regime. During the 1960s, exchanges between the evolving independence movement on the island and U.S. organizations such as the SNCC opened new avenues for activity within a growing anticolonial and Black internationalist sentiment.

I have deployed racial imbrication throughout the book as an alternative theoretical concept to the failed method of comparison in the study of race. Most importantly, the study of racial imbrication in Puerto Rico opens up possibilities for thinking about diaspora and race outside of conservative and minority nationalisms that erase the work, ideas, and contributions of marginalized groups. Hence racial imbrication captures the overlapping histories of racialization, colonialism, and exploitation even as it reckons with what remains hidden or concealed in those zones of political and social exchange.

The overlooked group of cultural workers and activists who labored within the connective spaces of imbrication coupled seemingly disparate racial regimes and imagined new possibilities. Each case study of imbrication shares a common history of marginalization within dominant Puerto Rican historiography. At times, as with Rosskam and the 1960s anticolonial activities on the island, these people and movements further marginalized and excluded certain subjects, especially women and members of the diaspora.

Beginning in the 1970s and early 1980s a more concerted effort developed on the island focused on filling in the gaps of Puerto Rican racial history. Referred to as the "new historicism," in Puerto Rico this movement arose primarily at the UPR and among professors deeply affected by the international and U.S. social movements of the previous decade. This era saw the publication of several monumental texts about Puerto Rican Black (working-class) life by intellectuals such as Eduardo Seda Bonilla, Rosario Ferré, Lydia Milagros González, Ángel Quintero Rivera, Isabelo Zenón Cruz, José Luis González, and Edgardo Rodríguez Julia, to name but a few. For example, Lydia Milagros González and Ángel Quintero Rivera's photo-book, *La otra cara de la historia*, sought to give a new face to "the Puerto Rico that has little to do with the idyllic image of our past that appears daily on television ads."[1]

Combined, these writers represented a significant shift away from the U.S. academics who directed many of the earlier studies at UPR. This group of intellectuals, many of whom spent considerable time outside Puerto Rico, reexamined the question of Puerto Rican national identity through intersectional studies that placed class, race, and gender at the center of their analyses. *La generación de los setenta* (the seventies generation), as they came to be known, even found institutional support through the establishment of various centers, such as the Centro para el Estudio de la Realidad Puertorriqueña (1970) and the Center for Puerto Rican Studies

(Centro) at Hunter College in New York (1973), which coalesced with the demands of popular social movements.[2]

These new institutional spaces served as significant sources for re-claiming and acknowledging blackness and its importance on the island and in the diaspora. As historical sociologist Roderick Ferguson reminds us, however, the university as an archive encapsulates radical possibilities that challenge state practices but ultimately can also be used by the state to regulate and manage difference. But the incorporation of these movements demonstrates how they also help to shape state and economic impulses that restrict the radical and dynamic possibilities for analyzing race, class, and gender that many of these studies in Puerto Rico and New York undertook.[3] In other words, we should not be surprised to see that the recognition and incorporation of race in Puerto Rican life did not pro-duce significant changes in the ways Puerto Ricans understand race but instead only strengthened the state's use of race-neutral tropes such as ra-cial democracy and the racial triad. Anthropologist Arlene Dávila teaches us that these practices are nicely packaged and literally marketed and sold back to us as forms of identity.[4] The continued growth of the Puerto Ri-can diaspora in the mainland United States makes these neoliberal modes of incorporation simultaneously even more desirable, profitable, and troubling.

Yet the diaspora's liminal position within the nation and its relation-ship to other racial and ethnic groups in the United States has taken on added significance in recent years with the island's continued economic problems and increasingly radicalized labor and student movements. In early 2014 the island's economic outlook worsened as the major credit agencies downgraded the Puerto Rican government's credit rating to junk status. Labor unions representing teachers and other public workers orga-nized as the government implemented new laws and austerity measures to bring the island's spending in line with the demands of investors and major lending agencies.

Given Puerto Rico's bleak economic outlook, the number of Puerto Ri-cans leaving the island has continued to rise over the last two decades such that by the 2010 census more than 4.7 million Puerto Ricans lived outside of Puerto Rico. Relatedly, the island's population has dropped by a little more than 2 percent since 2010, and there are now more Puerto Ricans living off the island than on it. Whereas in the past Puerto Ricans generally resettled in large urban centers in the northern United States, this no longer holds true. To avoid the harsh winters and high cost of living in cities like Chicago, Philadelphia, and New York, Puerto Rican migrants are opting to move to Florida, for example, where 744,473 persons of Puerto Rican origin had settled by 2008.[5]

Given these trends, Puerto Rican scholars are shifting their academic gaze away from the northern urban belt and toward the American South. A recent special edition of CENTRO Journal, for example, documented the migration trends, living conditions, and cultural practices of the Puerto Rican diaspora in the Sunshine State.[6] The growing presence of Puerto Ricans in Florida even dramatically reshaped the federal electoral landscape in 2012. Puerto Ricans, who traditionally tend to vote Democratic, offset the predominantly Republican Cuban American community in the south of the state.[7] The growing influence of Puerto Ricans in the American South requires rethinking the possibilities for grassroots alliances and new political opportunities among different groups in the region.

The growing presence of other Latin American migrants in the South, coupled with the striking migration trends among the Puerto Rican diaspora, have even led scholars to speak of the "Nuevo New South."[8] This term encapsulates the ways in which the presence of Puerto Ricans (and other Latina/os) ruptures traditional black-and-white paradigms about race in the region. Yet, despite its appeal, the term "Nuevo New South" directly conceals the larger social and political history of the region. Even the term "New South" is saturated with contradictory meanings given its repeated use throughout history by both the old southern aristocracy and southern liberals. Historian Julie Weise has recently shown that Latino immigration is not a particularly new phenomenon to the region but is rather the "[product] of scholarly and popular imaginations."[9] Just as the presence of Latina/o migrants is not particularly new, the region's simplistic black-and-white racial binary does not sufficiently capture the South's deeper and richer racial history within Latin America, as this book has shown.

Puerto Rico offered African American observers Deton Brooks and George Little an ideal model for the types of land reforms they imagined in the American South following the failure of Reconstruction. Similarly, in his journalism Harold Preece turned to the island, and to Latin America more generally, as a conceptual archetype that he imbricated with the

South in order to think more critically about the types of class, racial, and labor alliances that could benefit his native South. Undoubtedly, Preece would have had no problem with extending the geographic borders of his New South down to the Caribbean and to the southern cone of Latin America. Even the radical race work conducted by Ana Livia Cordero in Puerto Rico cannot be divorced from her substantial intellectual exchanges with SNCC, James Forman, and Robert Williams in the South.

To return to Weise's point, part of the desire to theorize about and name the changes in Florida and other parts of the U.S. South as the beginnings of a Nuevo New South arises from an academic milieu that rewards such thinking. But the academic desire for ingenuity is only a small piece of the problem. After all, it would be naïve and irresponsible not to encourage the dynamic study of changing social phenomena wherever they occur. The real problems emerge within the fields of Puerto Rican and Latina/o studies when we as multidisciplinary scholars succumb so fully to such forms of reductionism that we combine a long list of unquestioned narratives into a distorted historiography of partial truths or myths. These oversimplifications matter because they limit our respective fields to the parameters of history delineated by the nation-state, canonical formations, and those subjects the state considers most worthy of attention.

The overlapping anticolonial and antiracism work of the cultural brokers studied here raises larger questions about the possibilities for Puerto Rican sovereignty and citizenship. On one hand their work reaffirms recent calls by some members of the Puerto Rican Left for a radical statehood approach.[10] This approach advocates for using statehood and its corresponding civil rights to bring together similarly situated subaltern groups within the larger U.S. racial regime to demand a radical transformation in the conditions of their everyday lives. This political alliance draws upon the larger history of radical possibilities imagined by most of the writers in the preceding pages.

On the other hand, the writers and activists discussed also remained skeptical of allowing the state to be the ultimate arbiter of civil rights. These political actors knew better than most academics and government officials that civil rights and citizenship do not necessarily translate into a better quality of life. Recent U.S. census data support such skepticism: the percentage of Puerto Ricans who live in poverty in the United States (28 percent) nearly matches the percentage for African Americans

(27.4 percent) almost a full century after the imposition of U.S. citizenship on Puerto Ricans.[11] In these ways, the histories and futures of both groups remain intimately bound. In spite of these abysmal statistics, calls for Puerto Rican statehood continue unabated. Perhaps, as Rosskam's work reminds us, we should ask why it is not possible to see the detrimental effects of a haunting we have, in fact, been trained to see and to understand for so long. Sovereignty matters. Shrewdly questioning the myths that scaffold such calls for sovereignty—in whatever forms they might appear—matters more than the calls for sovereignty themselves.

# Notes

## Introduction

1. Vargas, "Júbilo ciudadano," 8.

2. "How Mississippi Is Catching Up—and Puerto Rico Is Not." *Puerto Rico Report*, October 15, 2012, www.puertoricoreport.com/how-mississippi-is-catching-up-and-puerto-rico-is-not. Puerto Rico's poverty relative to every state in the American union does not deter proponents of uneven economic development strategies from making further comparisons. Despite Puerto Rico's colonial status, they compare its development with that of the rest of Latin America and use those figures as evidence of progress and growth.

3. Marquez and Marquez, "Federal Funds Expenditure in Puerto Rico."

4. A. Gordon, "'Who's There?': Some Answers to Questions About Ghostly Matters" (speech presented at United Nations Plaza, Berlin, for Seminar 6, 2007). Gordon notes that ordinary people like Seguinot have the capacity to "ascertain these evidentiary things not also, but more often than professional seers . . . a vision that can not only regard the seemingly not there, but can also see that the not there is a seething presence. Seething, it makes a striking impression; seething, it makes everything we do see just as it is, charged with the occluded forgotten past." A. Gordon, *Ghostly Matters*, 195.

5. Under the Jones-Shafroth Act of 1917, all Puerto Ricans born on the island are granted a second-class form of U.S. citizenship. In protest several Puerto Ricans have renounced their U.S. citizenship in favor of Puerto Rican citizenship, even though the U.S. government does not recognize this status and there is no Puerto Rican passport. In addition to Marcano García, the late Juan Mari Brás—founder of the Puerto Rican Socialist Party—is perhaps the most notable Puerto Rican to renounce his American citizenship.

6. Marcano García, "Carta al presidente de Estados Unidos."

7. Rivera Schatz, "Igualdad: Come Home!" 24–25. Rivera Schatz's conflation of Puerto Ricans and Hispanics in his discussion of the island's decolonization is notable.

8. On the history of Black radicalism see Cedric Robinson's *Black Marxism*.

9. Robinson, *Forgeries of Memory and Meaning*, vi.

10. Kim, *Bitter Fruit*. Kim shows, for example, that our obsession with racial scapegoating or black irrationality allows white racial power to permeate throughout society without ever having to speak of it.

11. Lowe, "Insufficient Difference," 410. Within sociology, ideal types are the most common theoretical tools used to organize comparative analysis. First theorized by Max Weber, an ideal type is "the one-sided *accentuation* of one or more points of view" into *"concrete individual* phenomena which are arranged according to those one-sidedly emphasized viewpoints into a unified *analytical* construct." Weber, "Objectivity," 90; emphasis in original. As analytic constructions in their most extreme form, ideal types are comparative reference points used to generate knowledge about the differences and similarities between seemingly distinct social formations. For a more complete discussion see Hong and Ferguson, *Strange Affinities*, 3–4. For another outstanding critique of the comparative method see Seigel, "Beyond Compare."

12. See, for example, Briggs, *Reproducing Empire*; Findlay, *Imposing Decency*; Guerra, *Popular Expression and National Identity in Puerto Rico*.

13. Political cartoons appearing before and after the Spanish-American War are just one example of this. For a collection of some examples of these political cartoons see "Puerto Rican Independence Movement and the Status Issue under Spanish Rule."

14. Jordan, *Imperial Democracy*, 5.

15. Ibid., 32.

16. Jung, "Constituting the U.S. Empire State," 2–3, 9.

17. This book's primary focus is not centered on the question of whether or not Puerto Rico is a racially democratic nation. There now exists an extensive and exciting volume of literature that thoroughly debunks this nationalist mythology. See, for example, Dinzey-Flores, *Locked In, Locked Out*; Godreau, *Scripts of Blackness*; Guerra, *Popular Expression and National Identity in Puerto Rico*; Rivera-Rideau, *Remixing Reggaetón*, Rodríguez-Silva, *Silencing Race,* and Zenón Cruz, *Narciso descubre su trasero*.

18. In *Popular Expression and National Identity in Puerto Rico* Lillian Guerra discusses the deployment of the mythical Puerto Rican white *jíbaro* (peasant from the countryside) among Puerto Rico's elite and popular classes. At the turn of the twentieth century the *jíbaro* emerged as the quintessential symbol of national identity in Puerto Rico. Guerra argues that Puerto Rican elites undertook

this process of mythmaking in order to bring Puerto Rico's popular classes in line with their own interests as U.S. colonialism transformed the island's racial and class order.

19. In her recent book *Silencing Race*, Ileana Rodríguez-Silva wonderfully demonstrates the ways in which these forms of racial disavowals are historically produced through various practices of silencing, including avoidance and ambivalence.

20. Barbosa, *La obra de José Celso Barbosa*, 34. All translations from Spanish are my own. The full quotation reads, "En Puerto Rico, pues, no ha existido, ni existe, y Dios hará que nunca exista el problema del color tal cual existe en algunos Estados de la Unión, para vergüenza y oprobio de la nación más democrática del mundo." Although some scholars have described Barbosa's interest in Puerto Rican annexation and U.S. racial history as both contradictory and accommodationist, I do not wish to support such a reading here. As a Black medical doctor trained in the United States who admired the writings of Frederick Douglass and W.E.B. Du Bois, Barbosa also understood racial power as more than a unidirectional force. Barbosa admired the ways in which African Americans challenged their subjugation and used them to frame his own anti-colonial politics. "The history of the Negro in the United States is an inspiration for all men of color," noted Barbosa (87).

21. In Pedreira's case, this is hardly surprising, given that he admired Barbosa greatly and even penned Barbosa's biography.

22. Pedreira, *Insularismo*, 29.

23. For more on the ICP see Dávila, *Sponsored Identities*; Duany, *Puerto Rican Nation on the Move*; and Godreau, "Changing Space, Making Race.

24. Quoted in Duany, *Puerto Rican Nation on the Move*, 126–27. Duany's text is also one of the better contemporary studies to analyze both the deployment of cultural nationalism by Puerto Rican elites and the ways in which this has produced various forms of state-sanctioned exclusions, especially among migrants on the island.

25. Godreau, "Folkloric Others," 172.

26. Seigel, "Beyond Compare."

27. Robinson, *Forgeries of Memory and Meaning*, vi.

28. Seda Bonilla, "Dos modelos de relaciones raciales."

29. Seda Bonilla, "El racismo en dos culturas."

30. Seda Bonilla, "Un nuevo racismo es amenaza a la continuidad del pueblo puertorriqueño en la historia," 7–8.

31. A. Gordon, *Ghostly Matters*, 195, 8.

32. Quintero-Rivera, *Puerto Rico*; Rodríguez Juliá, *Puertorriqueños: álbum de la Sagrada Familia puertorriqueña*.

33. Among authors who used the family as a national trope are Manuel Zeno Gandía (*La Charca*) and particularly the members of *la generación del treinta*: Antonio Pedreira, Emilio Belaval, Enrique Laguerre, and Tomás Blanco. See also René Marqués, *Docile Puerto Rican*. For a criticism on this literature see Juan Gelpí, *Literatura y paternalismo en Puerto Rico*. I also want to make special note of Marisel Moreno's recent book, *Family Matters: Puerto Rican Women Authors on the Island and the Mainland* as an excellent study that both problematizes the trope of the family and ruptures the problematic separation between Puerto Rican writers on the island and those in the continental United States.

34. Micol Seigel calls for a similar shift away from comparative method, demanding that questions of comparison "become not just unanswerable, but also unaskable." *Uneven Encounters*, xi.

35. Ferguson, *Aberrations in Black*, 2–4. I am especially indebted to the queer of color critique for helping me to conceptualize this tension. While cautiously approaching culture, queer of color critique does not abandon culture but treats it "as a material site of struggle" where previously concealed forms of intersectionality might be revealed. In this way, queer of color critique treats race, gender, sexuality, and class not as isolated or hidden deviations constructed by the state but as intimately connected social formations.

36. Stuart Hall, "Notes on Deconstructing 'the Popular.'"

37. Lowe, "Insufficient Difference," 412.

38. Du Bois, *Souls of Black Folk*, 5.

## Chapter 1. The Puerto Rican Blueprint

1. Brooks, "Jim Crow at America's Air Crossroads," 1.

2. Ibid.

3. Ibid.

4. Ibid.

5. Dooley, "Wartime San Juan, Puerto Rico," 922.

6. Lefebvre, "Puerto Rico: Quiet Participant," 92–97. Despite its ideological and material support of the axis countries, Spain remained a formally neutral (non-belligerent) nation during World War II.

7. Du Bois, *Black Reconstruction in America*, 580–636. See, especially, the chapter "Counter-Revolution of Property."

8. Ibid., 670.

9. Baldwin, *Chicago's New Negroes*, 14.

10. Ibid.

11. Robinson, *Black Marxism*, 18; Collins, *Black Feminist Thought*.

12. See, for example, Du Bois, *The Souls of Black Folk*, and *Black Reconstruction in America*; or Wells Barnett, *On Lynchings*.

13. Foner, "The IWW and the Black Worker," 58.

14. Foner, *Organized Labor and the Black Worker,* 121.

15. Kelley, *Race Rebels*, 106–10.

16. Kelley, *Hammer and Hoe,* and *Race Rebels.*

17. Kelley, *Race Rebels*, 108.

18. Ibid.

19. On internal colonialism as a model for understanding Black subjugation see, for example, R. Allen, "Reassessing the Internal (Neo)Colonialism Theory"; Calderón-Zaks, "Domestic Colonialism"; Cruse, *Rebellion or Revolution*; K. Clark, *Dark Ghetto*; and Robert Blauner, "Internal Colonialism and Ghetto Revolt."

20. J. Allen, *Negro Question in the United States*, 15.

21. Kelley, *Race Rebels*, 108.

22. Von Eschen, *Race against Empire*, 3.

23. Wright, "Blueprint for Negro Literature."

24. Ibid.

25. Ibid. Wright refers to the agents of Black nationalism as "salesmen" and "preachers."

26. Ibid. On the history of Western racial capitalism, see Robinson, *Black Marxism.*

27. Wright, "Blueprint for Negro Literature," section 4.

28. Ibid., section 5.

29. Robinson, *Black Marxism*, 292.

30. Wright, "Blueprint for Negro Literature." "[Perspective] means that Negro writers must learn to view the life of a Negro living in New York's Harlem or Chicago's South Side with the consciousness that one sixth of the earth's surface belongs to the working class. It means that Negro writers must create in their readers' minds a relationship between a Negro woman hoeing cotton in the South and the men who loll in swivel chairs in Wall Street and take the fruits of her toil" (section 5).

31. Robinson, *Black Marxism*, 183.

32. Johnson, *Spaces of Conflict, Sounds of Solidarity*, 6.

33. Wright, "Blueprint for Negro Literature," section 5.

34. See, for example, Washburn, *African American Newspaper*; Buni, *Robert L. Vann of the* Pittsburgh Courier.

35. Washburn, *African American Newspaper*, 80.

36. Baldwin, *Chicago's New Negroes.*

37. Ibid., 37.

38. Washburn, *African American Newspaper*, 83–84. The *Chicago Defender* generated scandalous front-page headlines, "printed in bright red ink and each one larger than the one before." (83).

39. Buni, *Robert L. Vann of the* Pittsburgh Courier, 46–49.

40. Von Eschen, *Race against Empire*, 8.

41. Washburn, *African American Newspaper*, 140.

42. Buni, *Robert L. Vann of the* Pittsburgh Courier, 325.

43. Von Eschen, *Race against Empire*, 192, n. 3.

44. Cited in Washburn, *African American Newspaper*, 140.

45. Ibid., 143–44.

46. Abbott also visited Uruguay, Bolivia, Chile, and Argentina during his Latin American tour.

47. Abbott's reports appeared between March 31 and October 20, 1923. See for example, Abbott, *"Defender* Head Made Welcome by Brazilians," and "My Trip through South America."

48. Abbott, "My Trip Through South America."

49. Washburn, *African American Newspaper*, 132.

50. Von Eschen, *Race against Empire*, 14.

51. Patricia Lowry, "Places: Women Recall Homestead's 'Herstory,'" *Pittsburgh Post-Gazette*, March 21, 2006, www.post-gazette.com/life/lifestyle/2006/03/21/Places-Women-recall-Homestead-s-herstory/stories/200603210277.

52. See, for example, Schalk, "Toki Types."

53. Brooks, "Puerto Rico Up in Arms."

54. P. Wood, "Deton Brooks: Poverty Fighter," 22.

55. Ibid.

56. Brooks, "Negro Fate in U.S. Tied to Puerto Rico Freedom."

57. Ibid.

58. Little, "Puerto Rico, Island of Peace, Beauty and Contrasts."

59. "Rethinking Our Policy," emphasis added.

60. Ibid., emphasis added.

61. Little, "Pittsburgher Describes Puerto Rico."

62. Lemert, *Social Things*, 174–79. I am thinking here about Ana Julia Cooper's theorization of manners in "The Colored Woman's Office." Importantly, Cooper notes that manners are crucial in the creation of a truly radical project of racial justice because manners push one to think about the feelings of others, moving beyond individualism and toward collective goals.

63. Von Eschen, *Race against Empire*.

64. Cited in Robinson, *Black Marxism*, 255.

65. Padmore, "Atlantic Charter and the British Colonies."

66. Ibid.

67. Kaplan, *Anarchy of Empire in the Making of U.S. Culture*, 137.

68. Espiritu, *Home Bound*, 60.

69. Burnett and Marshall, *Foreign in a Domestic Sense*, 5.

70. Fowles, *Down in Porto Rico*.

71. Ibid., foreword.

72. Ibid., 60–61.

73. Rep. James Harvey Davis, *A Civil Government for Porto Rico: Hearings on H.R. 8501*, House Committee on Insular Affairs, 64th Cong., 1st Sess. 82 (January 26, 1916), 59–60.

74. Badger, "Regionalism in the Caribbean," 13.

75. Burnett and Marshall, *Foreign in a Domestic Sense*.

76. Badger, "Future of Africa," 15.

77. Bolden, "'Recognition of Color Problem,'" 12.

78. Brooks, "Puerto Rican One-Crop System," 13.

## Chapter 2. Dispatches from the Colonial Outpost

1. Brooks, "Rise of Puerto Rico 'Populars,'" 5.

2. Roosevelt, "Remarks in San Juan, Puerto Rico," American Presidency Project, www.presidency.ucsb.edu/ws/?pid=14722. Roosevelt's speech indicates that he visited Puerto Rico thirty years earlier before he formally entered political life.

3. Muñoz Marín, "To the President of the United States," 247.

4. Ibid., 248.

5. Roosevelt advocated for much larger sugar quotas for Puerto Rico and Hawaii but was ultimately unsuccessful in gaining the support of senators from sugar-producing regions in the continental United States.

6. "Sugar Quotas Set for Cuba, Islands."

7. Ibid.

8. Ayala, *American Sugar Kingdom*.

9. Information Research Section, PRRA, "Facts about the Puerto Rico Reconstruction Administration." Puerto Rico Reconstruction Administration report, 1938, http://newdeal.feri.org/pr/pr10.htm.

10. Puerto Rico provided for less of its subsistence needs because U.S. economic policy dictated an increased reliance on U.S. food products and materials. In this sense, Puerto Rico exemplifies one of the earliest neoliberal models of "economic development" later implemented throughout the Global South.

11. Santiago-Valles, *"Subject People,"* 170.

12. Ayala and Bernabé, *Puerto Rico in the American Century*, 102.

13. Ayala, *American Sugar Kingdom*.

14. Tydings, "Expenditure of Relief Funds in Puerto Rico."

15. Brooks, "Sugar Trusts Get Congress Aid."

16. Muñoz Marín, "El Plan Chardón se llevará a efecto."

17. Winship, "Washington to Make Philippine Mistake," S5287.

18. Ibid.

19. Ibid., S5288.

20. Ibid.

21. Brooks, "Negro Fate in U.S. Tied to Puerto Rico Freedom."

22. Muñoz Marín, "Democracy Would Be a Hoax," 321.

23. Brooks, "Congress Is Threat to Puerto Rico Reform."

24. Sanson, *Louisiana during World War II*, 266.

25. J. B. Williams, "Late Honorable Dan R. McGehee."

26. Lawson, *Commonwealth of Hope*. See, for example, McGehee's thoughts on Will Alexander, who openly discussed segregation and white supremacy in the South. McGehee referred to Alexander as a "bird who concocted all this rot" and therefore "should be kicked into Kingdom Come" (211).

27. Domengeaux resigned from the committee in 1944 to enter the military and was replaced by Representative John S. Gibson from Georgia.

28. Maldonado, *Luis Muñoz Marín*, 222.

29. McCabe, "Cole demanda en el Congreso la sustitución inmediata de Tugwell."

30. "Comité Bell cree que el gobierno de la isla tiende a un control completo."

31. "Comité Bell preocupado con gobierno insular."

32. Glossing over the fact that Puerto Ricans were U.S. citizens, the committee suggested that Puerto Ricans look to other countries in Central and South America that were experiencing labor shortages and move there instead.

33. Maldonado, *Luis Muñoz Marín*, 222–23.

34. Fernandez, *Disenchanted Island*, 144. Note that Fernandez incorrectly identifies the Louisiana representative as Carl, not James, Domengeaux. Congressional records show James Domengeaux was the only representative to Congress from Louisiana at the time.

35. Von Eschen, *Satchmo Blows Up the World*.

36. Santiago-Valles, *"Subject People,"* 57.

37. Brooks, "Puerto Rico a Test Tube for Atlantic Charter." On Puerto Rico's population problems, see Brooks, "Puerto Rico Suffers from Over-Population."

38. "Independence for Puerto Rico."

39. Brooks, "Negro Fate in U.S. Tied to Puerto Rico Freedom."

40. Brooks, "Puerto Rican One-Crop System Needs Reform."

41. Ibid.

42. Little, "Puerto Rico, Island of Peace, Beauty and Contrasts."

43. Little, "Pittsburgher Describes Puerto Rico." Little notes the efforts of the PPD to provide a more balanced diet for the people.

44. Brooks, "Rise of Puerto Rico 'Populars.'"

45. Ayala, *American Sugar Kingdom*, 199.

46. Brooks, "Puerto Rican One-Crop System Needs Reform."

47. Ibid.

48. "Alas, the Poor Puerto Ricans!"

49. See, for example, Brooks, "Negro Fate in U.S. Tied to Puerto Rico Freedom," "Puerto Rican One-Crop System Needs Reform," and "Congress Is Threat to Puerto Rico Reform"; and Little, "Puerto Rican National Pride and Democracy."

50. Brooks, "Puerto Rico Up in Arms."

51. Brooks, "Negro Fate in U.S. Tied to Puerto Rico Freedom."

52. Ibid.

53. Ibid.

54. "Independence for Puerto Rico."

55. T. Smith, "Changing Racial Labels," 497–98. Smith notes that *Colored* started to lose currency beginning in the early decades of the twentieth century, especially among prominent Black intellectuals including Booker T. Washington and W.E.B. Du Bois. Nonetheless, the term remained in use through the 1940s.

56. Burns, "2,000,000 Demand Labor Drop Jim Crow," and "Negro Nations Well Represented at Paris Meet."

57. "Do You Know?"

58. Brooks, "Negro Fate in U.S. Tied to Puerto Rico Freedom."

59. While respecting the sovereignty of Puerto Ricans living on the island, very few articles in the *Defender* and the *Pittsburgh Courier* at that time openly advocated for Puerto Rican statehood.

60. Badger, "Number One U.S. Colony."

61. Brooks, "Puerto Rico Has No Big Race Problems."

62. Godreau, "Changing Space, Making Race," 283.

63. Brooks, "Puerto Rico Has No Big Race Problems."

64. Brooks, "Jim Crow at America's Air Crossroads," 4.

65. Brooks does mention a few prominent Black Puerto Ricans, including Ramos Antonini and the head of the Department of Social Sciences at the University of Puerto Rico, Pilar Barbosa. Barbosa was also the daughter of Dr. Jose Celso Barbosa, a founding figure of the modern statehood movement.

66. Brooks, "Puerto Rico Has No Big Race Problems."

67. Little, "Puerto Rican National Pride and Democracy."

68. Ibid.

69. Holloway, "Puerto Rico Will Choose," 6.

70. I do not mean to imply that the "white" Puerto Rican woman is not also racialized within the U.S. racial regime. Rather, what I mean to show here are the points of convergence and departure between U.S. and Latin American racial configurations in Puerto Rico.

71. A. Gordon, *Ghostly Matters*.

72. Ayala and Bernabé, *Puerto Rico in the American Century*, 154.

73. Muñoz Marín, "Prólogo," 16–17.

74. Ayala and Bernabé, *Puerto Rico in the American Century*, 150.

75. Ibid.

76. Santiago-Valles, *"Subject People,"* 199.

77. See, for example, his collected writings and speeches in the Fundación Luis Muñoz Marín and the publication *Palabras de Luis Muñoz Marín: 1945–1948.*

78. Muñoz Marín, "En defensa del Partido Popular y su posición sobre *status*," 216.

79. Pettis Perry, "The Case of Puerto Rico and the Fight for Its Independence," 1951, Pettis Perry Papers, Schomburg Center for Research in Black Culture, Box 3, Folder 11, p. 5.

80. Ibid., 4–5.

81. Ibid., 15.

82. On the potential of Puerto Rico as a republic for people of color see Buck, "Porto Rico Colonization," 4.

## Chapter 3. The Living Negro in Latin America

1. Myrdal, *American Dilemma*, lxix.

2. Ibid., lxviii, lv.

3. Ibid., xxxv.

4. Myrdal's large team of researchers included prominent American social scientists, such as urban sociologists Franklin Frazier and Louis Wirth.

5. Myrdal, *American Dilemma*, 466, emphasis in original.

6. Blanco, *El prejuicio racial en Puerto Rico*, 2–3.

7. Ibid., 4. Blanco defined Puerto Rico's middle class as "everything that is not proletariat."

8. Ibid., 44; "En todo caso, nuestro llamado prejuicio racial . . . podrá tener otros componentes adjetivos . . . pero su base fundamental es algo que, a falta de vocablo más exacto, podríamos denominar con el puertorriquezismo (*sic*) changuería. Substantivo que evoca imitativas afectaciones del chango y los incongruentes y ridículos remilgos del tití" (61–62).

9. Ibid., 47.

10. Ibid., 62.

11. Blanco, *Prontuario histórico de Puerto Rico*, 147.

12. Preece, "Confessions of an Ex-Nordic," 232. Preece does not admit to ever having participated in these racially violent attacks or in bullying African Americans as a child. That said, he also recollected that his aversion to violence did not mean that he considered African Americans his equals or even as humans.

13. Harold Preece to Tevis Clyde Smith, March 27, 1931, Harold Preece Papers, Robert E. Howard Foundation.

14. Preece, "Confessions of an Ex-Nordic," 232.

15. Ibid., 233.

16. Preece, "Living South: Tomcats and Pollcats."

17. Ibid. The use of "ex-Nordic" here can also be read as an allusion to James Weldon Johnson's 1912 story, *Autobiography of an Ex-Colored Man*. After dropping out of college, Preece struggled to find steady employment and held jobs as a salesman, a secretary, and even a preacher. Preece to Clyde Smith, July 26, 1928, Preece Papers. The Robert E. Howard Foundation. Preece attended Texas Christian University in 1926–27. In 1932, Preece returned to college at the University of Texas at Austin, where he studied writing. Mooney, "Texas Centennial 1936," 41.

18. Preece to Clyde Smith, November 5, 1928. At times, Preece described himself as a "radical," in other instances as a socialist or a communist, and on rare occasions he adamantly denied having anything to do with the Communist Party. In a September 1928 letter to Clyde Smith, Preece refers to himself as "Austin's town radical." In another letter to Smith three years later, Preece clarified that his "communism is not simply youthful exuberance." This 1931 letter discussing Preece's founding of a political club describes his Marxist analysis of social relations: "More and more, class-conscious workers are going to have to adopt a definitely Left wing attitude. Class collaboration isn't going to get us anywhere." Preece to Clyde Smith, March 27, 1931.

19. Kevin Mooney reports that Preece began working as a cub reporter as early as 1922 for his local newspaper, the *Austin Statesmen*.

20. For example, in 1936 John Gibbs St. Clair Drake took exception to Preece's disapproval of African Americans fighting in World War II because Preece believed they had been "hoodwinked . . . by a specious patriotism." St. Clair Drake accused Preece of ignoring the risks of pacifism for African Americans especially given the ever-looming threat of violence against them by white laborers. St. Clair Drake dismissed Preece's communism as a "Utopian" project that overlooked intra-class differences in the Black community. Drake, *Communism and Peace Movements*," 44. Dismissing St. Clair Drake as a bourgeois black intellectual alienated from class struggle, Preece admitted that he "would rather entrust [his] hope of life to [CPUSA presidential candidate] Mr. Browder and his followers than to Mr. Drake and his allies." Preece, "From Mr. Preece."

21. Preece, "The Living South: Southern Liberals."

22. Preece, "The Living South: Beaumont vs. Nashville."

23. Davey and Clark, *Remember My Sacrifice*, xv.

24. Ibid., xxxviii.

25. Clark, "Likes Column by Harold Preece."

26. Preece, "The Living South: New Year Decision."

27. Though first organized in 1935 as the Committee of Industrial Organizations, the Congress of Industrial Organizations was not formally established until 1938.

28. Cohen, *Making a New Deal*, 291–92.

29. The CIO succeeded in the Black community because of its efforts to prioritize labor organizing over other political commitments such as CPUSA party work. On the CIO's efforts in the U.S. South, see Kelley, *Hammer and Hoe*; and Congress of Industrial Organizations, "Working and Fighting Together."

30. See, for example, Preece's "Living South" articles "Southern Liberals," "New Year Decision," and "Marcantonio vs. Pollcats."

31. *Solid South* is not a term exclusive to the work of Preece. The solid South was a common designation of the region's lack of modernity. Gunnar Myrdal, for example, devotes a section of *American Dilemma* to the "Solid South."

32. Preece, "The Living South: Judgment on June'Teenth."

33. Preece, "The Living South: Captain Charlie."

34. There are some discrepancies in the record between the dates Preece gives for the publication of some of his pieces and their actual publication dates. See, for example, Preece, "The Negro in Latin America: What Mexico Thinks of Jackie Robinson."

35. Preece, "The Negro in Latin America: Cooking Makes Friends." In addition to his readers in the United States, Preece and his editors acknowledged that readers in Latin America were among the series' loyal audience. It is not clear where Preece got his statistics on readership.

36. Despite being written from the continental United States, "The Negro in Latin America" challenged traditional understandings of Latin America as a region. Common practice in the United States was to treat Latin America as either a separate geographic space (everything south of the Rio Grande and Florida) or a linguistically bound region (Spanish-speaking countries). The series clouded these cultural and material borders by including different cultural and geographic spaces, like Haiti and the Anglophone Caribbean. It also encompassed regions within the borders of the United States, like maroon settlements in Florida. Preece, "The Negro in Latin America: Sewanee Republic." This example of Preece's hemispheric vision of the Americas focused on runaway slaves from Georgia who assimilated into indigenous communities, most prominently the Muskogee Seminole nation in Florida. Preece also discussed Texan and Mexican history in several reports.

37. Preece wrote almost the entire series from his homes in Tennessee and

Texas. Several stories were also written during frequent trips to New York to attend conferences on this topic or to meet with informants.

38. Preece, "The Negro in Latin America." It appears that Preece did read Spanish.

39. Ortiz even invited Blanco to Cuba to be one of the first speakers during the inaugural year of the Sociedad de Estudios Afro-Cubanos. During this talk before his peers, Blanco lectured on his not yet published book. Showing intellectual reciprocity and respect, Blanco dedicated *El prejuicio racial en Puerto Rico* to Ortiz when he published it five years later, in 1942. Blanco honored Ortiz as the "teacher and creator of dynamic *antillanismo*." On intellectual reciprocity, see Rúa, *Grounded Identidad*, 138. For more on the relationship between Blanco and Ortiz see Frank Guridy's excellent study on the exchanges between Cuban and African American intellectuals, *Forging Diaspora*, 167–168.

40. Seigel, "Beyond Compare," 75.

41. Preece, "The Negro in Latin America."

42. The encyclopedia was never published in its entirety, though a preliminary sketch of the project was eventually published in 1945. See Du Bois and Johnson, *Encyclopedia of the Negro.* The exchanges among Pattee, Du Bois, and Logan are available in the W.E.B. Du Bois Papers, MS-312, Special Collections and University Archives, University of Massachusetts–Amherst Libraries.

43. Pattee, "Efforts Made in Latin America to Document the History of the Negro," 57. The ASNLH meetings in New York also attracted prominent anthropologists and race scholars such as Carter Woodson, Melville Herskovits, and Ralph Bunche.

44. Seigel, "Beyond Compare," 75.

45. Pattee, "Efforts Made in Latin America to Document the History of the Negro," 63.

46. Ibid., 62.

47. Pattee, "Prontuario histórico de Puerto Rico, by Tomás Blanco."

48. Preece, "The Negro in Latin America."

49. Ibid.

50. Preece, "The Negro in Latin America: Cooking Makes Friends."

51. Preece, "The Negro in Latin America: Brazil."

52. Sánchez Korrol, *From Colonia to Community*, 25, 28.

53. Preece, "The Negro in Latin America: Latin American Negroes Make Good Citizens."

54. See, for example, Piri Thomas's 1967 memoir, *Down These Mean Streets.*

55. Preece, "The Negro in Latin America: Puerto Rico Faces Revolution. Preece incorrectly identifies Ramón Emeterio Betances as Emilio Betances.

56. The remaining rights of free men included freedom of speech, religion,

the press, the inviolability of the citizen, and the rights to bear arms and elect one's own authorities.

57. Preece, "The Negro in Latin America: Puerto Rico Faces Revolution."

58. Moral, *Negotiating Empire*, 8. For more on education as colonial practice in Puerto Rico, see García Blanco and Colon Morera, "Community-Based Approach to Educational Reform in Puerto Rico"; and Navarro Rivera, "Imperial Enterprise and Educational Policies."

59. Bonafoux, *Literatura de Bonafoux*, 26.

60. Sheller, *Consuming the Caribbean*, 23–26. See, for example, her discussion on indemnification and the larger abolitionist movement that reinforced colonial arrangements between the Caribbean and Europe.

61. Preece, "The Negro in Latin America: The Spirituals Come to Salvador."

62. Mooney, "Texas Centennial 1936," 41. The Works Progress Administration Federal Writers' Project hired Preece in 1937 as an editorial assistant for John A. Lomax. Working together, the two men collected popular Texan folk songs and legends. In the same year, Preece also officially joined the Texas Folklore Society, for which he helped to organize several musical and cultural festivals.

63. Preece, "Negro Folk Cult," 35.

64. Ibid., 37. Preece believed that "northern Negroes" shared his criticism of Hurston, and undoubtedly, it is they that he is characterizing as the "critical members of the race." Cultural critic Eve Dunbar contends that his misreading of Hurston is driven by the "underlying assumptions made by the dichotomous but stagnant ways of describing black cultural production of the period as versions of either the 'New Negro' or the 'primitive.'" More simply, by working at the seams of these tropes in her ethnographic work, Hurston described the development of an active and class-conscious form of Black cultural citizenship (Dunbar, *Black Regions of the Imagination*, 43).

Preece not only misread Hurston's study, his criticisms of her were driven by a long history of misogyny in his work and thinking. In one letter to Tevis Clyde Smith, for example, he commented that women were "nothing, at heart, but mentally deficient extraverts. One gets sated with their kitchen-range caresses and banal babblings. Catty, mean, and narrow—the majority of them" (Preece to Smith, July 26, 1928).

65. Ashby, *Organized Labor and the Mexican Revolution*, 93. For more on the founding of the CTAL, see Alexander, *Organized Labor in Latin America,* and *International Labor Organizations and Organized Labor.*

66. Lombardo Toledano, *C.T.A.L., the War and the Postwar*, 74–75.

67. Ashby, *Organized Labor and the Mexican Revolution*, 94.

68. Fletcher, "Imperative of Black Worker Mobilization," 19; Draper, *Conflict*

*of Interests.* Black workers often had to establish auxiliary unions to the AFL where they paid dues but often were not allowed to vote on key union matters.

69. Fletcher, "Imperative of Black Worker Mobilization," 21.

70. Preece, "The Negro in Latin America: The AFL Tries to Aryanize Latin America."

71. In 1933, Berle published his highly acclaimed *The Modern Corporation and Private Property,* which detailed in part the increase in the levels of corporate wealth concentration.

72. The CIT also played a crucial role in the fracturing of the Chilean Left. Drake, "International Crises and Popular Movements in Latin America," 131.

73. Nodín Valdés, *Organized Agriculture and the Labor Movement,* 61–63; Dietz, *Historia Económica de Puerto Rico,* 240–41.

74. Preece, "The Negro in Latin America: Sugar Lumps in the Ballot Box."

75. Preece, "The Negro in Latin America: Latin America Welcomes Negro Workers."

76. See, for example, Preece, "The Negro in Latin America: Why Negroes Should Learn Spanish" and "So You Want to Go to Jail." For both practical and political reasons, Preece recognized that getting a marginalized population with already limited resources to various countries in Latin America would be difficult if not impossible.

77. This figure is especially staggering given that it does not include military interventions in the rest of Latin America. See B. Wood, *Making of the Good Neighbor Policy,* 5.

78. Additionally, as historian Greg Grandin aptly notes, the powerful forms of nationalism expressed during the Mexican Revolution of 1910–20 and the Sandino insurgency in Nicaragua in the late 1920s served as significant examples of the types of resistance the United States faced as it continued to pursue interventionist policies in the region. Grandin, *Empire's Workshop,* 37–42.

79. Preece, "The Negro in Latin America: Colored People and the Good Neighbor Policy."

80. Ibid.

81. McEniry, "Infant Mortality," 37.

82. Ibid., 8.

83. Preece, "The Negro in Latin America: Sugar Lumps in the Ballot Box," 7.

84. Pfau, "Rationing."

85. Preece, "The Negro in Latin America: OPA in Puerto Rico."

86. Preece, "The Negro in Latin America: Puerto Rico—America's First Ally."

87. Preece, "The Negro in Latin America: Puerto Rico Faces Revolution," 7.

88. Ibid.

89. Tugwell, *Stricken Land*, 501; see also Tugwell's description of his discussions with Muñoz Marín about independence on pp. 486–97.

90. Ayala and Bernabé, *Puerto Rico in the American Century*, 154. The addition of the Taft-Hartley Act to the Federal Labor Relations Act and its extension to Puerto Rico in 1947 severely crippled labor unions on the island.

91. Preece, "The Negro in Latin America: Puerto Rico Faces Revolution," 7.

92. Ibid.

93. Friedman, "Exploiting the North-South Differential," 329. This is also an important illustration of the ways in which New Deal legislation produced unequal outcomes for African American and Latina/o versus white workers.

94. Silén, *Historia de Puerto Rico*, 223.

95. Nodín Valdés, *Organized Agriculture and the Labor Movement before the UFW*, 82–83.

96. Ibid., 85.

97. Preece, "The Negro in Latin America: Cooking Makes Friends," 7.

98. Mooney, "Texas Centennial 1936," 41.

99. See, for example, Preece, *Living Pioneers*, and *The Dalton Gang*.

100. In his later years, Preece also developed Alzheimer's disease and had to move into a group home. See Damon Sasser, "Harold and Winona: A Romance for the Ages," R.E.H. Two-Gun Raconteur, June 9, 2013, http://rehtwogunracon teur.com/harold-winona-a-romance-for-the-ages/.

101. Bogle, *Cold War*, 4.

102. Texas State Historical Association, "Wesley, Carter Walker," www.tsha online.org/handbook/online/articles/fwe28.

103. Harold Preece to W.E.B. Du Bois, August 3, 1947, W.E.B. Du Bois Papers, Special Collections and University Archives, University of Massachusetts–Amherst Libraries.

104. W.E.B. Du Bois to Harold Preece, August 12, 1947, MS-312, W.E.B. Du Bois Papers. It is not clear if Du Bois intended this passage as a critique of Wesley and Preece. As a southern progressive who had spent the last two decades working as a journalist, it would have been difficult for Preece not to see himself in some of Du Bois's pointed language.

105. Ibid.

106. Preece, "The Negro in Latin America: Sugar Lumps in the Ballot Box."

107. Preece, "The Negro in Latin America: Cooking Makes Friends."

## Chapter 4. The Republic of the Penniless

1. Rosskam, *Alien*, 13.

2. Ibid., 11.

3. Lipsitz, *Possessive Investment in Whiteness*, 2–4.

4. Chapman, *Point 4 in Action*, 2.

5. Grosfoguel, *Colonial Subjects*, 107–9. The use of Puerto Rico as a testing ground for U.S. medicine, including the forced sterilization of and administration of birth control pharmaceuticals to Puerto Rican women, serves as a case in point. See, for example, Lopez, *Matters of Choice;* and Briggs, *Reproducing Empire.*

6. For example, in his study of Puerto Rico, Earl Parker Hanson, the director of the Puerto Rico Reconstruction Administration, recalled a discussion with a diplomat from an unidentified African country about the competition between capitalist and socialist models of development:

> He could see no way in which his country could effectively improve its standard of living without borrowing from the socialism which is so often anathema to the democratic West. I replied that the Puerto Rican experience shows the main problem to be not that of adhering strictly to this or that doctrine. . . . The task in hand is to keep the job's twin goals—that of raising standards of living and that of strengthening democracy—always in mind and unseparated.

Hanson, *Puerto Rico*, 3.

7. Hansen and Wells, *Puerto Rico*, 112. This trend continued to accelerate such that by January 1964 "there had been 23,000 such visitors: teachers, engineers, public health and sanitation officials, economists, and many other professionals from 137 underdeveloped countries." Senior, *Our Citizens from the Caribbean*, 4.

8. Lauria-Perricelli, "Study in Historical and Critical Anthropology," 18. Directors of the CIS included prominent government officials and academics such as Rexford Tugwell (1946–47), Clarence Senior (1947–48), Simon Rottenberg (1948–49), and Millard Hansen (1949–65).

9. Hansen and Wells, foreword to *Puerto Rico*, vii. Wells assisted the PPD in two important respects: he helped draft Puerto Rico's first constitution and was a strong supporter of the PPD's modernization efforts via industrialization. See, for example, his 1969 book *Modernization of Puerto Rico.*

10. Steward, *People of Puerto Rico*, v. The chapters of this book contain dissertations of graduate students who later played a significant role in the formation of American anthropology, including Sidney Mintz, Elena Padilla, and Eric Wolf.

11. Santiago-Valles, *"Subject People,"* 224. Though Santiago-Valles's assertion is certainly valid, the colonialist narratives of "subject peoples" were nothing new and, in fact, extend back to the Spanish colonial regime in Puerto Rico. See, for example, Lillian Guerra's wonderful study *Popular Expression and National Identity in Puerto Rico.*

12. For example, People of Puerto Rico project researcher Elena Padilla was ultimately "kicked out" (*botada)* of the UPR due to her campus activism and political opposition to the PPD-supported university administration. Additionally, the claim that Padilla worked on a colonialist project speaks to the patriarchal

relationships within the university and the nation regarding who was allowed to represent and study the nation (i.e., White Puerto Rican men) and who was not (Latina women). See Rúa, *Latino Urban Ethnography and the Work of Elena Padilla*.

13. Ayala and Bernabé, *Puerto Rico in the American Century*, 181. See also Moscoso, "Industrial Development in Puerto Rico," 67–68.

14. Steward, *People of Puerto Rico*, 486–88, 497. Millard Hansen explicitly wrote against this strand of thought in his special issue. "In yet another sense Puerto Rico exhibits a not uncommon modern problem: that of accommodating a long-established culture . . . to the unsettling forces of rapid Americanization. . . . The impact of these influences has increased each year, but the conflict between the old culture and the new has gradually lessened as patterns of adjustment have worked themselves out." Hansen and Wells, *Puerto Rico*, vii.

15. Lauria-Perricelli also demonstrates that pro-PPD chancellor Jaime Benítez kept a very close watch on Steward and his team of researchers. Benítez even went so far as to delay the manuscript's publication because many of the project's findings implicitly countered central tenets of the PPD platform. Lauria-Perricelli, "Study in Historical and Critical Anthropology," 369, 214.

16. Whalen, *From Puerto Rico to Philadelphia*, 25.

17. Dietz, *Puerto Rico*, 172.

18. OIPR, "Little Mud," 8.

19. Both cited in Tyrrell, "Colonizing Citizens" 259–60.

20. "Puerto Rico: Senate Investigating Committee."

21. OIPR, "Little Mud," 8.

22. Foster, *Crime of El Fanguito*, 5. Truman's travel log of his trip to Puerto Rico briefly mentions his passing of the "notorious El Fanguito slums."

23. Ibid., 22.

24. Foster, *Respaldo a Puerto Rico*, 8.

25. Ibid., 7, 11.

26. J. Allen, *Negro Question in the United States*, 10, 171.

27. Ibid., 174.

28. Foster, *Crime of El Fanguito*, 13.

29. Padilla, "Nocorá," 291.

30. Wolf, "San José," 227. "A third [worker] mentions that the sugar fields offer an opportunity for a man able and willing to work, but he is afraid of the Negroes who live on the coast: 'The people who go down to the coast to cut cane must be careful, always vigilant. The people there are witches. They are waiting for a chance to offer a man a meal, but they put something in the food. Then you sicken and die."

31. Mintz, "Cañamelar," 348, 411–12.

32. M. Gordon, "Race Patterns and Prejudice in Puerto Rico," 297–98.

33. For an outstanding study of the life of Louise Rosskam, especially her photography and the ways in which it has been historically marginalized relative to Edwin's work, see Katzman and Brannan, *Re-viewing Documentary*.

34. Ibid., 22–27. Like other progressives of her day, Louise Rosskam also flirted with communist politics. In an interview years later, Louise Rosskam noted, "I thought that communism must be wonderful, if that whole country was, this huge country [Russia], was turning everything to the workers. . . . And this idea of communism sounded as if everybody was going to be treated equally and everybody was going to have a job. . . . I just thought it was a great idea, but I took a long time to realize that it wasn't working, and that especially *in the United States* it wasn't working" (181 n. 45, emphasis added).

35. Rosskam struggled to accomplish this assignment given his limited competency in Spanish and lack of connections on the island. Prior to departing for Puerto Rico, Rosskam met with Congressman Vito Marcantonio from East Harlem. A Leftist and advocate of Puerto Rican independence, Marcantonio was well connected in Puerto Rico through his dealings with the growing Puerto Rican constituency in his district. Saretzky, "Interview with Louise Rosskam."

36. Rosskam had a general fascination with islands. Years earlier, he visited the West Indies on his way to Tahiti and Raiatea. Rosskam admitted that his stop in Martinique and his three years in French Polynesia initiated his fascination with islands and "had some bearing on all the rest of his life." Saretzky, "Interview with Louise Rosskam"; Richard Doud, "Interview with Edwin and Louise Rosskam," Archives of American Art, Smithsonian Institution, August 3, 1965, www.aaa.si.edu/collections/interviews/oral-history-interview-edwin-and-louise-rosskam-13112 (accessed August 21, 2015).

37. Doud, "Interview with Edwin and Louise Rosskam."

38. Edwin Rosskam to Luis Muñoz Marín, May 14, 1976, Fundación Luis Muñoz Marín, Section: Memorias, Folder 1131, Document 18. In a 1965 interview Rosskam confirmed that he and Muñoz Marín shared a mutual love of brandy. Doud, "Interview with Edwin and Louise Rosskam."

39. Finnegan, *Picturing Poverty*, 27–33.

40. Natanson, *Black Image in the New Deal*, 60–62.

41. Ibid., 71.

42. Saretzky, "Interview with Louise Rosskam."

43. La Farge and Post, *As Long As the Grass Shall Grow*, 134–40. In his early years as a photographer, Rosskam provided extended and detailed captions for his photographs, unlike the short phrases that typically accompanied photos during the era.

44. Doud, "Interview with Edwin and Louise Rosskam."

45. Natanson, *Black Image in the New Deal*, 158.

46. Tugwell balked at Rosskam's request due to various unnamed "political complications." Doud, "Interview with Edwin and Louise Rosskam."

47. For analyses of DIVEDCO's work see Kennerley, "Cultural Negotiations"; Lauria-Perricelli, "Images and Contradictions"; and Thompson, "Film Music and Community Development in Rural Puerto Rico."

48. The Rosskams' police file made special mention of the "5,280 aerial negatives of all the towns, cities, neighborhoods, and strategic points of the island" that the couple "took ownership of." Combas Guerra, "En torno a la fortaleza."

49. The Rotkins were already under surveillance by the Puerto Rican Police Department. As early as 1948 the department observed that the Rotkins hosted a going-away party for Puerto Rican communist writer José Luis González attended by a number of prominent American and Puerto Rican radicals. The insular police also documented the "official and social relationships" between the Rosskams and other known communists, including Jules Korchein and suspected Soviet spies Mary Jane Keeney and Phillip Olin Keeney. See Salvador Roig to Luis Muñoz Marín, with attachments, March 12, 1951, Fundación Luis Muñoz Marín, Section V; Series 1, Folder 218, Documents 2, 5, and 6.

50. Muñoz Marín's displeasure led to the film being sent back to DIVEDCO for extensive revisions and editing prior to its wider release. Combas Guerra, "En torno a la fortaleza."

51. Even after Edwin Rosskam left the island in 1952, he returned intermittently to do special projects, and to him the island became an important literal and symbolic space for thinking about his personal feelings of alienation. Katzman and Brannan, *Re-viewing Documentary*, 107, 145.

52. In Trenton, located less than a half hour from Roosevelt, six young Black men were accused on trumped-up evidence of the murder of a local white shopkeeper and sentenced to death in 1948. Following their swift convictions, the CPUSA intervened and provided legal counsel for the "Trenton Six." Five of the six men were eventually released. Knepper, *Jersey Justice*.

53. Mumford, *Newark*, 98.

54. Katzman and Brannan, *Re-viewing Documentary*, 145.

55. Edwin Rosskam to Inés Mendoza Rivera de Muñoz Marín, November 16, 1960, Fundación Luis Muñoz Marín, Section VII, Series 1, Folder 524, Document 4.

56. Edwin Rosskam to Luis Muñoz Marín, December 26, 1960, Fundación Luis Muñoz Marín, Section VII, Series 1, Folder 524, Document 5.

57. Saretzky, "Interview with Louise Rosskam."

58. Rosskam, *Alien*, i–ii.

59. Doud, "Interview with Edwin and Louise Rosskam."

60. Rosskam, *Alien*, 114.

61. Ibid., 114–16.

62. Ibid., 11.

63. Ibid., 52.

64. Consider, for example, one of the quotations most frequently cited to understand Pedreira's thinking about race: "During transcendental historical moments when the martial rhythms of our European blood blossom in our acts we are capable of the grandest and most heroic feats. But when these actions are drenched under the waves of African blood we are indecisive, almost stupefied by the colors and threatened by the cinematic visions of witches and ghosts." Pedreira, *Insularismo*, 29.

65. Onís's theorization about the relationship between the frontier and culture is strikingly similar to Frederick Jackson Turner's classic treatise, *The Significance of the Frontier in American History* (1893). Even more interesting is how Onís conjoins the history of Spain and of the American South in his scholarship without discussing race. Onís, "España y el sudoeste de Estados Unidos," 25–31.

66. Pedreira, *Insularismo*, 27–28.

67. Ibid., 12.

68. Reuter, *Race and Culture Contacts*, 6–14.

69. Park, *Race and Culture*, 356.

70. For example, Reuter does not present any evidence to validate his assertions about the supposedly different values and attitudes of "medieval" Puerto Ricans versus "modern" Americans. Instead, he depends on racialized assumptions about Puerto Rican difference. Reuter, "Culture Contacts in Puerto Rico," 96.

71. Park, "Mentality of Racial Hybrids," 534.

72. Reuter, "Superiority of the Mulatto," 133. A decade after his time in Puerto Rico, Reuter published "Culture Contacts in Puerto Rico," which rehashed many of his earlier conclusions about the cultural and social disorganization produced by economic development. Such repetitive presentations of old arguments plagued Reuter's career. In 1940, the anthropologist Melville Herskovits took Reuter to task for re-presenting the same conclusions in his newest edition of *The American Race Problem* while ignoring recent breakthroughs in labor relations and writings about race. See Herskovits, "*The American Race Problem,* by E. B. Reuter."

73. Reuter, "Culture Contacts in Puerto Rico," 98.

74. Reuter also labeled Blacks "culturally retarded" in his earlier work, measuring their cultural development according to their capacity to adopt European and White American culture and values. However, unlike Pedreira, Reuter considered northern European culture as the benchmark. He did not consider Spain to be an example of economic progress and modernity, calling it instead

"increasingly backward." See, for example, Reuter, *American Race Problem*, 12, 26, and "Culture Contacts in Puerto Rico," 94.

75. Persons, *Ethnic Studies at Chicago*, 101.

76. Feagin and McKinney, *Many Costs of Racism*, 24. See also T. Williams, "Homestead Act," 1–5, 8–10. For more on the correlations among race, wealth, and asset accumulation see Lipsitz, *Possessive Investment in Whiteness*.

77. On transformative assets see Shapiro, *Hidden Cost of Being African American*.

78. Ayala and Bernabé, *Puerto Rico in the American Century*, 194–95.

79. Mills, Senior, and Goldsen, *Puerto Rican Journey*, viii.

80. Rosskam, *Alien*, 1–4.

81. Ibid., 5.

82. Ibid., 8–9.

83. Ibid., 5, 198.

84. Ibid., 198.

85. Ibid., 199.

86. OIPR, "Little Mud," 8.

87. Dinzey-Flores, "Temporary Housing, Permanent Communities," 468–69. See also her excellent history and ethnography of public housing and gated communities in Puerto Rico, *Locked in, Locked Out*.

88. Rosskam, *Alien*, 199, emphasis added.

89. Ibid., 208.

90. Edwin Rosskam to Inés Mendoza Rivera de Muñoz Marín, November 16, 1960, Fundación Luis Muñoz Marín.

91. Rosskam, "But This Family I Know," 11, 4. Fundación Luis Muñoz Marín, Section VII, Series 1, Folder 524, Document 6.

92. Negrón-Muntaner and Grosfoguel, *Puerto Rican Jam*, 169.

93. Lissner, "Terrorists Here Set Off 5 Bombs," 1.

94. Kihss, "20,000 Rally Here."

95. Edwin Rosskam to Luis Muñoz Marín and Inés Mendoza Rivera de Muñoz Marín, November 4, 1974, Fundación Luis Muñoz Marín, Section VII, Series 1, Folder 524, Document 14.

96. Ibid.

97. Rosskam, *Alien*, 1.

## Chapter 5. You Are Here to Listen

1. Prashad, *Darker Nations*, xv.

2. In February 1936, for example, two nationalists shot and killed Puerto Rican police commissioner Francis E. Riggs, an American, in response to police violence that included the killing of fellow nationalists. One year later, the Puerto

Rican police responded by killing nineteen Puerto Ricans at a Nationalist Party march in Ponce commemorating the abolition of slavery on the island. Ayala and Bernabé, *Puerto Rico in the American Century*, 109.

3. Ibid., 104. On Albizu Campos's conservative views about women see Briggs, *Reproducing Empire*.

4. According to Juan Mari Brás, Ana Livia Cordero participated in this strike; he named her as a "leading figure of the 1948 Puerto Rican university genera-tion." Mari Brás, "Sexta Asamblea MPI," 4. The lack of a clear and strategic vision combined with severe police repression brought down the student strike not long after it began. Silén, *Historia de la nación puertorriqueña*, 344–45.

5. Truman was temporarily residing at Blair House while the White House underwent renovations. Ayala and Bernabé, *Puerto Rico in the American Century*, 165–66.

6. Silén, *Historia de la nación puertorriqueña*, 402.

7. Arroyo Muñoz, *Rebeldes al poder*, 37–38. See also Silén, *Historia de la nación puertorriqueña*, 270–80.

8. For Juan Mari Brás's take on the MPI's separation from the PIP see "La salida del P.I.P."

9. On the consolidation of multiple strands of political independence see, for example, Mari Brás, "Los logros obtenidos por la vanguardia señalan el masivo despertar del pueblo como objetivo ya."

10. For example, chapter XI ("Declaration Regarding Non-Self-Governing Territories") in the UN founding charter required the United States and other colonial powers to report to the UN on the steps they were taking to facilitate self-government in their colonies. Charter of the United Nations, "Chapter XI: Declaration Regarding Non-Self-Governing Territories," http://www.un.org/en/sections/un-charter/chapter-xi/index.html.

11. UN General Assembly, Eighth Session, "Cessation of the transmission of information under Article 73 e of the Charter in respect of Puerto Rico," no. 6, November 27, 1953.

12. UN General Assembly, Fifteenth Session, "Declaration on the granting of independence to colonial countries and peoples," December 14, 1960.

13. In his recollection of the general debate over Resolution 1514 Juan Mari Brás noted that Cuban foreign minister Raúl Roa made an "extensive, accurate, and eloquent reference to the colonial situation of Puerto Rico." Mari Brás, *El independentismo en Puerto Rico*, 136.

14. Founding figures of NAM included Gamal Abdel Nasser from Egypt, Yu-goslavia's Josip Broz Tito, India's Jawaharlal Nehru, and Ghana's Kwame Nkru-mah. Prashad, *Darker Nations*, 95–96; see also Willetts, *Non-Aligned Movement*.

15. Mari Brás notes the fairly casual and friendly relationship between Maura

and his arresting officer: the man took Maura "to his home and even made him Croatian-style roasted pork." Mari Brás, *El independentismo en Puerto Rico,* 139.

16. James, *Nkrumah and the Ghana Revolution,* 62.

17. Gaines, "African-American Expatriates in Ghana," 65, 68. A member of the CPUSA for a short time, Mayfield is best known in literary circles for his novels about Black urban life, including *The Hit* (1957) and *The Long Night* (1958). I am deeply saddened by the recent passing of Maya Angelou as I write these pages.

18. Friends and family members disapproved of the Cordero-Mayfield union from the outset. Mayfield's friends "felt that [he] was copping out of the U.S. urban class struggle because they had decided to live in Puerto Rico." Mayfield's career as a writer also unsettled Cordero's parents, who remained skeptical of Mayfield's ability to earn a reasonable living in Puerto Rico. Mayfield, "La Borinqueña," 2, Julian Mayfield Papers, Schomburg Center for Research in Black Culture, New York Public Library.

Federal and local authorities closely monitored Mayfield's and Cordero's political activities in Puerto Rico. Sometimes, however, police struggled to make sense of their movements and were often dumbfounded by Mayfield's tendency to be a homebody. In a cold war era when redbaiting and persecution prevailed, local police appeared disappointed when they could only dryly report that Mayfield "stays at home most of the day and appears to do a lot of typing" (Gaines, *American Africans in Ghana,* 145).

19. Cordero met and befriended many African American expatriates and visitors, including Shirley Graham, W.E.B. Du Bois, Maya Angelou, and Malcolm X, to name just a few.

20. The Cordero–Du Bois friendship is especially noteworthy given the extreme persecution Du Bois experienced throughout his life, which made him extremely reluctant to confide in others during his final years. Lewis, *W.E.B. Du Bois,* 568–70.

21. Mari Brás, *El independentismo en Puerto Rico,* 140.

22. Ibid., 141. See also Ana Livia Cordero, "Letter to Ambassadors Attending Conference in Cairo," Ana Livia Cordero personal papers, courtesy of Efraín Negrón and Rafael Mayfield.

23. On the significance of Cuba and the Tricontinental Conference see Rodríguez, "De la esclavitud yanqui a la libertad cubana"; and Gronbeck-Tedesco, "Left in Transition."

24. These notes also discuss the delegation's goal to create a broader alliance of Caribbean countries impacted by (neo)colonialism. Cordero, "Informe sobre la Conferencia Tricontinental," 1. Ana Livia Cordero personal papers. For the M.P.I's take on the Tricontinental Conference see also Mari Brás, *Puerto Rico y la Tricontinental.*

25. Cordero, "Informe sobre la Conferencia Tricontinental," 5A.

26. Mari Brás, "Sexta Asamblea MPI," 4, 6.

27. Gaines, *American Africans in Ghana*, 224.

28. For Nkrumah's recollections of the coup and how his thinking evolved thereafter, see Nkrumah, *Dark Days in Ghana*.

29. "Ghana: Releases and Revelations," 697.

30. Pietri's speech at the Tricontinental Conference is reprinted in Manrara, *Tricontinental Conference*, 15–19. See also Mari Brás, "Puerto Rico y la Tricontinental," 5.

31. Mari Brás, "Los logros obtenidos por la vanguardia," 3. Cordero moderated town hall meetings in various communities on the island about the plebiscite as an MPI representative throughout the year. See, for example, *La Carta Semanal* from January to May 1968.

32. Efraín Negrón, personal communication, June 3, 2014.

33. Mari Brás, "Carmichael condena servicio militar."

34. For examples of *Claridad*'s coverage of U.S. racial violence see Don Pancho, "De negros y puertorriqueños"; Denis, "Ejemplo generoso"; and M. Blanco, "El concepto del poder negro." Mari Brás also wrote about colonialism in Africa and devoted several book reviews and articles to the work of Frantz Fanon. See, for example, Reyes, "Por la revolución africana."

35. "Stokely Carmichael: What Black Power Struggle Is All About," 805. Somewhat ironically, Cordero and Mayfield were part of a large political contingent that received Malcolm X when he traveled to Ghana in 1964. In his autobiography Malcolm X alludes to the "beautiful dinner which had been prepared by Julian Mayfield's pretty Puerto Rican wife, Ana Livia." Haley, *Autobiography of Malcolm X*, 353."

36. "Notes on Puerto Rico for SNCC," in "Communist Threat," 1361.

37. Gaines, *American Africans in Ghana*, 145–47.

38. Forman, *Making of Black Revolutionaries*, 158–60.

39. Williams was later charged with kidnapping a white couple that he actually helped to rescue from an angry Black mob. Cordero and Mayfield eventually helped to smuggle Williams and his family from Monroe to Cuba via Canada to prevent his being arrested by officials who had been ordered to "shoot him on sight." Gaines, *American Africans in Ghana*, 147.

40. Forman, *Making of Black Revolutionaries*, xiv.

41. "People with Purpose: Revolution," *San Juan Star,* 3, in Ana Livia Cordero personal papers.

42. "Description of Project," Doc. No. 3, Ana Livia Cordero personal papers.

43. This is a striking contrast to Ana Livia Cordero herself whose father was an established politician high within the ranks of the PPD and whose mother

taught at the UPR. According to some members whom I spoke with, this class disparity between Cordero and project workers did not go unnoticed: many often felt attacked or shamed by Cordero for any personal failings that she attributed to their investment in bourgeois ideology.

44. Kelley, *To Make Our World Anew,* 487; Zinn, *SNCC.*

45. Proyecto Piloto, "Description of Project," 3.

46. Mari Brás, "Misión nacional acuerda reorganización de la JMPI," 2.

47. Elizam Escobar, who also left the MPI and later joined FALN, becoming a well-known political prisoner, explained: "a lot of the factious FUPIs went to work with Ana Livia Cordero" after being "kicked out" by the MPI leadership. Gil, "Artist, Writer, and Political Prisoner," 233.

48. Proyecto Piloto, "Declaración sobre la crisis del MPI," 4, Ana Livia Cordero personal papers.

49. Ibid.; emphasis in original.

50. Mari Brás, "Hay un plan maestro."

51. Briggs, *Reproducing Empire,* 75.

52. Miguel Rodríguez López, interview with the author, June 27, 2012.

53. Lydia Milagros González García, interview with the author, June 29, 2012.

54. Rubén Sánchez, interview with the author, June 22, 2012.

55. Mari Brás, "Hay un Plan Maestro, 4.

56. Efraín Negrón and Luis Rivera, interview with the author, June 24, 2012.

57. Cordero and Elinson very likely crossed paths around this time, which would explain why Elinson described Cordero as "an internist and former student" in an article published years later. Elinson, "End of Medicine?" 271.

58. The Harvard Medical School Department of Internal Medicine determined consensus and authority in the United States. Cordero, "Determination of Medical Care Needs," 95, emphasis added.

59. In response, Cordero proposed "minimal adequate care" as a concept that more accurately measured local needs for screening, diagnosis, and treatment. Using this measurement Cordero discovered that while Puerto Rico had a paltry overall physician-to-patient ratio of 1 to 1,245; the ratio in rural communities such as Comerio was an even more dismal 1 to 7000. Ibid.

60. Proyecto Piloto, "Description of Project," 7A–7B.

61. Ibid., 8.

62. Negrón, "Prefacio," 4. Efraín Negrón personal papers, courtesy of Efraín Negrón.

63. Lydia Milagros González García, interview with the author, June 29, 2012.

64. Proyecto Piloto, "Description of Project," 4.

65. Rubén Sánchez, interview with the author, June 22, 2012.

66. Miguel Rodríguez López, interview with the author, June 27, 2012.

67. Dietz, *Puerto Rico*, 172.

68. "Nos vimos como un pueblo latino americano y un pueblo negro." Miguel Rodríguez López, interview with the author, June 22, 2012.

69. Efraín Negrón and Luis Rivera, interview with the author, June 24, 2012.

70. E. Williams, *Capitalism and Slavery*.

71. Proyecto Piloto, "Description of Project," 5.

72. "People with a Purpose: Revolution," *San Juan Star*. Photocopy in Ana Livia Cordero personal papers. A number of Proyecto Piloto members also indicated that Barrio Tortugo was selected in part due to its proximity to the home of Cordero's parents, located directly across the highway.

73. Proyecto Piloto, "Informe final de historia del Bo. Tortugo," 1, Ana Livia Cordero personal papers.

74. "People with a Purpose: Revolution." As Carlos Vargas-Ramos notes, in Puerto Rico *trigueño* is a fluid racial signifier whose use is "situational, contextual, and slippery." The term is most often used to refer to people within the Black-white racial spectrum, although it can also be used innocuously to refer to a Black person or a white person with a dark tan. Vargas-Ramos, "Black, Trigueño, White . . . ?" 270. See also Godreau, "La semántica fugitiva, raza, color y vida cotidiana en Puerto Rico," and Duany, *Puerto Rican Nation on the Move*.

75. Proyecto Piloto, "Informe final de historia del Bo. Tortugo," 6. Ana Livia Cordero personal papers.

76. Ibid., 1–3.

77. Ibid. According to the report, de Jesús called Rivas an asshole (*pendejo*).

78. Dietz, *Economic History of Puerto Rico*, 79.

79. Proyecto Piloto, "La importancia de ser negro: análisis del conflicto racial en Puerto Rico," 3. Ana Livia Cordero personal papers.

80. Ibid., 5.

81. Ibid., 4.

82. Contemporary scholarship has challenged this tendency on the island. See, for example, Negrón-Muntaner and Grosfoguel, *Puerto Rican Jam*; Duany, *Puerto Rican Nation on the Move*; Flores, *Diaspora Strikes Back*; and L. Thomas, *Puerto Rican Citizen*.

83. Proyecto Piloto, "Liberación: Puerto Rican Youth Project for National Liberation, Will You Help?" 1968; emphasis added. Ana Livia Cordero personal papers.

84. Efraín Negrón and Luis Rivera, interview with the author, June 24, 2012.

85. "El conflicto: primero sociodrama," 1–2, Ana Livia Cordero personal papers.

86. Jim Crow segregation limited the numbers of Puerto Ricans and African Americans who faced combat in the first two world wars. This changed during

the Vietnam War, when both groups saw action on the front lines. Not surprisingly, the exact number of Puerto Rican and Chicano soldiers killed in the Vietnam War is difficult to ascertain given the shoddy recordkeeping practices at the Pentagon. Recent studies suggest that Hispanics filled the front lines after African American leaders pressured the Pentagon to address the disproportionate number of African American deaths in combat. Gifford, "Combat Casualties and Race." See also Franqui-Rivera, "National Mythologies"; Marshal and Sánchez Korrol, "Military Service."

87. Arbona, "Las ataduras se rompen"; Ayala and Bernabé, *Puerto Rico in the American Century*, 229–30.

88. Proyecto Piloto, "Época del saqueo: máquina del tiempo," 1. Ana Livia Cordero personal papers.

89. Efraín Negrón and Luis Rivera, interview with the author, June 24, 2012.

90. Proyecto Piloto, "Soy yo," accompanying "Manela," Ana Livia Cordero personal papers.

91. Proyecto Piloto, "¿Y tu abuela, donde está? El conflicto racial en Puerto Rico," 2, Ana Livia Cordero personal papers.

92. Proyecto Piloto, *Federico,* Ana Livia Cordero personal papers.

93. Ibid., 6.

94. Ibid., 7.

95. Miguel Rodríguez, interview with the author, June 27, 2012.

96. "Que hace esa blanca vestida de africana o de negra?" Rubén Sánchez, interview with the author, Interamerican University of Puerto Rico School of Law, June 22, 2012.

97. Maldonado Trinidad was appointed as Puerto Rico's police superintendent in December 1976. However, after it came to light that he accepted a $7,000 loan from the owner of a furniture store whose warehouse had been destroyed in a suspicious fire, Maldonado Trinidad quickly resigned ("After 2½ Months, 2 in Puerto Rico's Cabinet Quit Under Pressure and a Third Is Out as Governor Is Vexed," *New York Times,* March 20, 1977, 23).

98. Hearings before the Subcommittee to Investigate the Administration of the Internal Security Act and Other Internal Security Laws of the Committee of the Judiciary, "Communist Threat to the United States through the Caribbean," 1323.

99. Miguel Rodríguez, interview with the author, June 27, 2012.

100. Although the police did not produce a search warrant on the day of the raid, they produced one the following day. Proyecto Piloto, "Resumen de la evidencia presentada en relación al proyecto," Ana Livia Cordero personal papers.

101. Proyecto Piloto, "Trabajo de muertos en Barrio Tortugo," Ana Livia Cordero personal papers.

102. Ángel Fret, "CIC alega Dra. Cordero Rehúsa sar datos sobre fuego en casa," *El Mundo*, March 15, 1971, 1, 18. Members of the Comandos Armados de Liberación claimed that the CIA also played a part in the arson of the Barrio Tortugo home. Cordero rejected this insinuation and distanced her group from CAL, stating she "did not agree with the way CAL was trying to use what happened in Tortugo to justify its [violent] actions." ("Rechazan versión CAL sobre quema de hogar").

103. "Rechazan versión CAL sobre quema de hogar."

104. Miguel Rodríguez, interview with the author, June 27, 2012.

105. Lydia Milagros González García, interview with the author, June 29, 2012.

106. The romantic involvements that produced children also became a point of contention in the group. Because Proyecto Piloto members believed that children born within the community were of the community, they mandated that anyone wishing to leave the group had to leave the child behind with the remaining partner. Several group members challenged these policies and sought custody of their children through the courts, with the most famous case making its way up to the Puerto Rican Supreme Court. An already difficult situation became worse when several fathers in the group took their children and went into hiding after the courts ruled against them and ordered the children returned to their mothers. See Moya, "Te recuerdo, Esther."

107. Cordero, *Cerro Maravilla: estudio del informe del Departamento de Justicia.*

**Conclusion**

1. González and Quintero Rivera, *La otra cara de la historia*, iii. For more on González and Quintero Rivera's photo-book and alternative take on Puerto Rican history see Quintero Rivera, "La otra cara de la historia y el teatro popular puertorriqueño."

2. Ayala and Bernabé, *Puerto Rico in the American Century*, 251.

3. Ferguson, *Reorder of Things.*

4. Dávila, *Sponsored Identities.*

5. Duany and Silver, "'Puerto Ricanization' of Florida," 4.

6. "Puerto Rican Florida," special issue, *CENTRO Journal* 22, no. 1 (Spring 2010).

7. See for example, Charles Babington, "Puerto Ricans Are Key in Florida Presidential Vote," November 4, 2012, www.huffingtonpost.com/2012/11/04/puerto-ricans-florida-presidential-vote_n_2072496.html. (Puerto Ricans who reside in the continental United States are allowed to vote in federal elections.)

8. Mohl, "Globalization, Latinization, and the Nuevo New South." For more scholarship utilizing the "Nuevo New South" terminology, see Silver,

184 NOTES TO PAGES 152–154

"Latinization, Race, and Cultural Identification in Puerto Rican Orlando"; Odem and Lacy, *Latino Immigrants and the Transformation of the U.S. South*; and Smith and Furuseth, *Latinos in the New South*.

9. Weise, "Dispatches from the 'Viejo' New South," 42.

10. Grosfoguel, *Colonial Subjects*, 72–73.

11. Anna Brown and Eileen Patten, "Hispanics of Puerto Rican Origin in the United States," Pew Research Hispanic Trends Project, June 19, 2013, www. pewhispanic.org/2013/06/19/hispanics-of-puerto-rican-origin-in-the-united-states-2011/ and National Poverty Center, "Poverty in the United States: Frequently Asked Questions," National Poverty Center, www.npc.umich.edu/poverty/. For a similar critique of radical statehood see José Fusté, "Unsettling Citizenship/Circumventing Sovereignty," 167–68.

# Bibliography

Abbott, Robert. "*Defender* Head Made Welcome by Brazilians." *Chicago Defender*, March 31, 1923, 3.

———. "My Trip through South America." *Chicago Defender*, October 20, 1923, A1.

"Alas, the Poor Puerto Ricans!" *Pittsburgh Courier*, October 16, 1943, 6.

Alexander, Robert J. *International Labor Organizations and Organized Labor in Latin America and the Caribbean: A History*. Santa Barbara, CA: ABC-CLIO, 2009.

———. *Organized Labor in Latin America*. New York: Free Press, 1965.

Allen, James S. *The Negro Question in the United States*. New York: International, 1936.

Allen, Robert L. "Reassessing the Internal (Neo)Colonialism Theory." *Black Scholar* 35, no. 1 (2005): 2–11.

Arbona, Ramón. "Las ataduras se rompen." In *Frente a la torre: ensayos del centenario de la Universidad de Puerto Rico, 1903–2003*, edited by Silvia Álvarez-Curbelo. San Juan: Editorial de la Universidad de Puerto Rico, 2005.

Arroyo Muñoz, José Carlos. *Rebeldes al poder: los grupos y la lucha ideológica (1959–2000)*. San Juan, PR: Isla Negra, 2002.

Ashby, Joe C. *Organized Labor and the Mexican Revolution under Lázaro Cárdenas*. Chapel Hill: University of North Carolina Press, 1967.

Ayala, César J. *American Sugar Kingdom: The Plantation Economy of the Spanish Caribbean, 1898–1934*. Chapel Hill: University of North Carolina Press, 1999.

Ayala, César J., and Rafael Bernabé. *Puerto Rico in the American Century: A History since 1898*. Chapel Hill: University of North Carolina Press, 2007.

Badger, John Robert. "The Future of Africa." *Chicago Defender*, World View section, October 30, 1943.

———. "Number One U.S. Colony." *Chicago Defender*, World View section, September 4, 1943, 15.

———. "Regionalism in the Caribbean." *Chicago Defender*, World View section, May 20, 1944.

Baldwin, Davarian L. *Chicago's New Negroes: Modernity, the Great Migration, and Black Urban Life*. Chapel Hill: University of North Carolina Press, 2007.

Barbosa de Rosario, Pilar, ed. *La obra de José Celso Barbosa*. Vol. 3, *Problema de Razas*. San Juan: Imprenta Venezuela, 1937.

Berle, Adolf A., Jr. *The Modern Corporation and Private Property*. New York: Harcourt, Brace & World, 1968.

Blanco, Mario. "El concepto del poder negro." *Claridad*, July 9, 1967, 4.

Blanco, Tomás. *El prejuicio racial en Puerto Rico*. San Juan: Instituto de Literatura Puertorriqueña, 1943.

———. *Prontuario histórico de Puerto Rico*. Madrid: Imprenta de Juan Pueyo, 1935.

Blauner, Robert. "Internal Colonialism and Ghetto Revolt." *Social Problems* 16, no. 4 (1969): 393–408.

Bogle, Lori Lyn. *The Cold War: Cold War Culture and Society*. New York: Routledge, 2001.

Bolden, Frank E. "'Recognition of Color Problem Will Save United States Future Embarrassment'—Bolden." *Pittsburgh Courier*, April 4, 1942.

Bonafoux y Quintero, Luis. *Literatura de Bonafoux*. San Juan: Instituto de Cultura Puertorriqueña, 1989.

Briggs, Laura. *Reproducing Empire: Race, Sex, Science, and U.S. Imperialism in Puerto Rico*. Berkeley: University of California Press, 2002.

Brooks, Deton J. Jr. "Congress Is Threat to Puerto Rico Reform." *Chicago Defender*, September 4, 1943, 13.

———. "Jim Crow at America's Air Crossroads Sabotages Latin Good Neighbor Policy." *Chicago Defender*, July 3, 1943, 1, 4.

———. "Negro Fate in U.S. Tied to Puerto Rico Freedom." *Chicago Defender*, July 31, 1943, 7.

———. "Puerto Rican One-Crop System Needs Reform." *Chicago Defender*, August 21, 1943, 13.

———. "Puerto Rico a Test Tube for Atlantic Charter." *Chicago Defender*, September 11, 1943, 13.

———. "Puerto Rico Has No Big Race Problems." *Chicago Defender*, August 14, 1943, 13.

———. "Puerto Rico Suffers from Over-Population." *Chicago Defender*, August 28, 1943.

————. "Puerto Rico Up in Arms against Colonial Status." *Chicago Defender*, August 7, 1943, 13.

————. "Rise of Puerto Rico 'Populars' a Saga of People's Democracy." *Chicago Defender*, July 3, 1943, 5.

————. "Sugar Trusts Get Congress Aid to Enforce Puerto Rico Poverty." *Chicago Defender*, July 10, 1943, 7.

Buck, William. "Porto Rico Colonization: A Suggestion That the Colored People of America Be Given a Dhauce [*sic*] to Buy That Island." *Fair Play*, June 17, 1898.

Buni, Andrew. *Robert L. Vann of the* Pittsburgh Courier: *Politics and Black Journalism*. Pittsburgh, PA: University of Pittsburgh Press, 1974.

Burnett, Christina Duffy, and Burke Marshall. *Foreign in a Domestic Sense: Puerto Rico, American Expansion, and the Constitution*. Durham, NC: Duke University Press, 2001.

Burns, Ben. "Negro Nations Well Represented at Paris Meet." *Chicago Defender*, October 27, 1945, 5.

————. "2,000,000 Demand Labor Drop Jim Crow." *Chicago Defender*, October 20, 1945, 1.

Calderón-Zaks, Michael. "Domestic Colonialism: The Overlooked Significance of Robert L. Allen's Contributions." *Black Scholar* 40, no. 2 (2010): 39–48.

"Cessation of the transmission of information under Article 73E of the Charter in respect of Puerto Rico." United Nations General Assembly, Eighth Session, no. 6, November 27, 1953.

Chapman, Oscar L. *Point 4 in Action: Interior Department's Role*. Washington, DC: GPO, 1951.

Clark, Clinton. "Likes Column by Harold Preece." *Chicago Defender*, September 11, 1943, 14.

Clark, Kenneth. *Dark Ghetto: Dilemmas of Social Power*. New York: Harper and Row, 1965.

Cohen, Lizabeth. *Making a New Deal: Industrial Workers in Chicago, 1919–1939*. Cambridge: Cambridge University Press, 1990.

Collins, Patricia Hill. *Black Feminist Thought: Knowledge, Consciousness, and the Politics of Empowerment*. Boston: Unwin Hyman, 1990.

Combas Guerra, Eliseo. "En torno a la fortaleza: no satisfecho." *El Mundo*, March 22, 1967, 2.

"Comité Bell cree que el gobierno de la isla tiende a un control completo, como en Italia." *El Mundo*, May 3, 1945, 7.

"Comité Bell preocupado con gobierno insular." *El Mundo*, May 2, 1945, 6.

"Communist Threat to the United States through the Caribbean." *Hearings before the Subcommittee to Investigate the Administration of the Internal Security Act and Other Internal Security Laws of the Committee of the Judiciary*. Washington, DC: GPO, 1970.

Congress of Industrial Organizations. *Working and Fighting Together Regardless of Race, Creed, Color, or National Origin*. Washington, DC: CIO Committee to Abolish Racial Discrimination, 1943.

Cooper, Ana Julia. "The Colored Woman's Office." In *Social Theory: The Multicultural and Classic Readings*, ed. Charles Lemert, 178–84. 4th ed. Boulder, CO: Westview Press, 2010.

Cordero, Ana Livia. *Cerro Maravilla: estudio del informe del Departamento de Justicia*. San Juan: Colegio de Abogados de Puerto Rico, 1979.

———. "The Determination of Medical Care Needs in Relation to a Concept of Minimal Adequate Care: An Evaluation of the Curative Outpatient Services of a Rural Health Centre." *Medical Care* 2, no. 2 (1964): 95–103.

Cruse, Harold. *Rebellion or Revolution*. New York: Morrow, 1968.

Davey, Elizabeth, and Rodney Clark, eds. *Remember My Sacrifice: The Autobiography of Clinton Clark, Tenant Farm Organizer and Early Civil Rights Activist*. Baton Rouge: Louisiana State University Press, 2007.

Dávila, Arlene M. *Sponsored Identities: Cultural Politics in Puerto Rico*. Philadelphia, PA: Temple University Press, 1997.

"Declaration on the granting of independence to colonial countries and peoples." United Nations General Assembly, 15th sess., December 14, 1960.

Del Moral, Solsiree. *Negotiating Empire: The Cultural Politics of Schools in Puerto Rico, 1898–1952*. Madison: University of Wisconsin Press, 2013.

Denis, Manuel Maldonado. "Ejemplo generoso." *Claridad*, July 2, 1967, 2.

Dietz, James L. *Economic History of Puerto Rico: Institutional Change and Capitalist Development*. Princeton, NJ: Princeton University Press, 1986.

———. *Historia económica de Puerto Rico*. Río Piedras, Puerto Rico: Ediciones Huracán, 1989.

———. *Puerto Rico: Negotiating Development and Change*. Boulder, CO: Lynne Rienner, 2003.

Dinzey-Flores, Zaire Zenit. *Locked In, Locked Out: Gated Communities in a Puerto Rican City*. Philadelphia: University of Pennsylvania Press, 2013.

———. "Temporary Housing, Permanent Communities: Public Policy and Housing in Puerto Rico." *Journal of Urban History* 33, no. 3 (2007): 467–92.

"Do You Know?" *Chicago Defender*, April 17, 1943, 15.

Dooley, Edwin L. "Wartime San Juan, Puerto Rico: The Forgotten American Home Front, 1941–1945." *Journal of Military History* 63, no. 4 (1999): 921–38.

Drake, Paul. "International Crises and Popular Movements in Latin America." In *Latin America in the 1940s: War and Postwar Transitions*, edited by David Rock. Berkeley: University of California Press, 1994.

Drake, John Gibbs St. Clair. "Communism and Peace Movements." *The Crisis*, February 1936.

Draper, Alan. *Conflict of Interests: Organized Labor and the Civil Rights Movement in the South, 1954–1968*. Ithaca, NY: ILR Press, 1994.

Duany, Jorge. *The Puerto Rican Nation on the Move: Identities on the Island and in the United States*. Chapel Hill: University of North Carolina Press, 2002.

Duany, Jorge, and Patricia Silver. "The 'Puerto Ricanization' of Florida: Historical Background and Current Status." *CENTRO Journal* 22, no. 1 (2010): 4–31.

Du Bois, W.E.B. *Black Reconstruction in America, 1860–1880*. New York: Free Press, 1935.

———. *The Souls of Black Folk*. New York: Bantam Books, 1989.

Du Bois, W.E.B., and Guy Benton Johnson, eds. *Encyclopedia of the Negro*. New York: Phelps-Stokes Fund, 1945.

Dunbar, Eve. *Black Regions of the Imagination: African American Writers between the Nation and the World*. Philadelphia, PA: Temple University Press, 2013.

Elinson, Jack. "The End of Medicine and the End of Medical Sociology?" *Journal of Health and Social Behavior* 26, no. 4 (1985): 268–75.

Espiritu, Yen Le. *Home Bound: Filipino American Lives across Cultures, Communities, and Countries*. Berkeley: University of California Press, 2003.

Feagin, Joe R., and Karyn D. McKinney. *The Many Costs of Racism*. Lanham, MD: Rowman & Littlefield, 2002.

Ferguson, Roderick A. *Aberrations in Black: Toward a Queer of Color Critique*. Minneapolis: University of Minnesota Press, 2004.

———. *The Reorder of Things: The University and Its Pedagogies of Minority Difference*. Minneapolis: University of Minnesota Press, 2012.

Fernandez, Ronald. *The Disenchanted Island: Puerto Rico and the United States in the Twentieth Century*. 2nd ed. Westport, CT: Praeger, 1996.

Findlay, Eileen J. Suárez. *Imposing Decency: The Politics of Sexuality and Race in Puerto Rico, 1870–1920*. Durham, NC: Duke University Press, 1999.

Finnegan, Cara A. *Picturing Poverty: Print Culture and FSA Photographs*. Washington, DC: Smithsonian Institution Press, 2003.

Fletcher, Bill, Jr. "The Imperative of Black Worker Mobilization in Renewing Organized Labor in the United States." In *Race and Labor Matters in the New U.S. Economy*, edited by Manning Marable, Immanuel Ness, and Joseph Wilson, 17–26. Lanham, MD: Rowman & Littlefield, 2006.

Flores, Juan. *The Diaspora Strikes Back: Caribeño Tales of Learning and Turning*. New York: Routledge, 2008.

Foner, Philip Sheldon. "The IWW and the Black Worker." *Journal of Negro History* 55, no. 1 (1970): 45–64.

———. *Organized Labor and the Black Worker, 1619–1973*. New York: International, 1974.

Forman, James. *The Making of Black Revolutionaries*. Seattle: University of Washington Press, 1972.

Foster, William Z. *The Crime of El Fanguito: An Open Letter to President Truman on Puerto Rico*. New York: New Century, 1948.

———. *Respaldo a Puerto Rico*. San Juan, PR: Librería Estrella Roja, 1948.

Fowles, George Milton. *Down in Porto Rico*. New York: Eaton & Mains, 1906.

Franqui-Rivera, Harry. "National Mythologies: U.S. Citizenship for the People of Puerto Rico and Military Service." *Memorias: revista digital de historia y arqueología desde el Caribe* 21 (September–December 2013): 5–21.

Friedman, Tami J. "Exploiting the North-South Differential: Corporate Power, Southern Politics, and the Decline of Organized Labor after World War II." *Journal of American History* 95, no. 2 (2008): 323–48.

Fusté, José. "Unsettling Citizenship/Circumventing Sovereignty: Reexamining the Quandaries of Contemporary Anti-Colonialism in the US Through Black Puerto Rican Anti-Racist Thought." *American Quarterly* 65, no. 4 (2014): 161–69.

Gaines, Kevin K. "African-American Expatriates in Ghana and the Black Radical Tradition." *Souls* 1, no. 4 (1999): 64–71.

———. *American Africans in Ghana: Black Expatriates and the Civil Rights Era*. Chapel Hill: University of North Carolina Press, 2006.

García Blanco, Ana Maria, and José Javier Colon Morera. "A Community-Based Approach to Educational Reform in Puerto Rico." In *Colonial Dilemma: Critical Perspectives on Contemporary Puerto Rico*, edited by E. Meléndez and E. Meléndez. Boston: South End Press, 1993.

Gelpi, Juan. *Literatura y paternalismo en Puerto Rico*. San Juan: Editorial de la Universidad de Puerto Rico, 1993.

"Ghana: Releases and Revelations," *West Africa*, June 18, 1966, 696–97.

Gifford, Brian. "Combat Casualties and Race: What Can We Learn from the 2003–2004 Iraq Conflict?" *Armed Forces and Society* 31, no. 2 (2005): 201–25.

Gil, Carlos. "Artist, Writer, and Political Prisoner: An Interview with Elizam Escobar." In *The Puerto Rican Movement: Voices from the Diaspora*, edited by Andrés Torres and José E. Velázquez. Philadelphia, PA: Temple University Press, 1998.

Godreau, Isar. *Scripts of Blackness: Race, Cultural Nationalism, and Colonialism in Puerto Rico*. Urbana: University of Illinois Press, 2015.

———. "Changing Space, Making Race: Distance, Nostalgia, and the Folklorization of Blackness in Puerto Rico." *Identities* 9, no. 3 (2002): 281–304.

———. "Folkloric Others: 'Blanqueamiento' and the Celebration of Blackness as an Exception in Puerto Rico." In *Globalization and Race: Transformations in the Cultural Production of Blackness*, edited by Deborah Thomas and Kamari Clarke, 171–87. Durham, NC: Duke University Press, 2006.

———. "La semántica fugitiva, raza, color y vida cotidiana en Puerto Rico." *Revista de Ciencias Sociales, Nueva Época* 9: 52–71.

González, Lydia Milagros, and Ángel G. Quintero Rivera. *La otra cara de la historia: la historia de Puerto Rico desde su cara obrera, 1800–1925*. San Juan, PR: CEREP, 1970.

Gordon, Avery F. *Ghostly Matters: Haunting and the Sociological Imagination*. Minneapolis: University of Minnesota Press, 1997.

Gordon, Maxine W. "Race Patterns and Prejudice in Puerto Rico." *American Sociological Review* 14 (1949): 294–301.

Grandin, Greg. *Empire's Workshop: Latin America, the United States, and the Rise of the New Imperialism*. New York: Metropolitan Books, 2006.

Gronbeck-Tedesco, John. "The Left in Transition: The Cuban Revolution in U.S. Third World Politics." *Journal of Latin American Studies* 40, no. 4 (2008): 651–73.

Grosfoguel, Ramón. *Colonial Subjects: Puerto Ricans in a Global Perspective*. Berkeley: University of California Press, 2003.

Guerra, Lillian. *Popular Expression and National Identity in Puerto Rico: The Struggle for Self, Community, and Nation*. Gainesville: University Press of Florida, 1998.

Guridy, Frank Andre. *Forging Diaspora: Afro-Cubans and African Americans in a World of Empire and Jim Crow*. Chapel Hill: University of North Carolina Press, 2010.

Haley, Alex. *The Autobiography of Malcolm X*. New York: Random House, 1965.

Hall, Stuart. "Notes on Deconstructing 'the Popular.'" In *People's History and Socialist Theory*, edited by Raphael Samuel, 227–40. Boston: Routledge & Kegan Paul, 1981.

Hansen, Millard, and Henry Wells, eds. *Puerto Rico: A Study in Democratic Development*. Special issue, *Annals of the American Academy of Political and Social Science* 285 (January 1953).

Hanson, Earl Parker. *Puerto Rico: Ally for Progress*. Princeton, NJ: Van Nostrand, 1962.

Herskovits, Melville J. "The American Race Problem, by E. B. Reuter." *American Journal of Sociology* 45, no. 5 (1940): 801–4.

Holloway, Wilbert L. "Puerto Rico Will Choose." *Pittsburgh Courier*, June 16, 1945.

Hong, Grace Kyungwong, and Roderick Ferguson. *Strange Affinities: The Gender and Sexual Politics of Comparative Racialization.* Durham, NC: Duke University Press, 2011.

"Independence for Puerto Rico." *Pittsburgh Courier,* June 19, 1943, 6.

James, C.L.R. *Nkrumah and the Ghana Revolution.* Westport, CT: Lawrence Hill, 1977.

Johnson, Gaye Theresa. *Spaces of Conflict, Sounds of Solidarity: Music, Race, and Spatial Entitlement in Los Angeles.* Berkeley: University of California Press, 2013.

Jordan, David Starr. *Imperial Democracy.* New York: Garland, 1972.

Jung, Moon-Kie. "Constituting the U.S. Empire State and White Supremacy." In *State of White Supremacy: Racism, Governance, and the United States,* edited by Moon-Kie Jung, João H. Costa Vargas, and Eduardo Bonilla-Silva. Stanford, CA: Stanford University Press, 2011.

Kaplan, Amy. *The Anarchy of Empire in the Making of U.S. Culture.* Cambridge, MA: Harvard University Press, 2002.

Katzman, Laura, and Beverly Brannan. *Re-Viewing Documentary: The Photographic Life of Louise Rosskam.* Washington, DC: American University Museum, 2011.

Kelley, Robin D. G. *Hammer and Hoe.* Chapel Hill: University of North Carolina Press, 1990.

———. *Race Rebels.* New York: Free Press, 1994.

———. *To Make Our World Anew: A History of African Americans to 1880.* Oxford: Oxford University Press, 2005.

Kennerley, Cati Marsh. "Cultural Negotiations: Puerto Rican Intellectuals in a State-Sponsored Community Education Project, 1948–1968." *Harvard Educational Review* 73, no. 3 (2003): 416–48.

Kihss, Peter. "20,000 Rally Here for Puerto Rican Independence." *New York Times,* October 28, 1974, 35.

Kim, Claire Jean. *Bitter Fruit: The Politics of Black-Korean Conflict in New York City.* New Haven, CT: Yale University Press, 2000.

Knepper, Cathy. *Jersey Justice: The Story of the Trenton Six.* New Brunswick, NJ: Rivergate Books, 2011.

La Farge, Oliver. *As Long as the Grass Shall Grow.* Photographs by Helen M. Post. New York: Alliance Book Corporation, 1940.

Lauria-Perricelli, Antonio. "Images and Contradictions: DIVEDCO's Portrayal of Puerto Rican Life." *CENTRO Journal* 3, no. 1 (1990): 92–96.

———. "A Study in Historical and Critical Anthropology: The Making of the People of Puerto Rico." PhD diss., New School for Social Research, New York, 1989.

Lawson, R. Alan. *A Commonwealth of Hope: The New Deal Response to Crisis*. Baltimore, MD: Johns Hopkins University Press, 2006.

Lefebvre, Andrew. "Puerto Rico: Quiet Participant." In *Latin America during World War II*, edited by Thomas M. Leonard and John F. Bratzel. Lanham, MD: Rowman & Littlefield, 2007.

Lemert, Charles. *Social Things: An Introduction to Sociological Life*. 5th ed. Lanham, MD: Rowman & Littlefield, 2012.

Lewis, David Levering. *W.E.B. Du Bois: Biography of a Race, 1868–1919*. New York: Henry Holt, 1993.

Lipsitz, George. *The Possessive Investment in Whiteness: How White People Profit from Identity Politics*. Philadelphia, PA: Temple University Press, 2006.

Lissner, Will. "Terrorists Here Set Off 5 Bombs at Business Sites." *New York Times*, October 27, 1974.

Little, Dr. George. "Pittsburgher Describes Puerto Rico as 'Land of Shops, Rum, Sugar, Flowers.'" *Pittsburgh Courier*, February 28, 1942, 14.

———. "Puerto Rican National Pride and Democracy are Real World Models." *Pittsburgh Courier*, March 7, 1942, 14.

———. "Puerto Rico, Island of Peace, Beauty and Contrasts, Described by Physician." *Pittsburgh Courier*, February 21, 1942, 14.

Lombardo Toledano, Vicente. *The C.T.A.L., the War and the Postwar*. Mexico: Universidad Obrera de México, 1945.

Lopez, Iris Ofelia. *Matters of Choice: Puerto Rican Women's Struggle for Reproductive Freedom*. New Brunswick, NJ: Rutgers University Press, 2008.

Lowe, Lisa. "Insufficient Difference." *Ethnicities* 5, no. 3 (2005): 409–13.

Maldonado, A. W. *Luis Muñoz Marín: Puerto Rico's Democratic Revolution*. San Juan: Universidad de Puerto Rico, 2006.

Manrara, Luis V. *The Tricontinental Conference: A Declaration of War*. Miami: Truth about Cuba Committee, 1966.

Marcano García, Pablo. "Carta al presidente de Estados Unidos enviada por el artista puertorriqueño Pablo Marcano García." *El Nuevo Día*, June 14, 2011, 47.

Mari Brás, Juan. "Carmichael condena servicio militar." *Claridad*, January 29, 1967, 1.

———. *El independentismo en Puerto Rico: su pasado, su presente y su porvenir*. San Juan, PR: Editorial CEPA, 1984.

———. "Hay un plan maestro para romper al movimiento pro independencia." *La Carta Semanal*, October 13, 1967, 3–4.

———. "La salida del P.I.P." *Claridad*, May 7, 1966, 4.

———. "Los logros obtenidos por la vanguardia señalan el masivo despertar del pueblo como objetivo ya." *La Carta Semanal*, December 21, 1967, 2–5.

———. "Misión nacional acuerda reorganización de la JMPI." *La Carta Semanal*, September 5, 1967, 2.

———. "Puerto Rico y la Tricontinental." *Claridad*, February 5, 1966, 5.

———. "Sexta asamblea MPI dedicada a Evangelista González y Ana Livia Cordero: militantes del año." *Claridad*, Segunda Quincena de Marzo, 1965, 4.

Marqués, René. *The Docile Puerto Rican: Essays*. Philadelphia, PA: Temple University Press, 1976.

Marquez, Carlos, and James Marquez. "Federal Funds Expenditure in Puerto Rico Compared to Four Other States, Fiscal Year 2009." *Caribbean Business* 38, no. 48 (December 9, 2010), 26.

Marshal, Pamela J., and Virginia Sánchez Korrol. "Military Service." In *Latinas in the United States: A Historical Encyclopedia*, edited by Vicki Ruiz and Virginia Sánchez Korrol, 473–75. Bloomington: Indiana University Press, 2006.

Mayfield, Julian. *The Hit*. New York: Vanguard Press, 1957.

———. *The Long Night*. New York: Vanguard Press, 1958.

McCabe, Charles. "Cole demanda en el Congreso la sustitución inmediata de Tugwell." *El Mundo*, February 1, 1945.

McEniry, Mary. *Infant Mortality during the 1920s–1940s in Puerto Rico and the Health of Older Puerto Rican Adults*. CDE Working Paper No. 2009-03. Madison: University of Wisconsin Center for Demography and Ecology, 2009.

Mills, C. Wright, Clarence Senior, and Rose Kohn Goldsen. *The Puerto Rican Journey*. New York: Harper and Brothers, 1950.

Mintz, Sidney. "Cañamelar: The Subculture of a Rural Sugar Plantation Proletariat." In *The People of Puerto Rico: A Study in Social Anthropology*, edited by Julian Haynes Steward, 314–417. Urbana: University of Illinois Press, 1956.

Mohl, Raymond A. "Globalization, Latinization, and the Nuevo New South." *Journal of American Ethnic History* 22, no. 4 (2003): 31–66.

Mooney, Kevin. "Texas Centennial 1936: African-American Texans and the Third National Folk Festival." *Journal of Texas Music History* 1, no. 1 (2001): 36–43.

Moral, Solsiree del. *Negotiating Empire: The Cultural Politics of Schools in Puerto Rico, 1898–1952*. Madison: University of Wisconsin Press, 2013.

Moreno, Marisel. *Family Matters: Puerto Rican Women Authors on the Island and the Mainland*. Charlottesville: University of Virginia Press, 2012.

Moscoso, Teodoro. "Industrial Development in Puerto Rico." *Annals of the American Academy of Political and Social Science* 285 (January 1958): 60–69.

Moya, Iris Jackson. "Te recuerdo Esther." *Claridad*, December 7, 2010, 24.

Mumford, Kevin. *Newark: A History of Race, Rights, and Riots in America*. New York: New York University Press, 2008.

Muñoz Marín, Luis. "Democracy Would Be a Hoax." In *Palabras de Luis Muñoz Marín, 1941–1944*, 321–23. San Juan, PR: Fundación Luis Muñoz Marín, 2005.

———. "El Plan Chardón se llevará a efecto y no podrá ser traicionado." In *Palabras de Luis Muñoz Marín, 1931–1935*, 283–85. San Juan, PR: Fundación Luis Muñoz Marín, 2005.

———. "En defensa del Partido Popular y su posición sobre status." In *Palabras de Luis Muñoz Marín, 1945–1948*: 216–17. San Juan, PR: Fundación Luis Muñoz Marín, 2005.

———. "Prólogo." In *Palabras de Luis Muñoz Marín, 1936–1940*: 11–20. San Juan, PR: Fundación Luis Muñoz Marín, 2005.

———. "To the President of the United States." In *Palabras de Luis Muñoz Marín, 1931–1935*, 247. San Juan, PR: Fundación Luis Muñoz Marín, 2005.

Myrdal, Gunnar. *An American Dilemma: The Negro Problem and Modern Democracy*. New York: Harper & Row, 1969.

Natanson, Nicholas. *The Black Image in the New Deal: The Politics of FSA Photography*. Knoxville: University of Tennessee Press, 1992.

Navarro Rivera, Pablo. "The Imperial Enterprise and Educational Policies in Colonial Puerto Rico." In *Colonial Crucible: Empire in the Making of the Modern American State*, edited by Alfred W. McCoy and Francisco A. Scarano, 163–74. Madison: University of Wisconsin Press, 2009.

Negrón-Muntaner, Frances, and Ramón Grosfoguel, eds. *Puerto Rican Jam: Rethinking Colonialism and Nationalism*. Minneapolis: University of Minnesota Press, 2008.

Nkrumah, Kwame. *Dark Days in Ghana*. New York: International, 1968.

Nodín Valdés, Dionicio. *Organized Agriculture and the Labor Movement before the UFW: Puerto Rico, Hawai'i, and California*. Austin: University of Texas Press, 2011.

Odem, Mary, and Elaine Lacy, eds. *Latino Immigrants and the Transformation of the U.S. South*. Athens: University of Georgia Press, 2009.

OIPR (Office of Information for Puerto Rico). *The Little Mud* (brochure). San Juan: OIPR, 1943.

Onís, Federico de. "España y el sudoeste de Estados Unidos." In *Bases culturales del entendimiento continental*. Austin: Institute of Latin American Studies, University of Texas, 1942.

Padilla, Elena. "Nocorá: The Subculture of Workers on a Government-Owned Sugar Plantation." In *The People of Puerto Rico: A Study in Social Anthropology*, edited by Julian Haynes Steward. 265–313. Urbana: University of Illinois Press, 1956.

Padmore, George. "The Atlantic Charter and the British Colonies." *Chicago Defender*, September 26, 1942, B9.

Pancho, Don. "De negros y puertorriqueños." *Claridad*, February 12, 1967, 2.

Park, Robert Ezra. "Mentality of Racial Hybrids." *American Journal of Sociology* 36, no. 1 (1931): 534–51.

———. *Race and Culture*. Glencoe, IL: Free Press, 1950.

Pattee, Richard. "The Efforts Made in Latin America to Document the History of the Negro." *Journal of Negro History* 24, no. 1 (1939): 57–64.

———. "Prontuario histórico de Puerto Rico, by Tomás Blanco." *Hispanic American Historical Review* 16, no. 2 (1936): 240–42.

Pedreira, Antonio Salvador. *Insularismo: ensayos de interpretación puertorriqueña*. San Juan, PR: Editorial Plaza Mayor, 2002.

Persons, Stow. *Ethnic Studies at Chicago, 1905–1945*. Urbana: University of Illinois Press, 1987.

Pfau, Wade. "Rationing." In *The Home Front Encyclopedia: United States, Britain, and Canada in World Wars I and II*, edited by James Ciment, contributing editor Thaddeus Russell, 1000–1001. Santa Barbara, CA: ABC-CLIO, 2007.

Prashad, Vijay. *The Darker Nations: A People's History of the Third World*. Edited by Howard Zinn. New York: New Press, 2007.

Preece, Harold. "Confessions of an Ex-Nordic: The Depression Not an Unmixed Evil." *Opportunity Journal of Negro Life* 13, no. 8 (1935): 232–33.

———. *The Dalton Gang: End of an Outlaw Era*. New York: Hastings House, 1963.

———. "From Mr. Preece." *The Crisis*, April 1936, 123.

———. *Living Pioneers: The Epic of the West by Those Who Lived It*. Cleveland, OH: World Publishing, 1952.

———. "The Living South: Beaumont vs. Nashville." *Chicago Defender*, July 10, 1943, 15.

———. "The Living South: Captain Charlie." *Chicago Defender*, November 25, 1944, 11.

———. "The Living South: Judgment on June'Teenth." *Chicago Defender*, June 17, 1944, 11.

———. "The Living South: Marcantonio vs. Pollcats." *Chicago Defender*, August 26, 1944, 13.

———. "The Living South: New Year Decision." *Chicago Defender*, January 8, 1944, 11.

———. "The Living South: Southern Liberals." *Chicago Defender*, June 19, 1943, 15.

———. "The Living South: Tomcats and Pollcats." *Chicago Defender*, January 27, 1945, 11.

———. "The Negro Folk Cult." In *Mother Wit from the Laughing Barrel: Readings in the Interpretation of Afro-American Folklore*, edited by Alan Dundes, 34–38. Englewood Cliffs, NJ: Prentice-Hall, 1973.

———. "The Negro in Latin America." *Plaindealer*, June 23, 1944, 7.

———. "The Negro in Latin America: The AFL Tries to Aryanize Latin America." *Plaindealer*, March 24, 1944, 11.

———. "The Negro in Latin America: Brazil." *Plaindealer*, November 26, 1943, 7.

———. "The Negro in Latin America: Colored People and the Good Neighbor Policy." *Plaindealer*, March 3, 1944, 7.

———. "The Negro in Latin America: Cooking Makes Friends." *Plaindealer*, February 15, 1946, 7.

———. "The Negro in Latin America: Latin America Welcomes Negro Workers." *Plaindealer*, May 26, 1944, 7.

———. "The Negro in Latin America: Latin American Negroes Make Good Citizens." *Plaindealer*, June 8, 1945, 11.

———. "The Negro in Latin America: OPA in Puerto Rico." *Plaindealer*, February 2, 1945, 7.

———. "The Negro in Latin America: Puerto Rico—America's First Ally." *Plaindealer*, August 17, 1945, 7.

———. "The Negro in Latin America: Puerto Rico Faces Revolution." *Plaindealer*, July 20, 1945. 7.

———. "The Negro in Latin America: Sewanee Republic." *Plaindealer*, April 6, 1945, 7.

———. "The Negro in Latin America: So You Want to Go to Jail." *Plaindealer*, March 22, 1946, 7.

———. "The Negro in Latin America: The Spirituals Come to Salvador." *Plaindealer*, April 19, 1946, 11.

———. "The Negro in Latin America: Sugar Lumps in the Ballot Box." *Plaindealer*, April 21, 1944, 7.

———. "The Negro in Latin America: What Mexico Thinks of Jackie Robinson." *Plaindealer*, February 22, 1946, 7.

———. "The Negro in Latin America: Why Negroes Should Learn Spanish." *Plaindealer*, November 3, 1944. 7.

"The Puerto Rican Independence Movement and the Status Issue under Spanish Rule: Selected Sources, 1892–1897." Special issue, *CENTRO Journal* 20, nos. 1–2 (1998). http://centropr.hunter.cuny.edu/journal/journal-collections/journal-1998.

"Puerto Rico: Senate Investigating Committee Finds It an Unsolvable Problem." *Life*, March 8, 1943, 23.

Quintero-Rivera, Ángel G. "La otra cara de la historia y el teatro popular puertorriqueño: el tajo del alacrán de Lydia Milagros González." *CENTRO Journal* 20, no. 2 (2008): 175–91.

———. *Puerto Rico: identidad nacional y clases sociales*. Río Piedras, PR: Ediciones Huracán, 1981.

"Rechazan versión CAL sobre quema de hogar." *El Mundo*, May 2, 1971, 1A.

"Rethinking Our Policy." *Chicago Defender*, August 28, 1943, 14.

Reuter, Edward Byron. *The American Race Problem: A Study of the Negro*. New York: Thomas Y. Crowell, 1927.

———. "Culture Contacts in Puerto Rico." *American Journal of Sociology* 52, no. 2 (1946): 91–101.

———, ed. *Race and Culture Contacts*. New York: McGraw-Hill, 1934.

———. "The Superiority of the Mulatto." *American Journal of Sociology* 23, no. 1 (1917): 83–106.

Reyes, Alberto Batista. "Por la revolución africana." *Claridad*, September 10, 1967, 2.

Rivera-Rideau, Petra. *Remixing Reggaetón: The Cultural Politics of Race in Puerto Rico*. Durham, NC: Duke University Press, 2015.

Rivera Schatz, Tomás. "Igualdad: Come Home!" *El Nuevo Día*, June 14, 2011.

Robinson, Cedric J. *Black Marxism: The Making of the Black Radical Tradition*. Chapel Hill: University of North Carolina Press, 2000.

———. *Forgeries of Memory and Meaning: Blacks and the Regimes of Race in American Theater and Film before World War II*. Chapel Hill: University of North Carolina Press, 2007.

Rodríguez, Besenia. "'De la esclavitud yanqui a la libertad cubana': U.S. Black Radicals, the Cuban Revolution, and the Formation of a Tricontinental Ideology." *Radical History Review* 92 (2005): 62–87.

Rodríguez Juliá, Edgardo. *Puertorriqueños: álbum de la sagrada familia puertorriqueña a partir de 1898*. Madrid: Editorial Playor, 1989.

Rodríguez-Silva, Ileana. *Silencing Race: Disentangling Blackness, Colonialism, and National Identities in Puerto Rico*. New York: Palgrave Macmillan, 2012.

Rosskam, Edwin. *The Alien*. New York: Grossman, 1964.

Rúa, Mérida. *A Grounded Identidad: Making New Lives in Chicago's Puerto Rican Neighborhoods*. Oxford: Oxford University Press, 2012.

———. *Latino Urban Ethnography and the Work of Elena Padilla*. Urbana: University of Illinois Press, 2011.

Sánchez Korrol, Virginia. *From Colonia to Community: The History of Puerto Ricans in New York City*. Berkeley: University of California Press, 1994.

Sanson, Jerry Purvis. *Louisiana during World War II: Politics and Society, 1939–1945*. Baton Rouge: Louisiana State University Press, 1999.

Santiago-Valles, Kelvin A. *"Subject People" and Colonial Discourses: Economic Transformation and Social Disorder in Puerto Rico, 1898–1947*. Albany: State University of New York Press, 1994.

Saretzky, Gary. "Interview with Louise Rosskam." In *Remembering the Twentieth*

*Century: An Oral History of Monmouth County*, edited by Flora T. Higgins. Manalapan, NJ: Monmouth County Library, 2002.

Schalk, Toki. "Toki Types." *Pittsburgh Courier*, May 15, 1943, 11.

Seda Bonilla, Eduardo. "Dos modelos de relaciones raciales: Estados Unidos y América Latina." *Revista de Ciencias Sociales* 12, no. 4 (1968): 569–97.

———. "El racismo en dos culturas y en la conciencia de la cultura." *Lares: Grito Cultural* 7, no. 2 (1998): 5–10.

———. "Un nuevo racismo es amenaza a la continuidad del pueblo puertorriqueño en la historia." *Lares: Grito Cultural*, 7, no. 1 (1998): 5–8.

Seigel, Micol. "Beyond Compare: Comparative Method after the Transnational Turn." *Radical History Review* 91 (2005): 62–90.

———. *Uneven Encounters: Making Race and Nation in Brazil and the United States*. Durham: Duke University Press, 2009.

Senior, Clarence. *Our Citizens from the Caribbean*. New York: McGraw-Hill, 1965.

Shapiro, Thomas M. *The Hidden Cost of Being African American: How Wealth Perpetuates Inequality*. Oxford: Oxford University Press, 2004.

Sheller, Mimi. *Consuming the Caribbean: From Arawaks to Zombies*. London: Routledge, 2003.

Silén, Juan Ángel. *Historia de la nación puertorriqueña*. Río Piedras, RP: Editorial Edil, 1973.

———. *Historia de Puerto Rico*. San Juan, PR: Distribuidora de Libros, 2003.

Silver, Patricia. "Latinization, Race, and Cultural Identification in Puerto Rican Orlando." *Southern Cultures* 19, no. 4 (2013): 55–75.

Smith, Heather, and Owen J. Furuseth, eds. *Latinos in the New South: Transformations of Place*. Burlington, VT: Ashgate, 2006.

Smith, Tom W. "Changing Racial Labels: From 'Colored' to 'Negro' to 'Black' to 'African American.'" *Public Opinion Quarterly* 56, no. 4 (1992): 496–514.

Steward, Julian Haynes. *The People of Puerto Rico: A Study in Social Anthropology*. Urbana: University of Illinois Press, 1956.

"Stokely Carmichael: What Black Power Struggle Is All About." *World Outlook* 5, no. 32 (October 6, 1967): 802–24.

"Sugar Quotas Set for Cuba, Islands." *New York Times*, June 1, 1934, 35.

Thomas, Lorrin. *Puerto Rican Citizen: History and Political Identity in Twentieth-Century New York City*. Chicago: University of Chicago Press, 2010.

Thomas, Piri. *Down These Mean Streets*. New York: Vintage Books, 1997.

Thompson, Donald. "Film Music and Community Development in Rural Puerto Rico: The DIVEDCO Program (1948–91)." *Latin American Music Review* 26, no. 1 (2005): 102–14.

Tugwell, Rexford G. *The Stricken Land: The Story of Puerto Rico*. Garden City, NJ: Doubleday, 1947.

Tydings, Millard. "Expenditure of Relief Funds in Puerto Rico." 74 Congressional Record, S4896–S4980. April 3, 1935.

Tyrrell, Marygrace. "Colonizing Citizens: Housing Puerto Ricans, 1917–1952." PhD diss., Northwestern University, 2009.

Vargas, Daniel Rivera. "Júbilo ciudadano: esperan que todo transcurra con normalidad." El Nuevo Día, June 14, 2011.

Vargas-Ramos, Carlos. "Black, Trigueño, White . . . ?: Shifting Racial Identification among Puerto Ricans." Du Bois Review 2, no. 2 (2005): 267–85.

Von Eschen, Penny M. Race against Empire: Black Americans and Anticolonialism, 1937–1957. Ithaca, NY: Cornell University Press, 1997.

———. Satchmo Blows Up the World: Jazz Ambassadors Play the Cold War. Cambridge, MA: Harvard University Press, 2004.

Washburn, Patrick Scott. The African American Newspaper: Voice of Freedom. Evanston, IL: Northwestern University Press, 2006.

Weber, Max. "'Objectivity' in Social Science and Social Policy." In Max Weber on the Methodology of the Social Sciences, edited by Edward Shils and Henry Finch, 49–112. Glencoe: Free Press, 1949.

Weise, Julie M. "Dispatches from the 'Viejo' New South: Historicizing Recent Latino Migrations." Latino Studies 10, nos. 1–2 (2012): 41–59.

Wells, Henry. The Modernization of Puerto Rico: A Political Study of Changing Values and Institutions. Cambridge, MA: Harvard University Press, 1969.

Wells Barnett, Ida B. On Lynchings. Amherst, MA: Humanity Books, 2002.

Whalen, Carmen. From Puerto Rico to Philadelphia: Puerto Rican Workers and Postwar Economies. Philadelphia, PA: Temple University Press, 2001.

Willetts, Peter. The Non-Aligned Movement: The Origins of a Third World Alliance. New York: Nichols, 1978.

Williams, Eric. Capitalism and Slavery. Chapel Hill: University of North Carolina Press, 1944.

Williams, John Bell. "The Late Honorable Dan R. McGehee." 87 Congressional Record, H2987, February 27, 1962.

Williams, Trina. "The Homestead Act: A Major Asset-Building Policy in American History." Working Paper 00-9. St. Louis, MO: Center for Social Development, Washington University, 2000.

Winship, Blanton. "Washington to Make Philippine Mistake in Puerto Rico, Says Fajardo Sugar Executive." 74 Congressional Record, S5287–88, April 9, 1935.

Wolf, Eric. "San José: Subculture of a 'Traditional' Coffee Municipality." In The People of Puerto Rico: A Study in Social Anthropology, edited by Julian Haynes Steward, 171–264. Urbana: University of Illinois Press, 1956.

Wood, Bryce. The Making of the Good Neighbor Policy. New York: Columbia University Press, 1961.

Wood, Percy. "Deton Brooks: Poverty Fighter." *Chicago Tribune*, December 27, 1964.

Wright, Richard. "Blueprint for Negro Literature." *ChickenBones: A Journal for Literary & Artistic African-American Themes*, http://nathanielturner.com/blueprintfornegroliterature.htm (accessed August 29, 2008).

Zenón Cruz, Isabelo. *Narciso descubre su trasero: el negro en la cultura puertorriqueña*. Humacao, PR: Editorial Furidi, 1975.

Zinn, Howard. *SNCC, the New Abolitionists*. Cambridge, MA: South End Press, 1964.

# Index

Page numbers in *italics* refer to illustrations.

ABB. *See* African Blood Brotherhood
Abbott, Robert, 26, 27–28, 69
Abolish Peonage Committee, 68
Abolition, 72, 73–74, 98, 168n60, 172n2
Act for International Development, 88
AFL. *See* American Federation of Labor
African Americans: in FSA photographs, 99; Great Migration of, 26, 100; MPI and, 124–26; poverty of, 153–54; Puerto Rican political alliance with, 52; Puerto Rican U.S. citizenship followed by, 34–37, 52; sovereignty sought by, 19, 23, 35; in Vietnam War, 181n86; in World War I, 20–21; in World War II, 165n20; Wright on writing by, 24–25, 159n30. *See also* Black; Black press
African Blood Brotherhood (ABB), 21–22
"The Age of Plunder: The Time Machine" (comic), *138*, 139–40
*Agredados* (sharecroppers), 49, 50
Agricultural Adjustment Act, 67
Albizu Campos, Pedro, 119–20, 128
*The Alien* (E. Rosskam), 15–16, 86, 103–6, 109–14, 115
Alienation, 97–98, 106, 110, 174n51

Allen, James, 94–95
*An American Dilemma* (Myrdal), 61–62, 85, 166n31
American Federation of Labor (AFL), 76–77, 78, 82, 168n68
Andreu Iglesias, César, 94
Angelou, Maya, 122, 178n17, 178n19
*Annals of the American Academy of Political and Social Science*, 89
Anticolonialism, 13, 16, 117, 119–20, 122–24, 126
Anti-Imperialist League, 6
Antonini, Ernesto Ramos, 46, 163n65
Article 73, UN, 121
*As Long as the Grass Shall Grow* (La Farge), 99–100, 173n43
Association for the Study of Negro Life and History (ASNLH), 70
Atlantic Charter, 33, 35–36
Ayala, César J., 49, 119

Badger, John Robert, 35–36, 52
Baldwin, James, 3
Barbosa, José Celso, 8, 157n20, 163n65
Barrio Tortugo, 132–34, 142–43, 145–46, 181n72, 183n102
Bell, Charles Jasper, 44–45
Bell Committee, 43–46, 50–51
Benítez Rexach, Jaime, 30, 119, 145–46, 172n15

Betances, Ramón Emeterio, 73–74

Black Belt theory, 23, 36

Black internationalism, 14, 19, 22–24, 37, 125

Black Leftists, 14, 22–23, 52, 59

*Black Metropolis* (Cayton), 100

Black nation, Puerto Rico as, 51, 131–32

Black nationalism, 22, 24, 143, 159n25

Blackness: coastal region linked to, 53, 96, 142, 172n30; Proyecto Piloto's support of, 134–35, 136–37

Black Power, 117, 124–25

Black press: *Chicago Defender* as, 26–27, 28, 51–52, 60, 159n38, 163n59; history of, 25–28; imbrication by, 19, 33, 35, 39, 60, 149; Muñoz Marín's betrayal and, 59; *Pittsburgh Courier* as, 26, 28, 49, 51–52, 60, 163n59; Puerto Rico's influence on, 19–20, 33–34; racism, colonialism and capitalism linked in, 20, 28, 32–34; racism addressed by, 26–28; on World War II, 27. *See also* Brooks, Deton; Little, George

Black radicalism, 14, 20–25, 118

*Black Reconstruction in America* (Du Bois), 20

Blanco, Tomás, 8, 62–63, 69–71, 85, 167n39

*Blanqueamiento* (whitening), 9, 135–36, 140

"Blueprint for Negro Literature" (Wright), 24, 159n30

Brooks, Deton, 14–15, 17, 29, 31–32, 35–36; on Bell Committee, 50–51; on colonialism and poverty, 47–49; on Crawford, 43–44; on land reforms, 39, 41, 43, 50–51, 152; Muñoz Marín and, 30, 38, 60; on poverty despite U.S. citizenship, 49–50; on racism, 53–57; on sugar industry, 47–48

"But This Family I Know" (script), 113–14

CAL. *See* Comandos Armados de Liberación (Armed Commandos of Liberation)

Capitalism: colonialism and racism linked with, 20, 28, 32–34, 118. *See also* Racial capitalism

Carmichael, Stokely, 124–25

Cayton, Horace, 100

Center for Puerto Rican Studies, Hunter College, 150–51

Central Aguirre, 48

Centro de Investigaciones Sociales (Social Science Research Center) (CIS), 88–89

Centro para el Estudio de la Realidad Puertorriqueña, 150

CGT. *See* Confederación General de Trabajadores

*Chicago Defender*, 26–27, 28, 51–52, 60, 66, 159n38, 163n59. *See also* Brooks, Deton

Chicago School of Sociology, 100, 108, 110

Churchill, Winston, 33, 35–36

CIO. *See* Congress of Industrial Organizations

CIS. *See* Centro de Investigaciones Sociales (Social Science Research Center)

CIT. *See* Inter-American Confederation of Workers

Citizenship, U.S.: African American interest in Puerto Rico's, 34–37, 52; Jones-Shafroth Act on, 21, 35, 139, 155n5; poverty despite, 46–47, 49–50

Clark, Clinton, 66, 67

Class: Blanco on, 63; racism linked to, 53–54, 65, 152–53

Class-based typologies, 15–16, 87, 99, 105, 115–16, 135

Coastal region, 53, 96, 132, 134, 142, 172n30

Colonialism: *The Alien* as indictment of, 104, 112–13; capitalism and racism linked to, 20, 28, 32–34, 118; CIS as, 89; comparative method and, 5–10; displaced workers created by, 87, 104; education as, 74, 168n58; internal, in U.S., 19, 23; medical care in, 129, 180n59; Padmore on, 32–33; poverty and sugar industry linked to, 47–49; Preece on, 72, 81; of Spain, 4, 18, 47, 132, 135–36; UN Special Committee on Decolonization regarding, 123

Comandos Armados de Liberación (Armed Commandos of Liberation) (CAL), 145, 183n102

Comics, 135–44, *138*, *141*

Commonwealth rule, 3, 5, 119, 121

Communism: Black internationalism and, 22–23; Point Four Program in response to, 88; Preece and, 65, 165n18, 165n20; of Proyecto Piloto, 144–45; Rosskam, Louise, and, 173n34. *See also* Marxism

Communist Party of the United States of America (CPUSA): Black Leftists marginalized by, 14, 22–23; on Negro Question, 94–95; Trenton Six and, 174n52

Comparative method, 5–10, 6, 149–50, 156n11, 158n34

Confederación General de Trabajadores (CGT), 77–78, 81–82, 83, 85

Confederation of Latin American Workers (Confederación de Trabajadores de América Latina) (CTAL), 76–78, 85

Congress of Industrial Organizations (CIO), 68, 82–83, 166n27, 166n29

Cordero, Ana Livia, *118*, 179n43; anticolonial work of, 13, 16, 122–24; death of, 147; Du Bois and, 122–23, 178nn19–20; Forman and, 125–26, 153; in Ghana, 16, 118, 122–23, 124; on Latin American racism, 123–24; Mari Brás's expelling of, 127–29; Mayfield and, 16, 122, 124, 125, 178n18, 179n35; medical care research of, 129, 180n59; Williams and, 125, 153, 179n39. *See also* Proyecto Piloto para Trabajo con el Pueblo (Pilot Project for Work with the Nation)

CPUSA. *See* Communist Party of the United States of America

Crawford, Fred, 43–44

Criminalization, of diaspora, 110–14, 115

*Criollo* (creole) elites, 7, 11

CTAL. *See* Confederation of Latin American Workers (Confederación de Trabajadores de América Latina)

Declaration Regarding Non-Self-Governing Territories, UN, 177n10

*Decline of the West* (Spengler), 106

De Jesús, Timoteo, 134–35

Delano, Irene, 99, 102

Delano, Jack, 99, 102

Democracy, racial, 6, 7–8, 72–73, 151, 156n17

Diaspora: Blackness valorized by, 136–37; in comics, 135–44, *138*, *141*; criminalization of, 110–14, 115; in Harlem, 72, 137, 142; marginalization of, 113–14, 150; "The Negro in Latin America" on, 15, 64, 69–76, 83, 84–85, 166n36; in southern U.S., 151–53; U.S. elections impacted by, 152

Dinzey-Flores, Zaire Zenit, 112

Displaced workers, 41, 87, 92, 99, 104–5, 107

División de Educación de la Comunidad (DIVEDCO), 101–2, 174n50

Domengeaux, James "Jimmy," 43, 44, 45–46, 50–51, 162n27

*Down in Porto Rico* (Fowles), 34–35

Draft, 139–40, 142–43, 145–46

Du Bois, W.E.B., 3, 70, 167n42; on "colored" terminology, 153n55; Cordero, Ana, and, 122–23, 178nn19–20; on double consciousness, 14; Khrushchev and, 122; on liberalism, 84, 170n104; NAACP founded by, 65; on reconstruction, 20–21

Education, 74, 79, 168n58

Elections: decline in, of Puerto Rican Left, 120; diaspora impacting U.S., 152. *See also* Voting

Elinson, Jack, 129, 180n57

Empire: and folk, 73–75; Global South response to, 117; Preece on, 72, 74, 81; race and, 3–6, 11, 39, 61, 76, 118, 142, 149

*Encyclopedia of the Negro* (Du Bois and Logan), 70, 167n42

Fair Labor Standards Act, 82

Fajardo Sugar Company, 42, 48

FALN. *See* Fuerzas Armadas de Liberación Nacional (Armed Forces for National Liberation)

El Fanguito slum (The Little Mud), 86, 92–93, 103–6, 109–10, 111, 115

Farm Security Administration (FSA), 15, 87, 98–99

Fascism, 27, 45, 46, 59

Federación de Universitarios Pro-Independencia (Federation of Pro-Independence University Students) (FUPI), 120–21, 124, 126–27, 147 180n47

Federación Libre de Trabajadores (Federation of Free Workers) (FLT), 77–78, 82

Federal Labor Relations Act, 170n90

*Federico* (play), 142–43

Ferguson, Roderick, 114, 151

FLT. *See* Federación Libre de Trabajadores (Federation of Free Workers)

Folk culture, 73–75, 143, 168n62

Food, Tobacco, Agricultural and Allied Workers of America union, 67

Foraker Act, 18–19, 34

Forman, James, 125–26, 153

Foster, William, 93–95, 97, 104

Fowles, George Milton, 34–35

FSA. *See* Farm Security Administration

Fuerzas Armadas de Liberación Nacional (Armed Forces for National Liberation) (FALN), 114–15

FUPI. *See* Federación de Universitarios Pro-Independencia (Federation of Pro-Independence University Students)

Gag law (*ley de la mordaza*), 119–20

Garvey, Marcus, 21–22, 64–65, 78

*La generación de los setenta* (the seventies generation), 150–51

*La generación del treinta*, 8, 62, 158n33

Ghana, 16, 118, 122–23, 124, 179n35

Global South, 32, 41, 88, 117, 121, 130, 161n10

Godreau, Isar, 9, 53

González, José Luis, 118, 132, 150, 174n49

González García, Lydia Milagros, 128, 130, 150

Good Neighbor Policy, 78–80

Gordon, Avery, 2, 10–11, 155n4

La gran familia puertorriqueña, 10–14, 158n33

Haiti, 11, 52, 142, 147, 166n36

Harlem, 72, 137, 142

Hauntings, 2, 10–14, 154, 158n33

Hearst, William Randolph, 26

Homestead Act, 109–10

House Committee on Un-American Activities (HUAC), 83–84

Housing, 112, 131
Houston Informer (newspaper), 84
HUAC. See House Committee on Un-
American Activities
Hurston, Zora Neale, 65, 75, 168n64

IASB. See International African Service
Bureau
Ibáñez, Bernardo, 77
ICP. See Institute of Puerto Rican
Culture
Imbrication: by Black press, 19, 33,
35, 39, 60, 149; of Preece, 83; racial,
12–13, 14, 16, 37, 149–50
Imperialism, 14, 20, 21, 22, 32, 37, 46, 81
Independence, 2, 49, 52, 57, 81, 95, 114–
15, 119, 124–25. See also Sovereignty
Independentistas, 63, 73, 78, 98, 117, 146,
147
India, 29–30, 31, 32, 35
Institute of Puerto Rican Culture (ICP),
8–9
Insularismo: ensayos de interpretación
puertorriqueña (Pedreira), 106–7,
175n64
Insularity, 106–10, 116
Intellectual imperialism, 46
Inter-American Confederation of Work-
ers (CIT), 77
Internal colonialism, of U.S., 19, 23
International African Service Bureau
(IASB), 32
Internationalism, Black, 14, 19, 22–24,
37, 125
International Labor Defense, 68
International Workers of the World
(IWW), 21–22
IWW. See International Workers of the
World

James, C.L.R., 3, 32
Jíbaros (peasants), 18, 156n18
Jim Crow. See Segregation

JMPI. See Juventud del Movimiento
Pro-Independencia (Youth of the
Pro-Independence Movement)
Jones-Costigan Act (Sugar Act), 39–46,
78
Jones-Shafroth Act of 1917, 21, 34, 35,
139, 155n5
Journal of Negro History (Woodson), 70
Juventud del Movimiento Pro-In-
dependencia (Youth of the Pro-
Independence Movement) (JMPI),
126–27

Kelley, Robin, 22–23
Koger, Harry, 66–67
Ku Klux Klan, 20, 66, 83

Labor movement: AFL in, 76–77, 78,
82, 168n68; CGT in, 77–78, 81–82,
83, 85; CIO in, 68, 82–83, 166n27,
166n29; CIT in, 77; CTAL in, 76–78,
85; Fair Labor Standards Act and,
82; labor unions in, 51–52, 67, 151;
"The Living South" series on, 15, 63–
64, 66–69, 75–76, 83, 85; Lombardo
Toledano on, 76–77; Preece on, 15,
64, 66–69, 75–85, 149; on racism,
94–95; Tugwell in, 81–83
La Farge, Oliver, 99–100, 173n43
Land reforms: Bell Committee opposing, 43–46, 50–51; Brooks on,
39, 41, 43, 50–51, 152; latifundios
in, 58; Little on, 39, 41, 152; Muñoz
Marín and, 18–19, 41–42, 57–59;
Plan Chardón for, 41; southern U.S.
threatened by, 52; of Tugwell, 43, 79
Lauria-Perricelli, Antonio, 91, 172n15
Lebrón, Lolita, 120, 128
Left: Black, 14, 22–23, 52, 59; Puerto
Rican, 98, 117, 119–24, 128, 132, 153,
154, 176n2
Lenin, Vladimir, 22, 23, 24
Lewis, David Levering, 122–23

Liberalism: alienation misread in, 110; class-based typologies in, 15, 115–16; Du Bois on, 84, 170n104; of Roosevelt, New Jersey, 102–3; of Rosskam, Edwin, 98; southern U.S., 61–62, 84, 85

Lincoln, Abraham, 2–3, 73

Little, George, 14–15, 29, 30–32, 35; on caste system, 54–55; on land reforms, 39, 41, 152; on racism in Puerto Rico, 53–57; on sugar industry, 48–49

"The Living Negro in Latin America" (Preece), 15

"The Living South" (Preece), 15, 63–64, 66–69, 75–76, 83, 85

Lombardo Toledano, Vicente, 76–77

Lowe, Lisa, 6, 12, 156n11

Malcolm X, 125, 178n19, 179n35

Maldonado Trinidad, Luis, 144–45, 182n97

"Manela" (comic), 140, 141, 142

Marcano García, Pablo, 2, 3, 16, 155n5

Marginalization, 110–12, 115, 150; of Black Leftists by CPUSA, 14, 22–23; gender, 113–14

Marginal man, 106–10

Mari Brás, Juan, 115, 119, 124–25, 127–29, 155n5

Marxism: of MPI, 121; in The People of Puerto Rico, 90–91; of Proyecto Piloto, 130, 133–34; Wright on, 24–25

Maura, Gabriel Vicente, 122, 177n15

Mayfield, Julian, 16, 122, 124, 125, 178nn17–18, 179n35

McGehee, Dan "Smiling Dan," 43, 44, 51, 162n26

Migration: Great Migration as, 26, 100; out-migration as, 45, 162n32

Military, U.S., 18, 51, 54, 58, 78–79

Mintz, Sidney, 95–97, 171n10

Movimiento Pro-Independencia (MPI), 117, 120, 121, 124–27, 129, 144

Mulattoes, 106, 107–9, 110, 135–36, 142

Muñoz Marín, Luis: Bell Committee opposed by, 45; betrayal by, 57–59; Brooks and, 30, 38, 60; CGT alignment of, 77–78, 81–82; on Crawford, 43; land reform goals of, 18–19, 41–42; Perry on, 59; on Roosevelt's visit, 38–39; Rosskam, Edwin, and, 98, 115; on sovereignty, 58–59

Myrdal, Gunnar, 61–62, 63–64, 85, 166n31

Myths: in racial regimes, 5, 6, 97, 136, 156n18; sovereignty and, 154

NAACP. See National Association for the Advancement of Colored People

NAM. See Non-Aligned Movement

National Association for the Advancement of Colored People (NAACP), 65, 125

National Labor Relations Act, 81

National Liberation Council (NLC), 124

"The Negro in Latin America" (Preece), 15, 64, 69–76, 83, 84–85, 166n36

Negrón, Efraín, 130, 132, 137

"The Negro Question," 22, 24, 94–95

New Deal, 38, 40, 43, 67, 80, 170n93

New historicism, 150–51

New York City, 72, 137, 142

Nkrumah, Kwame, 122, 123, 124, 177n14

NLC. See National Liberation Council

Nodín Valdés, Dionicio, 83

Non-Aligned Movement (NAM), 121–23, 177n14

Nuevo New South, 152, 153

Obama, Barack, 1–3

Office of Information for Puerto Rico (OIPR), 100–101, 103, 112

Office of Price Administration (OPA), 80

OIPR. See Office of Information for Puerto Rico

OPA. *See* Office of Price Administration
Organic Act of 1900 (Foraker Act), 19, 34
Ortiz, Fernando, 69–71, 167n39
Out-Migration, 45, 162n32

Padilla, Elena, 95, 171n10, 171n12
Padmore, George, 32–33, 36
"El país de cuatro pisos" (González, J.), 132
Pan-Africanism, 16, 22–23, 32, 35, 122
Park, Robert, 107–9
Partido Independentista Puertor- riqueño (Puerto Rican Independence Party) (PIP), 120
Partido Nuevo Progresista (PNP), 5
Partido Popular Democrático (PPD), 5, 8–9, 30, 89, 91, 119–20, 171n9, 172n15. *See also* Muñoz Marín, Luis
Patriarchy, 6, 7, 10, 11, 16, 106, 127, 128
Pattee, Richard, 70–71
Peasants (*Jíbaros*), 18, 156n18
Pedreira, Antonio Salvador, 106–8, 110, 114, 158n33, 175n64
*Peonage: 1940 Style Racism* (Preece), 68
*The People of Puerto Rico* (Steward), 89–92, 95, 130, 172n15
Perry, Pettis, 59
Perspective, 25, 28, 159n30
Photography, 15, 87, 90, 91, 92, 96, 97–103
Pietri Castellón, Norman, 123, 124
PIP. *See* Partido Independentista Puer- torriqueño (Puerto Rican Indepen- dence Party)
*Pittsburgh Courier*, 26, 27, 28, 49, 51–52, 60, 163n59. *See also* Little, George
Plan Chardón, 39–46, 50–51
PNP. *See* Partido Nuevo Progresista
Point Four Program, 88
Police surveillance, 101–2, 144–45, 146, 147, 174n48, 178n18
Ponce Massacre, 98, 104, 110, 176n2

Post, Helen, 99–100, 173n43
Post-racial subject, 103–6
Poverty, 1, 155n2; in *The Alien*, 104; colonialism linked to, 47–49; despite U.S. citizenship, 46–47, 49–50; as racialized, 131; sugar industry linked to, 39, 47–49, 91; Tugwell on, 49; in U.S., 153–54
PPD. *See* Partido Popular Democrático
Prashad, Vijay, 117, 121
Preece, Harold: on AFL, 76–77, 78; biographical sketch of, 64–65, 164n12, 165n17; on CGT, 78; class and racism linked by, 65, 152–53; on colonialism, 72, 81; communism and, 65, 165n18, 165n20; Du Bois and, 84, 170n104; on empire, 72, 74, 81; on folk culture, 75, 168n62; "The Living South" of, 15, 63–64, 66–69, 75–76, 83, 85; misogyny of, 168n62; "The Negro in Latin America" of, 15, 64, 69–76, 83, 84–85, 166n36; Ortiz and, 69–71; on price gouging, 80; on self-determination, 81; sources of, 69–70, 71, 73, 85; on Tugwell, 81; Wesley and, 84; on white scholar- ship about racism, 71–72
*El prejuicio racial en Puerto Rico* (Racial Prejudice in Puerto Rico) (Blanco), 62, 69, 167n39
PRERA. *See* Puerto Rico Emergency Relief Administration
PRLRA. *See* Puerto Rico Labor Rela- tions Act
Proletariat, 96–97, 117–18, 129–35
*Prontuario histórico de Puerto Rico* (Blanco), 71
Proyecto Piloto para Trabajo con el Pueblo (Pilot Project for Work with the Nation) (Proyecto Piloto), *118*, 183n106; anticolonialism of, 117, 126; arrest of, *133*, 145; Barrio Tor- tugo and, 132–34, 142–43,

Proyecto Piloto—*continued*
145–46, 181n72, 183n102; Blackness
supported by, 134–35, 136–37; comics
by, 135–44, *138*, *141*; communism
investigations about, 144–45; conflict
studied by, 126–27, 129–35; founding of, 126; housing concerns of, 131;
Marxism of, 130, 133–34; MPI and,
117, 129, 144; on mulattoes, 135–36;
Nicaraguan Sandinistas and, 147;
police surveillance and repression of,
144–45, 146; proletariat studied by,
117–18, 129–35; race, colonialism and
capitalism's links analyzed by, 118;
race studied by, 129–35; racialized
poverty and, 131; SNCC and, 117–18,
126; on UPR's research, 129–30;
Vietnam draft protested by, 139–40,
142–43, 145–46
PRPC. *See* Puerto Rico Policy
Commission
PRRA. *See* Puerto Rican Reconstruction
Administration
Puerto Rican Communist Party, 77, 94
Puerto Rican Partido Nacionalista, 98,
119–20, 176n2
Puerto Rican Reconstruction Adminis-
tration (PRRA), 40, 171n6
Puerto Rican Socialist Party, 115, 155n5
Puerto Rico. *See specific topics*
Puerto Rico Emergency Relief Adminis-
tration (PRERA), 40
"Puerto Rico Faces Revolution" (Pre-
ece), 73–74
Puerto Rico Labor Relations Act
(PRLRA), 81–82
"Puerto Rico One-Crop System Needs
Reform" (Brooks), 48
Puerto Rico Policy Commission (PRPC),
40–41
"Puerto Rico Will Choose" editorial, 55,
55–57

Queer of color critique, 158n35
Quintero Rivera, Ángel G., 150
Quotas, sugar industry, 40, 161n5

Race: in comics, 135–44, *138*, *141*; and
empire, 3–6, 11, 39, 61, 76, 118, 142,
149
*Race and Culture Contacts* (Reuter), 107
Racial capitalism, 15, 21, 24–25, 32, 48,
65, 76, 87, 94, 109, 115, 117; "Soy yo"
poem on, 140, 142
Racial democracy, 6, 7–8, 72–73, 151,
156n17
Racial imbrication, 12–13, 14, 16, 37,
149–50
Racialized poverty, 131
Racial power, 4, 16, 156n10, 157n20
Racial regimes: imbrication of, 149–50;
myth in, 5, 6, 97, 136, 156n18; Robinson on, 4
Racism: of AFL, 76–77, 78; of Bell Committee, 50–51; Black press addressing, 26–28; Blanco on, 62–63; Brooks
and Little on, 53–57; capitalism and
colonialism linked with, 20, 28,
32–34, 118; class linked to, 53–54, 65,
152–53; in Homestead Act, 109–10;
labor movement on, 94–95; Latin
American, 123–24; "The Living South"
series on, 15, 63–64, 66–69, 75–76,
83, 85; Myrdal on, 61–62, 63–64, 85,
166n31; as myth supporting slavery,
136; in Puerto Rico compared to U.S.,
62–63; southern liberals and, 61–62,
84, 85; in U.S. Military, 54; white
scholarship on, 71–72
Radicalism, Black, 14, 20–25, 118
Ramos, Arthur, 70, 71
Rankin, John, 83–84
Reconstruction, 20–25, 149, 152
Reform model, Puerto Rico as, 46–52,
60, 149, 152. *See also* Land reforms

Republicans, 43, 152
Research: medical care, 129, 180n59; social scientific, 89–92, 95, 129–30, 172n15
Research laboratory, Puerto Rico as, 88–97
Reserve Officer Training Corps (ROTC), 139, 145–46
Resolution 748, UN, 121
Resolution 1514, UN, 121, 123, 177n13
Reuter, Edward B., 107–8, 175n70, 175n72, 175n74
Robinson, Cedric, 4, 21, 25
Rodríguez López, Miguel, 128, 131–32, 144, 145
Roig, Salvador, 101–2
Roosevelt, Franklin, 33, 35–36, 38–40, 78–79, 161n5
Roosevelt, New Jersey, 102–3
Rosskam, Edwin, 101, 149, 154, 173n36; alienation of, 97–98, 106, 174n51; The Alien of, 15–16, 86, 103–6, 109–14, 115; class-based typologies of, 15–16, 87, 105, 115–16; diaspora criminalized by, 110–14, 115; in DIVEDCO, 101–2, 174n50; on FALN bombing, 115; marginalization by, 150; Muñoz Marín supported by, 98, 115; photography of, 15, 87, 90, 91, 92, 96, 97–103; police surveillance of, 101–2, 174n48
Rosskam, Louise, 98, 100, 101, 101–3, 173n33, 173n34
ROTC. See Reserve Officer Training Corps

Sánchez, Rubén, 128, 144
Santiago-Valles, Kelvin, 47, 58, 171n11
Schomburg, Arturo (Arthur), 2, 3
Seda Bonilla, Eduardo, 9–10, 150
Segregation, 17, 22, 24, 31, 62; Bell Committee interests in, 50; CPUSA on, 94–95; Domengeaux supporting,

44; Foster on, 94–95; McGehee on, 162n26; in proletariat, 96–97; slavery linked to, 142; in slums, 142; World Federation of Trade Unions and, 51–52; in World Wars I and II, 181n86
Seguinot, Juanita, 1–2, 3, 16, 155n4
Seigel, Micol, 70, 158n34
Self-determination, 22–23, 33, 36, 81
Senior, Clarence, 89, 110, 171n8
Sharecroppers, 39, 49–50, 59, 67
Slavery, 3, 32, 74, 132, 136, 142
Slums, 86, 92–93, 97, 103–6, 109–10, 111, 115, 142
Smith, Tevis Clyde, 64, 153n55, 165n18, 168n64
Smith Act, 119
Smith v. Allwright, 80
SNCC. See Student Nonviolent Coordinating Committee
Social scientific research, 89–92, 95, 129–30, 172n15
Sociedad de Estudios Afro-Cubanos (Society of Afro-Cuban Studies), 69, 70
Southern U.S.: Bell Committee members from, 50–51; diaspora in, 151–53; land reform threatening, 52; liberalism in, 61–62, 84, 85; "The Living South" on, 15, 63–64, 66–69, 75–76, 83, 85; as Nuevo New South, 152, 153; Puerto Rico equated with, 39, 46, 49–50; sharecroppers in, 39, 49–50, 59, 67
South Porto Rico Sugar Company, 48
Sovereignty, 2, 153; African Americans seeking, 19, 23, 35; Article 73 and Resolution 748 on, 121; Foster's speech about, 94; Muñoz Marin on, 58–59; myths in calls for, 154
Spain: colonialism of, 4, 18, 47, 132, 135–36; Reuter on, 108, 175n74; in World War II, 158n6

Spanish-American War, 33, 34

Spengler, Oswald, 106, 108

Statehood, 163n59; anti-Hispanics opposing, 3; Muñoz Marín's rejection of, 58–59; Puerto Rican Left on, 153, 154; Tydings Bill for, 55, 55–57, 58; voting allowed by, 51–52

St. Clair Drake, John Gibbs, 65, 100, 122, 165n20

Steward, Julian Haynes, 89–92, 95, 130, 172n15

Strikes, 49, 119, 177n4

Stryker, Roy, 98–99, 100

Student Nonviolent Coordinating Committee (SNCC), 117–18, 125–26, 149, 153

Student strike, 119, 177n4

Subsidies, sugar industry, 49

Sugar Act, 39–46, 78

Sugar industry: colonialism linked to, 47–49; poverty linked to, 39, 47–49, 91; PRLRA and, 81–82; quotas, 40, 161n5; slavery in, 142; strike, 49; xenophobia in, 83

Surveillance. See Police


Taft-Hartley Act, 170n90

Teller Amendment, 34

Torres, Arlene, 11

Tricontinental Conference, 123, 124

Trigueño (mixed race), 133, 181n74

Truman, Harry, 58, 88, 93, 95, 120

Tugwell, Rexford, 79; Bell Committee opposed by, 45–46; in FSA, 98; in labor movement, 81–83; land reform programs of, 43, 79; OIPR and, 100–101; on poverty, 49

12 Million Black Voices (Wright), 99–100

Tydings, Millard, 41, 55, 55–56

Tydings Bill, 55, 55–57, 58


UN. See United Nations

Unemployment, 40, 91–92, 140

UNIA. See Universal Negro Improvement Association

Unions, 51–52, 67, 151

United Nations (UN): Article 73 of, 121; Declaration Regarding Non-Self-Governing Territories of, 177n10; MPI and, 121; Resolution 748 of, 121; Resolution 1514 of, 121, 123, 177n13; Special Committee on Decolonization of, 123

United States (U.S.): diaspora impacting elections in, 152; as empire, 7; internal colonialism of, 19, 23; military of, 18, 51, 54, 58, 78–79; NAM influenced by, 122; poverty in, 153–54; Puerto Rico used by, in World War II, 18; racism in Puerto Rico compared to, 62–63. See also Citizenship, U.S.; Southern U.S.

Universal Negro Improvement Association (UNIA), 21–22

University of Puerto Rico (UPR), 70–71, 87, 88, 97, 150; Benítez Rexach at, 30, 119, 145–46, 172n15; Carmichael's speech at, 124–25; FUPI of, 120–21, 124, 126–27, 147 180n47; new historicism of, 150–51; Proyecto Piloto on research of, 129–30; student strike at, 119, 177n4; Vietnam draft protests at, 139, 145–46


Vandenberg, Arthur, 42–43

Vann, Robert, 26

Vecinos (film), 102

Vietnam War, 123, 124, 138, 139–40, 141, 142–43, 145–46, 181n86

Von Eschen, Penny, 28, 32

Voting: land reforms linked to, 51; Puerto Ricans denied, 35, 58, 139; of Puerto Ricans in Florida, 152; Smith v. Allwright on, 80; statehood allowing, 51–52

Wages, in sugar industry, 49

War. *See* Draft; Spanish-American War; Vietnam War; World War I; World War II

Washington, Booker T., 21, 73, 153n55

Washington, George, 73, 74

Weise, Julie, 152, 153

Wells, Henry, 89, 171n9

Wells, Ida B., 3, 21

Whitening (*blanqueamiento*), 9, 135–36, 140

Williams, Robert, 125, 153, 179n39

Wilson, Woodrow, 139

Winship, Blanton, 42, 98

Wirth, Louis, 164n4

Wolf, Eric, 95–97, 171n10, 172n30

Women, in Puerto Rican Left, 128

Woodson, Carter G., 70

World Federation of Trade Unions, 51–52

World War I, 20–21, 181n86

World War II, 18, 27, 48, 158n6, 165n20, 181n86

Wright, Richard, 3, 24–25, 28, 99–100, 159n25, 159n30

Xenophobia, 83

Zenón Cruz, Isabelo, 150

Carlos Alamo-Pastrana is interim dean of the college and associate professor of sociology and Latin American and Latina/o studies at Vassar College.

www.ingramcontent.com/pod-product-compliance
Lightning Source LLC
Chambersburg PA
CBHW020531270326
41927CB00006B/525